C.S. LEWIS
VIEWS FROM
WAKE FOREST

Collected Essays on C.S. Lewis

MICHAEL TRAVERS

EDITOR

C.S. Lewis Views From Wake Forest
Copyright © 2008 Zossima Press
Wayne, Pennsylvania

All rights reserved. Except in the case of brief quotations embodied in critical articles or reviews, no part of this book may be reproduced or transmitted in any form or by any means, electronic or mechanical, including photocopying, recording, or by any information storage or retrieval system, without written permission of the publisher. For information, contact Zossima Press www.Zossima.com

Zossima Press titles may be purchased for business or promotional use or special sales.

Book design by Robert Trexler

ISBN 0-9723221-5-9

Table of Contents

Preface and Acknowledgements	Bruce Little	
Introduction	Michael Travers	1
Editing C. S. Lewis	Walter Hooper	13

Part 1 CSL as Social Critic—Philosophy, Psychology, Science and Ethics

1. Culture & Public Philosophy: Another C.S. Lewis — James Como — 33

2. Hangman's Duty: — Justin Barnard — 51
   C.S. Lewis on Christian Citizenship in Wartime

3. Can Science be Saved?: — Michael P. Muth — 63
   C.S. Lewis on Science, Magic & Ethics

4. "The Colour of Things in Dark Places": — Byron Brown — 77
   C.S. Lewis & the "New Science" of Psychology

Part 2 Reasoned Truth and Truth Too Deep for Reason

5. Compulsion & Liberation: — Brad Mercer — 91
   God's Soveriegnty and Human Responsibility in CSL

6. *Reflections on the Psalms*: — Gregory M. Anderson — 105
   C.S. Lewis as Biblical Commentator

7. A Kneeling and Sceptered Love — Stephen D. Boyer — 125

8. Wilderness, Arcadia and Longing: — Kip Redick — 137
   Mythic Landscapes and the Experience of Reality

Part 3 The Baptized Cosmos—*Narnia* and *The Space Trilogy*

9.	The Spirit of Comedy in *The Chronicles of Narnia*	Samuel Joeckel	161
10.	A High and Lonely Destiny: Sources for Jadis, the White Witch	Elizabeth B. Hardy	169
11.	From Vampire to Venus: C.S. Lewis' Affirmation of the Human Body	David Rosenberg	185
12.	Why Wells is From Mars, Bergson From Venus: Mapping Evolution in the *Space Trilogy*	Sanford Schwartz	201

Part 4 Myths Retold—*The Discarded Image* and *Till We Have Faces*

13.	*The Discarded Image:* Patterns of Truth & Fantasy	David Hogg	225
14.	The Classical Sub-text to *Till We Have Faces*	Ian C. Storey	237
15.	Medieval Models of Loss in *Till We Have Faces*	Stephen Yandell	255
	Contributors		277
	Indexes		281

Preface

The "C. S. Lewis: The Man and His Work—a 21st Century Legacy" Conference was the first major conference hosted by the newly established L. Russ Bush Center for Faith and Culture which is housed on the campus of Southeastern Baptist Theological Seminary in Wake Forest, NC. The life and works of C. S. Lewis seemed the obvious choice as a proper way to introduce the spirit and vision of the Center. The vision of the Center is to place itself at the intersection of theology and culture forming a bridge between the two in order to bring faith and culture into an understanding relationship. The Center's aim is to be theological in nature, cultural in awareness, redemptive in orientation, and charitable in disposition. It is dedicated to bring a Christian voice to the questions of culture by providing an intellectual context and a charitable environment where an ongoing dialogue is possible between those who may have differing opinions.

Arguably, C. S. Lewis stands as one of the most noted Christian apologist of the 20th century who did precisely this. His life and works penetrated the academy, appealed to the man on the street, and challenged young and old alike. He used various literary genres by which he elucidated and defended Christian truths as well as engaged others on the difficult cultural issues facing those of his day. The Center hopes to mirror the standard exhibited by C. S. Lewis in pursuing truth, displaying intellectual honesty in addressing the issues, and developing well-formed arguments of one's position and to do so with intellectual humility. The Center counts it a privilege to have brought together some of the best Lewis scholars of our day which hopefully forwarded Lewis scholarship as well as introducing others to the work and vision of the Center. We are grateful for all those who participated in this conference, especially Walter Hooper, James Como, and Bruce Edwards.

Dr. Bruce Little
Director of the L. Russ Bush Center for Faith and Learning

Introduction

Michael E. Travers

The essays in this volume have been selected from those delivered at the "C. S. Lewis: The Man and His Works, a 21st Century Legacy" conference sponsored by the L. Russ Bush Center for Faith and Culture at Southeastern Baptist Theological Seminary in Wake Forest, North Carolina on October 26th and 27th, 2007. The conference brought together a varied group of C. S. Lewis scholars who spoke from multiple points of view. Speakers addressed Lewis from the standpoint of theology, philosophy, psychology, and literature—often in overlapping and mutually-beneficial ways; "Iron sharpens iron," the wise man said (Prov 27:17). Conferees naturally found common ground in their appreciation for Lewis and his Christianity, and the exchange of various outlooks on Lewis provided a full-orbed appreciation of the man and a sharpened understanding of his writings. Now, in this volume, selected essays from the conference are gathered together to provide a lasting record of this multi-stranded perspective for thoughtful readers of C. S. Lewis.

Introducing the essays is an account of the history of the posthumous publication of C. S. Lewis' works by the man best qualified to write the story—Walter Hooper. Walter Hooper is now the Literary Advisor to the C. S. Lewis Estate and has functioned very much in that capacity since the summer of 1963 when he served Lewis as his personal secretary. When Lewis died on November 22, 1963, Walter Hooper was home in the United States at the University of Kentucky and planning to re-join Lewis in January 1964. After Lewis' death and with the encouragement of Austin Farrer, Warden of Keble College at Oxford, and his wife, Hooper returned to England to edit Lewis' manuscripts. Hooper remains in Oxford to this day and is still performing the important duty of editing Lewis' works. The narrative Hooper provides in his address, "Editing C. S. Lewis," contains observations and insights that are available nowhere else in print. Hooper not only chronicles the major publications of Lewis' works, he also creates a warm account that he alone, with his intimate knowledge of the history of Lewis publications, could provide. Encouraged by the reminder that "every new book helps to sell the old ones," Hooper pressed to have Lewis' works published in the years following his death. It would have been a tragedy, he thought then (and thinks more so now) for Lewis to have passed into literary oblivion. He had so much to say that needs to be heard. For Hooper, C. S. Lewis has never been dated; he never could be because he speaks to the essential humanity we all share, whatever our gender, ethnicity, or religion. The huge volume of Lewis publications in the last five decades, numbering in the millions and in multiple languages, has proven Hooper to be something of a prophet; he certainly gauged Lewis' works accurately, for Lewis speaks to the issues of life with a refreshing—and at time unnerving—clarity. Readers of Lewis owe much to Walter Hooper, and here is his account of the publication of Lewis' writings.

The remainder of the volume is divided into four parts—"C. S. Lewis as Social Critic—Philosophy, Psychology, Science and Ethics"; "Reasoned Truth and Truth Too Deep for Reason"; "The Baptized Cosmos—Narnia and the Ransom Trilogy"; and "Myths Retold—*The Discarded Image* and *Till We Have Faces.*" In all, there are fifteen essays in these four sections which present a wide range of perspectives on Lewis. At the same time, the reader will be struck by the commonalities that tie the chapters together.

Part One looks outward. For many first-time readers of C. S. Lewis, Lewis may be primarily a writer of children's fantasy stories, science fiction, and mythological tales. Lewis did indeed write these kinds of stories, and he did so well. But this popular understanding of Lewis does not represent the whole man. There is more. In *An Experiment in Criticism*, published in 1961, Lewis says that imaginative literature helps us to see "with other eyes" (137), and thereby it enlarges our own moral sympathy and sharpens our own understanding. For those of us now who have the benefit of Lewis' "eyes," we can enlarge our sympathies and understand our condition from his perspective. In this first section, Lewis critiques public life and speaks to the public square. To be sure, Lewis wrote in the middle of the twentieth century, not in the twenty-first century, but much that is fruit in the culture of the early twenty-first century was seed in Lewis' day. And Lewis correctly identified the fruit in the seed. We can learn much about our contemporary culture and recognize our public responsibilities when we read Lewis' social criticism.

≈ *Introduction* ≈

This "public square" section begins with James Como's address, "Culture and Public Philosophy: Another C. S. Lewis." Como sees Lewis as a realist about the "great decline" and cultural idolatry of the mid-twentieth century. Lewis analyzed his culture in as clear-headed a manner as he explained the beliefs of "mere Christianity," and we can learn from his insights. In this chapter, Como looks through the eyes of the medieval monks who cultivated the wastelands of their day and, with this model in mind, presents a Lewisian guide for us as modern-day "monks" to civilize the cultural wasteland of our own day. For Como, Lewis is like a prophet who declares that we must be "emissaries" to the "ruined and ruinous" culture of our own day. The biblical admonition is to be salt and light (Matt 5:13-16), and Lewis proclaims that duty to us anew in the face of our own time and place. Como's comments on Lewis are a tonic, providing a bracing antidote to those who might merely enjoy Lewis' fiction for its own sake and not heed his cultural critique—a critique that resonates so singularly well in our own day. Lewis takes the long view and the outward view, Como demonstrates, and so should we.

In "The Hangman's Duty: C. S. Lewis on Christian Citizenship in Wartime," Justin Barnard offers an analysis of Lewis' thinking about a Christian's responsibilities in times of war. Lewis' observations about war, while grounded in the particular conflicts of his time, have an always-contemporaneous ring to them, for he thinks in terms of universal principles that apply to all warfare. Barnard analyzes Lewis' practical comments on a Christian's duty in war-time, making explicit a tacit principle in Lewis' thinking that is helpful to us today. Specifically, Barnard sees a principle of "epistemic moral certainty" in Lewis' writing on the subject that not only helps explain Lewis, but may be helpful to us today as well. In truth, Barnard's analysis of Lewis helps us get past the counter-productive impasse of those with differing positions who think the other party is merely stating ungrounded assumptions and drawing "conclusions" that are, in point of fact, merely personal preferences. Barnard's article looks in two directions—an understanding of C. S. Lewis and a helpful perspective on our own time.

Taking up Lewis' controversial position—and one that is opposed to the modernist orthodoxy of Lewis' day and our own—that we should be suspicious of science, Michael Muth draws on Lewis to think about the place of science in our own culture. "Can Science Be Saved? C. S. Lewis on Science, Magic, and Ethics" dares to think about the most entrenched idol of modern and post-modern times, science, and ask what its limits ought to be. For some people, particularly those with a naturalistic worldview that disavows any supernatural or transcendent realities (or those who regard such supernatural realities, if they exist, as irrelevant in any event to our lives here and now), we cannot ask moral questions of science. In fact, they say, we should not ask such questions. For others, science must be limited by certain ethical and moral parameters that address issues that are fundamental to our humanity. In his chapter on Lewis' comments on science, Muth provides a balanced analysis of what Lewis actually said about science and "scientism" and then considers how Lewis' thinking might offer a framework for us to think about science and its implications today. Because science and technology are even more pervasive today than in Lewis' time, the problem of science is more acute for us now. Lewis' characteristically clear thinking about science blows away the smokescreens and looks squarely at the issues themselves.

The final essay in the public square section is Byron Brown's "'The Colour of Things in Dark Places': C. S. Lewis and the New Science of Psychology." By the time Lewis was converted to Christianity, psychology had won the day in the academy and become the entrenched orthodoxy of modernism. The dominant strain of psychology in Lewis' day—and in our own—was one based on philosophical materialism and naturalism. For a "science" grounded in such presuppositions, the "real" was to be understood as what is material and temporal. But what if, alternately, the "real" were the spiritual and transcendent? Lewis asks. Brown develops the implications of such a reversal and examines them in Lewis' works, particularly those with an autobiographical element to them, and then considers how Lewis might provide perspective to those people today who believe in transcendence and yet wish to make sense of the human mind. As with the other chapters in the "C. S. Lewis as Social Critic" section, Brown "looks along" Lewis as Lewis "looks at" modern culture and by doing so finds helpful tools for our time.

From Lewis as social critic, Part Two turns our attention to Lewis as Christian theologian and apologist—Lewis presenting and defending "the faith that was once delivered unto the saints" (Jude 3). Lewis' defense of the faith ran along multiple tracks: he offered rational arguments, he pressed moral arguments, and he expressed the longing for God which is there in every human heart (Augustine 3). At the same time, Lewis himself never claimed to be a professional theologian; he protested on more than one occasion that he was simply a layman helping other laymen understand the basic tenets of "mere Christianity" (Preface, *Mere Christianity*, viii; Introduction, *Reflections on the Psalms*, 1). He claimed he did not wish to meddle in what he thought were the finer points of theology; these, he stated, were reserved for the "real experts" (Preface, *Mere Christianity*, viii). In fact, Lewis may have been more an apologist than a theologian. Even in his apologetics, however, he is conscious of his limitations and does not presume too far. He saw himself simply as a "translator—one turning Christian doctrine...into the vernacular, into language that unscholarly people would attend to and could understand" ("Rejoinder to Dr. Pittenger" 183; cf. "Christian Apologetics" 98). Lewis was acutely aware that apologetics could be dangerous to the apologist, for his pride might get the better of him and he might come to think that he actually understood profound spiritual truths when they still contained an element of mystery ("Christian Apologetics" 103; "The Founding of the Oxford Socratic Club" 128; letter of 2nd August 1946 to Dorothy Sayers, *The Collected Letters of C. S. Lewis*, Vol. 2, 730). Even granting Lewis' humility as an interpreter of Christianity and as an apologist, however, it is still this Lewis—the theologian and defender of the faith—whom many readers know. Without a doubt, C. S. Lewis is one of the twentieth century's most popular Christian writers, and he produced a major body of work in apologetics.

The section on C. S. Lewis as theologian and apologist begins with an unflinching and nuanced examination by Bradford Mercer of Lewis' understanding of divine sovereignty and human responsibility. In "Compulsion and Liberation: God's Sovereignty and Human Responsibility in the Writings of C. S. Lewis," Mercer considers the apparently conflicting claims that Lewis made at various times in his life on a subject that has divided great theologians and separated denominations. Mercer's analysis of Lewis' work is both representative and comprehensive, and it is faithful to the contexts in Lewis' works. The subject is a difficult one at best, and Lewis' writings on the matter cannot be reduced to a superficial sermon. He knew that the issue of divine sovereignty and human responsibility was a complex and ultimately mysterious one. Readers of this essay will come away refreshed in their appreciation of Lewis' articulation of Christianity at the center where, he claims, "her truest children dwell" (Preface, *Mere Christianity*, xii).

The second essay in this part is Gregory Anderson's "*Reflections on the Psalms*: C. S. Lewis as Biblical Commentator." *Reflections on the Psalms* (1958) is Lewis' only piece of biblical commentary. Because it comes late in Lewis' life, Anderson suggests that the claims of some scholars and biographers that Lewis gave up on apologetics and theology in 1947 appear to be unfounded, for Lewis' ability to make spiritual matters accessible to the general reader prove to be unabated in his commentary on the Psalms. In fact, *Reflections on the Psalms* gained him an invitation from Lambeth Palace to join The Commission to Revise the Psalter. While we may not agree with every claim that Lewis makes in *Reflections on the Psalms*, the work is a helpful antidote to those scholarly works which tend to atomize the biblical texts, for it begins where all effective studies on the Psalms arguably should begin—with the Psalms as coherent and unified poems. As poems, Lewis claims and Anderson demonstrates, the Psalms appeal to their readers by combining ethics, emotion, and logic. The point is that the Psalms employ more than reason to communicate, and this understanding is one of the contributions Lewis makes to their study. Anderson's study of Lewis' work on the Psalms opens up these three ways of entering the world of the Psalms and understanding them as they were composed. Christians throughout the ages have loved the Psalms, and Anderson explicates how Lewis "rehabilitates" the Psalms for modern Christians who may not know how to appreciate the Psalms appropriately.

The next chapter tackles a subject that, for many in our culture, is a social issue. For Lewis, however, it was a spiritual matter. How does Lewis understand hierarchy and how do his understandings of hierarchy help us today—or even fit our culture at all? These are the questions that Steve Boyer considers in "A Kneeling and a Sceptered Love: Lewis' Perilous Passion for Inequality." A superficial reading of Lewis has resulted in more heat than light on this subject, for his opponents brand him as a misogynist and see his claims about hierarchy as merely a smokescreen for male power over women. Boyer demonstrates, however, that Lewis' understanding of hierarchy is much larger and deeper than gender, for hierarchy is grounded in the created order—or, more properly stated, in the relationship of God and his creation. That relationship is, necessarily, unequal—and it is this inequality which is built into creation. Lewis celebrates this inequality and encourages modern people to do the same. Were Boyer (or Lewis) to leave it at that, however, might hierarchy not become dangerous? Could it not encourage political, social and sexual abuse? Of course; history is full of examples of such abuse. The abuse of hierarchy and inequality, however, is not a reason to reject it altogether. In this chapter, Boyer looks critically at Lewis' comments on inequality and hierarchy and offers perspective for us today on this vexed subject.

The last chapter in this section demonstrates the expansive scope of Lewis' spiritual view and the effectiveness of his Christian witness in his writings. In "Wilderness, Arcadia and Longing: Mythic Landscapes and the Experience of Reality," Kip Redick considers how the landscapes in Lewis' fiction evoke spiritual longing—what Lewis often called *Sehnsucht*—in the reader. Of course much has been written on Lewis' expression of "the argument from desire" or the spiritual longing for God inherent in all people of all times and in all places. In this chapter, Redick defines and explains spiritual longing, shows how Lewis' landscapes evoke it, and outlines the tradition in which Lewis is writing. Redick comments on the landscapes in the Space Trilogy,

Narnia, and *Till We Have Faces* which stir up the reader's spiritual longing. The only disappointment in this chapter is that Redick does not write more.

Part Three, "The Baptized Cosmos—Narnia and the Ransom Trilogy," explores some of what Lewis wrote on the longing we all share for something this world cannot satisfy. Lewis once wrote that "all the leaves of the New Testament are rustling with the rumour [sic]..." of a reality grounded in God Himself ("The Weight of Glory" 37). In a similar vein, he believed that all of nature and all of our experiences "rustle" with hints of God, attracting us to Himself. For Lewis, one way God draws us to Himself is by creating in us a desire that only He can satisfy. St. Augustine confesses his similar conviction that God made us in such a way as to be incomplete without Him—and we know it instinctively (*Confessions* 3). We sometimes call this notion "The Argument from Desire." The argument proceeds like this: there is a desire in the human heart which nothing in this world can satisfy; all desires were made to be satisfied; if nothing in this world can satisfy the desire in the heart, then it must be satisfied by something in another "world." Lewis came to understand that it is not "something" in another world that satisfies this spiritual desire, but it is God Himself who satisfies it (*Surprised by Joy* 221-227). He often referred to this desire that cannot be satisfied with such words as *longing, joy,* or *Sehnsucht*. To use another of Lewis' favorite images, we live in the "Shadowlands," and our real "home" is with God. He is the real Reality, and we long to be re-united with him. For writers like Lewis—and countless others—God provides hints of Himself in everyday objects and events. In the third section of the book, "The Baptized Cosmos," we look at longing and joy in Lewis' fiction.

Part Three begins with Samuel Joeckel's "The Spirit of Comedy in *The Chronicles of Narnia*." Starting from what some readers might think an unlikely source, the ancient Greek god Bacchus, Joeckel suggests that in *The Chronicles of Narnia* Lewis expresses wildness and laughter as good things. Now Bacchus in many ancient accounts is given to drunken revels and lewdness. Joeckel suggests, however, that Bacchus is tamed in Narnia and comes to represent a healthy impulse in the good characters of the stories. Laughter and joy in Narnia are cleansed of their impurities and become simply delightful expressions of goodness and joy; they are "baptized," as it were.

It is not all joy and laughter in Narnia, however. Even in these children's stories, Lewis faces squarely the evil side of things. Longing for God is good, but that same longing is often twisted into sinful desires that destroy the image of God in us, not build it up. Longing cuts both ways. It is this side of Narnia that Elizabeth Hardy considers in her essay, "A High and Lonely

Destiny: Sources for Jadis, the White Witch, in Milton's *Paradise Lost* and Spenser's *The Faerie Queene*." Hardy examines two English writers whom Lewis admired—Edmund Spenser and John Milton—and in their poetry she finds prototypes of Jadis and demonstrates the literary lineage of Lewis' White Witch. Despite her claims to power and priority, Jadis is a pretender to the throne of Narnia and a trickster. Like Satan in *Paradise Lost*, to choose one of the prototypes Hardy comments on, Jadis has twisted the naturally good longings for deity into a desire for her own divinity. Aslan does not fill her with joy as he does Peter, Susan, and Lucy Pevensie early in *The Lion, the Witch, and the Wardrobe*; rather, he fills her with hatred and fear. Hardy's analysis of the earlier analogues to Jadis in Spenser and Milton enriches our understanding of Jadis and our appreciation of what Lewis is doing with her character. Jadis and the other evil characters in *The Chronicles of Narnia* are the reasons why the cosmos must be "baptized" if it is to be joyful.

Too bad Philip Pullman does not see it that way. In his fantasy trilogy, *His Dark Materials*, Pullman offers an alternative to Narnia which inverts all that is good in Narnia. Taking his cue from Pullman's trilogy, David Rosenberg offers an incisive and up-to-date analysis of how Lewis presents the created order in *The Chronicles of Narnia*. Is the created order in Narnia evil or good? Is Pullman correct in his claims that Lewis denigrates the material world so as to elevate heaven? What is the relationship of God to his creation? These are Rosenberg's starting points. Rosenberg's essay goes in two directions, analyzing Pullman's *His Dark Materials* with singular clarity and explaining Lewis' appreciation of the created order as one of God's self-revelations. What better world than Narnia in which to come to such an appreciation? Rosenberg shows us one way in which Narnia helps us think afresh about our own world.

For the writer of the last chapter in this section, two of Lewis' novels in the science fiction trilogy, *Out of the Silent Planet* and *Perelandra*, not only suggest a baptized cosmos; they incarnate it. In "Why Wells is from Mars, Bergson from Venus," Sanford Schwartz demonstrates that Lewis removes us from earth to the other planets so that we can "re-view" the cosmos and our place in it from a thoroughly transformed perspective. In Schwartz's fresh reading of the science fiction trilogy, Lewis begins with the modern ideas of Darwinian evolution and Bergsonian cosmic development and transforms the natural into the spiritual. Readers go along for the inter-planetary ride, as it were, finding their own modernist assumptions challenged, shown to be wanting, and finally re-shaped in terms of the Christian tradition. What was it Lewis said about "smuggling theology past the watchful dragons"?

Introduction

Part Four reminds us that Lewis taught medieval and Renaissance English literature at Magdalen College, Oxford from 1925 to 1954 and at Magdalene College, Cambridge until a few months before he died in 1963. While he is known popularly for his apologetics and his fiction, he wrote scholarly works that were significant contributions to the field and, of course, he wrote fiction and poetry himself. We might say he was a practitioner as well as a scholar. Lewis' first work of literary scholarship, *The Allegory of Love* (1936), was an influential study of the allegorical love poetry of the Middle Ages. A few years later, he "rehabilitated" John Milton's important Christian epic for the modern reader with the publication of *A Preface to* Paradise Lost (1942)—still an accessible and helpful introduction to the great poem for modern students, many of whom know little about Milton's Christianity and who may even be hostile toward it. And in 1954 he published the magisterial *English Literature in the Sixteenth Century, Excluding Drama*—a comprehensive and fresh look at an important period of English literature. This final section looks in two directions—first to Lewis' understanding of the medieval worldview and then to his last novel, *Till We Have Faces*.

This last section begins with Lewis' explanation of the medieval model of reality. In "*The Discarded Image*: Patterns of Truth and Fantasy," David Hogg asks two questions. First, did the people of the European Middle Ages have a coherent model of reality? And, if so, did Lewis get it right? Lewis had good reasons for writing about the worldview of medieval Europe—not only to describe its great beauty, but also to help us see that we moderns also have a perspective from which we view our world. We would do well to take Lewis' hint and look at our own modern model of reality. We may not spend much time thinking consciously about the way we look at the world, but our understandings of it are framed in a largely naturalistic and materialistic way that excludes the transcendent; like others before us, we have certain blind spots. Hogg re-examines modern culture by seeing it alongside medieval culture with Lewis as his guide.

In "The Classical Sub-text in *Till We Have Faces*," Ian Storey helps us understand Lewis' last novel which was sub-titled, "A Myth Retold." To be sure, Lewis "re tells" the ancient Greek myth of Cupid and Psyche—this much is readily apparent. It should come as no surprise to us either then that he would suffuse allusions to classical literature and mythology throughout the novel, for one of his university degrees, we should remember, was in the "Greats"—classics, philosophy, and ancient history. Like countless other writers before him, Lewis "married" his Christianity with classical Greek and Roman literature, expressing the one through the other. He is in good company here, from Augustine and Aquinas to Luther and Calvin, and from Chaucer and Shakespeare to Dante and Milton. Storey's analysis mines one rich vein of Lewis' imagination and deepens our appreciation for *Till We Have Faces*.

Complementing Ian Storey's explanation of classical allusions in *Till We Have Faces*, Stephen Yandell explains the novel's medieval affinities. The idea that the novel would reflect medieval influences should not surprise us any more than finding its classical allusions, for Lewis was a medievalist by profession. Specifically, Yandell discovers motifs and patterns in the fourteenth-century anonymous *Pearl* poem which are paralleled in *Till We Have Faces*. The multiple layers in the novel, its loss-and-regain patterns, and even its dream-vision motif echo the *Pearl* poem, and understanding the earlier poem helps us understand the novel. Readers of Michael Ward's *Planet Narnia: The Seven Heavens in the Imagination of C. S. Lewis* will find in Stephen Yandell's study another layer to enrich their re-reading of Lewis's last work of fiction.

It has been said often, but that does not make it less true: C. S. Lewis was a man for all times. He wrote about matters that were universal in significance, and he did so in ways that made difficult issues accessible to all people of good will. Theology and philosophy, psychology and ethics—he spoke to their central issues with insight and clarity. He was truly a man for all seasons. He was also a man for all readers, for he communicated in multiple types and registers of writing—imaginative fiction, poetry, literary criticism, apologetics, biblical exegesis, social criticism, satire, and hundreds of letters. The essays in this volume reflect the breadth of Lewis' writings. At the same time, Lewis' Christian faith gave him a unified and coherent voice, so it comes as no surprise that the present essays demonstrate a remarkable coherence. When Lewis wrote social criticism, he did so from a Christian perspective. In his apologetics, he remembered what he had learned early in life as an atheist and provided Christian answers to universal questions. In his imaginative writings, Lewis incarnated a spiritual longing in his characters and evoked that same spiritual longing in his readers—certainly one of the reasons why his fiction is perennially popular. Finally, Lewis positions himself squarely in the great, central Christian tradition in Western literature, helping his readers think about the important issues of life from this perspective. Lewis' Christianity permeated every aspect of his character, unifying all he thought and wrote. "I believe in Christianity as I believe that the Sun has risen," Lewis said in "Is Theology Poetry?", "not only because I see it, but because by it I see everything else" (106).

WORKS CITED

Augustine. *Confessions*. 2nd Ed. Trans. F. J. Sheed. Introduction by Peter Brown. Ed. Michael P. Foley. Indianapolis: Hackett Publishing Co., Inc., 2006.

Lewis, C. S. "Christian Apologetics." *God in the Dock: Essays on Theology and Ethics*. Ed. Walter Hooper. Grand Rapids: Eerdmans, 1970. 89-103.

—. The Collected Letters of *C. S. Lewis: Books, Broadcasts, and the War, 1931-1949*. Ed. Walter Hooper. Vol. 2. New York: HarperSanFrancisco, 2004.

—. *An Experiment in Criticism*. Cambridge: Cambridge UP, 1961.

—. "The Founding of the Oxford Socratic Club." *God in the Dock: Essays on Theology and Ethics*. Ed. Walter Hooper. Grand Rapids: Eerdmans, 1970. 126-128.

—. Introductory. *Reflections on the Psalms*. San Diego: Harvest Books, nd. 1-8.

—. "Is Theology Poetry?" *"The Weight of Glory" and Other Addresses*. Ed. and with an Introduction by Walter Hooper. New York: Touchstone, 1996. 90-106.

—. Preface. *Mere Christianity*. New York: HarperCollins, 2001. vii-xvi.

—. *The Problem of Pain*. New York: Touchstone, 1996.

—. "Rejoinder to Dr. Pittenger." *God in the Dock: Essays on Theology and Ethics*. Ed. Walter Hooper. Grand Rapids: Eerdmans, 1970. 177-183.

—. *Surprised by Joy: The Shape of My Early Life*. New York: Harcourt Brace, 1956.

—. "The Weight of Glory." *"The Weight of Glory" and Other Addresses*. Ed. and with an Introduction by Walter Hooper. New York: Touchstone, 1996. 25-40.

Editing C. S. Lewis

Walter Hooper

I have been invited to write about the forty-five years I have spent editing the writings of C. S. Lewis, and I begin with a little background. I came originally from Reidsville, North Carolina, and I began corresponding with Lewis in 1954. While teaching at the University of Kentucky, I visited Lewis in Oxford during the summer of 1963. We became friends, and I moved into his house as his secretary. He wanted this to be a permanent arrangement and I agreed to give up my job in Kentucky and return to Oxford in 1964. When I got back to Kentucky I resigned my job and was preparing to rejoin Lewis in January 1964. Then, on 22 November 1963 President J. F. Kennedy was assassinated. Hours after learning of his death, I was told that C. S. Lewis had died the same hour. Even now, I can hardly bear to think about that terrible day.

Lewis had been the center of my life since I first came across his writings in 1953. And during the months we were together I had come to love him. Now everything seemed lost. However, as things settled down I received a letter from those friends of Lewis I had come to know best during the summer of 1963, Dr Austin Farrer, the Warden of Keble College, and his wife Katharine. They felt there was something for me to do in Oxford, and they urged me to come back and stay with them in Keble College.

I took them at their word, and returned to Oxford in January 1964. I was a guest of the Farrers in Keble College, and I soon came to know Lewis' brother, Warnie. To avoid confusion, I will give them the names their friends used. C. S. Lewis was called Jack, and Warren Lewis was known as Warnie. While my loss was perhaps nothing compared to Warnie's, we met as friends both of whom had lost a great deal. Over time I realized that, although Warnie was four years older than Jack, his dependence on Jack made him in some ways the younger of the two. Certainly what Jack said about the death of their mother when they were children was true—again—for Warnie: "There was to be... no more of the old security. It was sea and islands now; the great continent had sunk like Atlantis" (*Surprised by Joy* 15).

Warnie could have remained at The Kilns. This was the house bought jointly in 1930 by the Lewis brothers and Mrs. Jane Moore—the mother of Jack's friend, Paddy, who was killed in the First War, and whom Jack came to call his "adopted mother." It was agreed that The Kilns would be the home of the Lewis brothers as long as they lived, after which it would pass to Mrs. Moore's daughter, Maureen. So Warnie could have spent the rest of his life there. But he panicked. He feared he would not have enough to pay the taxes, and I arrived to find that he had already bought a small house a quarter of a mile away in 51 Ringwood Road. He thought this would be cheaper to run. When C. S. Lewis died his step-sons, David and Douglas, were aged 19 and 18. They were both away in college, but they were given a home with their mother's greatest friend, Miss Jean Wakeman. No one could have proved better at being a substitute-mother than this lovable woman who still lives in Oxford.

I had observed in Jack Lewis at moments an almost comical fear of going broke. It was something he shared with his father, despite the fact that none of the Lewises was ever close to such a catastrophe. It turned out that Warnie inherited all his brother's copyrights, but the Estate had not yet been settled, and Warnie feared the worst. Jack's Estate was evaluated at approximately £59,000 and the government took £20,000 in inheritance tax. As anyone in England can buy a copy of anyone's will, I see no harm in revealing that Jack left the copyrights in his books to Warnie for the rest of his life, after which they would go to his two step-sons. The Estate was settled after a few months, but royalties depend on the sale of books, and Warnie had no idea whether or not his brother's books would continue to sell. This uncertain state of affairs was still causing him terrible anxiety as late as 1 September 1964 when he wrote in his diary, *Brothers and Friends: The Diaries of Major Warren Hamilton Lewis*:

> My life continues very desolate, and I seem to miss my dear Jack more rather than less as time goes on...Whilst the perpetual ache of Jack's absence is the chief cause of my depression it is not the only one. He will soon have left me ten months ago, and still I haven't the smallest idea of the amount of my income or the extent of my liabilities. The thing is becoming a nightmare and is rarely out of my thoughts for an hour together. (254)

Meanwhile, in preparation for moving out of The Kilns and into the small house, Warnie was "downsizing" to an almost alarming degree. He knew it had to be done, and I remember that he gave all Joy's clothes to his housekeeper, Mrs. Molly Miller. Warnie had set aside those things in the brothers' lives which had a special significance for them, such as diaries and family mementoes, but the rest had to go. Warnie was a historian, not an English scholar, nor even a scholar of his brother's writings. He loved his brother's Christian apologetics, but I remember him picking up a copy of Jack's *English Literature in the Sixteenth Century* and saying, "I don't suppose anyone has ever read this." "I have," I replied. "*Really*?!" he said, "I thought it was the kind of things scholars *had* to write, but that no one read."

I have mentioned elsewhere the day I went out to The Kilns to learn from Lewis' gardener, Fred Paxford, that a bonfire had been burning for three days (*The Dark Tower and Other Stories* 7). Paxford knew I loved anything in C. S. Lewis' hand and he told me I had arrived just in time: that morning he had been instructed to add to the fire a mass of notebooks and other papers that had belonged to C.S.L. He urged Warnie to delay until I could see them. When I showed up Warnie told me I could have the papers so long as they were removed that very day.

What papers went into the fire I never discovered. George Sayer believed that Lewis had written a sequel to *Surprised by Joy*. If so, it was never found. I wondered then, as I still wonder now, what happened to the correspondence between Lewis and Joy. Was it destroyed in this fire? In any event, let me say that none of this surprised me. Neither of the brothers felt the reverence for their manuscripts which we feel. When I was getting to know Jack Lewis I asked what he did with his manuscripts and he told me that after writing a book, such as *The Lion, the Witch and the Wardrobe*, he turned the manuscript over and wrote another book on the other side. He then threw the manuscript away. I did not need to express my horror for he saw it in my face, and from that point on he began giving me the manuscripts of whatever he had published or was about to publish, the first of which was *Letters to Malcolm*, now in the Bodleian Library. When Warnie saw the delight I took in the notebooks and various papers he gave me—those originally destined for the fire—he was delighted that I cared so much for them.

One of the items saved from the fire was a blue folder of poems Jack had been working on in his Magdalene College rooms in Cambridge. When Jack sent me over to Cambridge in August 1963 to clear out his rooms he begged me to be sure I brought the folder back to Oxford and put it in his hands, so precious were the poems to him. When I explained to Warnie that his brother had been getting some of his poems together for publication, he invited me to become the editor of his brother's literary remains—thus setting the course of my life for the next forty-five years.

It was not, however, Warnie alone who could determine what would be published, but the Trustees of C. S. Lewis' literary estate, his old friends Owen Barfield and Cecil Harwood, Lewis' exact contemporaries. I had known both for some time, and if they felt any resentment about my being asked to edit their friend's writings I never detected it. They said they were pleased, and I believe they were because, while they were exactly Jack Lewis' age, they had been waiting for their retirement in order to pen the books they wanted to write. Barfield, the lawyer, was just beginning his "second life" as a speaker on American campuses, and he was to write many books from 1964 onwards. Cecil Harwood, who lives in my memory as one of the nicest men I ever met, was, as he had been for forty years, involved in Anthroposophy and teaching in a Rudolph Steiner school. In brief, responsibility for Jack's literary estate fell on them at an inconvenient time, and they welcomed the young man Jack had already asked to help him.

Another whom I met soon after arriving in Oxford was Tolkien, who could hardly have been kinder to me and who soon introduced me to his whole family. Tolkien helped me see why Lewis' Christian writings made him so unpopular with his unbelieving colleagues, and I remember him saying over and over, "Lewis was driven to write Christian apologetics by his *conscience*!" Some have argued that Lewis and Tolkien were no longer friends in the last years of Lewis' life. I could see nothing like that. They seemed devoted to one another.

What, then, about my reflections on editing Lewis? Well, Jack was gone, but not his literary estate. What could be done about it?

There are a number of things you can do about a literary estate. (1) You can do as Warnie was to do years later—have it settled by lawyers who do not have a clue about books and their proliferation, but who merely settle things. I do not think any of Warnie's books were reprinted after his estate was wound up. (2) You can pay the government what is owing to them and leave it to publishers to decide if they reprint your books. (3) Or you can do as Owen Barfield, Cecil Harwood and I did—fight with all our might to keep C. S. Lewis' books in print—and add more books to the list!

I am afraid I have been tamed by the English, and am not as aggressive with publishers as I once was. But in 1964 Barfield, Harwood and the Farrers liked my determination and they did whatever they could to cheer me on. But it was not as easy as I am making it sound.

I read somewhere that "Walter Hooper kicked off his career by publishing Lewis' *Poems*." I remember nothing like that. I remember, first, the bepuzzlement and anger I felt on seeing Lewis' books remaindered in various Oxford bookshops. It caused me to recall an argument I had with Lewis. He believed that when an author died his books usually stopped selling after about three years. I argued that this could not happen with his books! But as I was later to learn Lewis was right in thinking that the sales of most authors' books usual trail off to nothing when they die.

What everyone in England was conscious of at the time was the excitement caused by the publication of J. A. T. Robinson's *Honest to God* (1963), a chapter of which Lewis had criticized a few months before he died. At any other time the Bishop's book would have been disregarded. It 1963 it became a "media event"—a best seller. What was it all about? The Bishop said if Christianity is to mean anything in the future to more than "a tiny religious remnant" it would have to learn a new language in which "the most fundamental categories of our theology—of God, of the supernatural, and of religion itself—must go into the melting" (*Honest to God* 7-8). He suggested that we are even called to a "Copernican Revolution" in which "the God of traditional theology" must be given up "in any form" (17-18).

Asked to comment on the book, Lewis said calmly: "The Bishop of Woolwich will disturb most of us Christian laymen less then he anticipates. We have long abandoned belief in a God who sits on a throne in a localized heaven. We call that belief anthropomorphism, and it was officially condemned before our time. There is something about this in Gibbon" (Hooper, *C. S. Lewis: A Companion and Guide* 115).

It was nevertheless true that even the Bishop's drawing attention to the fact that the phrase "He came down From Heaven" is a metaphor—forgetting that there is no other way of talking except by metaphors—helped open up a gap between the new, secular mentality and the Churches. Lewis, as we all know, was unwilling to allow the smallest particle of traditional doctrine to be thrown overboard unexamined; Robinson, a man for the 1960's, was willing to de-mythologize almost anything of which modernity might be suspicious. When Bishop Robinson talked about the problem of theological language the papers made it sound as if he did not believe, and soon many theologians were deserting the ranks of the orthodox for the "New Reformation" as Robinson called it. Some of you may remember that it was not long before the States was involved in a similar movement—in this case the "Death of God" movement and its leader, Thomas Altizer, who was pictured on the cover of *Time* magazine on 8 April 1966.

While all this was going on the Second Vatican Council met in Rome from 1962 to 1965, and one of the most positive things to emerge from this Council was the Decree on Ecumenism. "Catholics," it said, "in their ecumenical work, must assuredly be concerned for their separated brethren, praying for them, keeping them informed about the Church, making the first approaches toward them" (4). I am sure that this led many Catholics to read Lewis for the first time. At the same time the Catholic Church began dialogues with many Protestant bodies. But years before the Second Vatican Council one Catholic bishop was reading *The Screwtape Letters* with his Polish students. He of course became Pope John Paul II who had a special regard for *The Four Loves*.

The world was thrown into confusion during the years immediately after Lewis' death, and what alarmed me more than anything was that publishers were torn between publishing the kind of orthodox Christianity that had been in vogue, or going for works on the New Reformation and the Demythologizing of the Gospel.

While waiting for things to settle down, I spent most of my time editing Lewis' volume of *Poems*. Some have wondered why I did not begin with a scholarly edition of the poems, showing all the variations the poems have undergone. But at that time this would have meant certain defeat as far as getting people to read the poems. You must remember that more than anything I wanted to keep Lewis' books in print and before the public. That was a battle we could not afford to lose.

The reason I began with the poems is because they meant so much to Lewis. But I was not alone in feeling this was the right way to begin. Austin and Katharine Farrer went over every version of every poem, trying to determine which version Lewis would have published. Not those we might prefer, but those the author preferred. I had the cooperation of Barfield and Harwood who loved their friend's poems and who, though they had seen many of them as they were being written, had never seen so many together.

I discovered from my time with Jack Lewis that he had forgotten many of his poems and other works, for no man I believe was so humble, so almost totally forgetful of himself. Except for the poems in the blue folder brought back from Cambridge, he had few, if any, of the poems published in various periodicals. I expect that most of those who read this will have better collections of Lewis First Editions than Lewis. I do not think he had more than half a dozen of his own books.

Because Lewis preserved so few of his own works, I spent much of my time in what is to me the most glorious of academic places—the Bodleian Library, the main library of Oxford University. There is still so very much I do not know about Lewis and his writings, but when I come within sight of that great library I always say to myself: "I may not find it, but what I want to know is in that building!" You should know that the Bodleian gets copies of everything published in Great Britain. I do not know how the staff could have been so patient with me for I know I was a great nuisance. I made out a list of publications I knew Lewis had published in, and a list of those he might have published in, and I would go through every copy of a weekly such as the church paper, *The Guardian*—the one in which *Screwtape* originally appeared—page by page from about 1930 to 1963. The only thing to do was begin at the beginning and look at each page.

I have mentioned elsewhere the only time when during these years of searching I wish I could have worn a mask. A young English don told me that he was almost certain Lewis had published an essay in a monthly called *Men Only*. I got it into my head that this must be a magazine about deep-sea fishing or hunting bears, in any event, the activities of the "outdoor man." And so I ordered up every copy of *Men Only* from 1930 to 1963.

As it turned out, I sat every day across the desk from a very tall Catholic priest who turned out to be Fr. Ian Boyd, later to become the distinguished editor of *The Chesterton Review*. You must imagine me sitting across from Fr. Boyd awaiting the arrival of those deep-sea fishing journals when one of the staff members arrived with a trolley piled high with copies of *Men Only*. "And there are many *more* copies," she said, "when you finish these." From the moment I opened the first issue of *Men Only* I could not look at Fr. Boyd, though I could feel his eyes on me. *Men Only* had nothing to do with deep-sea fishing or bear hunting. It was pure pornography of the most graphic kind. So why did I spend two solid weeks examining every issue of *Men Only*? Because, it did contain many articles by notable writers such as C. Day-Lewis, Robert Graves and others, but nothing, as it turned out, by C. S. Lewis. The best thing that came out of *Men Only* was that, after a rocky start, Fr. Boyd did finally believe my good intentions and we are now good friends. Those thousands of hours spent in the Bodleian led me to include in a pretty full Bibliography of Lewis' writings in the first volume of essays about him, *Light on C. S. Lewis* (1965), which contains valuable pieces by Owen Barfield, Nevill Coghill, John Lawlor and others who knew Lewis well.

Warnie could not move into the smaller house until May of 1964 and he was working furiously on what he intended to be a biography of his brother.

He had advertised for copies of his brother's letters and as there was no such thing as photocopying in Oxford, I took my typewriter up to The Kilns to help copy those letters various correspondents had lent. I regret now that I was not more vigilant about the letters we borrowed.

Because Warnie intended to write a biography, not edit a volume of letters, he spent his time copying what were really quotations from Jack's letters. While he worked with great speed, I plodded along typing entire letters. If only there had been a way of photocopying we might have preserved many letters that may be lost forever. In the end, about three-quarters of Warnie's book was made up of quotations from the letters, with only about a fourth being narrative. It did not have the makings of a biography and poor Warnie was heartbroken when Geoffrey Bles published it as *Letters of C. S. Lewis* with a Memoir by W. H. Lewis (1966).

But that was still two years away, and I was as excited as I have ever been in my life when I saw the latest C. S. Lewis book, *Letters to Malcolm*, appear in bookshop windows on 27 January 1964, to be followed by *The Discarded Image* on 7 May of that same year. They were followed in October by Lewis' *Poems*.

I have to admit to being an essentially lazy man. You will remember how much Lewis loved the great Italian epics by Ariosto and Boirdo and Tasso. In his *Allegory of Love* he described his "ideal happiness" would be "to be always convalescent from some small illness and always seated in a window that overlooked the sea, there to read those poems eight hours of each happy day" (304). I would choose the same method of happiness, except that I would be reading every work of Lewis' eight hours of each happy day.

What forced me to work harder with the editing was a chance comment I heard in a meeting with Lewis' publisher, Jock Gibb. He said, "Every *new* book by an author helps sell the old ones." It may not happen with every author but it certainly seems to be true of Lewis, and this has spurred me on as much as anything. "Every *new* book helps to sell the *old* ones."

It had become impossible to spend more than a few hours a day editing Lewis' papers because I was financially very insecure and needed to work. I had spent two years in an American seminary, and Austin Farrer wanted me to complete my studies in theology and be ordained an Anglican clergyman. I lived for a year with Warnie in the small house in Ringwood Road—The Kilns being rented at this time—while I read theology in Oxford. After being ordained I was appointed Chaplain of Wadham College, an appointment at that time always limited to two years. I loved the work, but it still did not pay the bills and I got some work teaching English literature in the local polytechnic college. From Wadham I went to Jesus College where I was Chaplain from 1967 to 1971. I was very homesick my first two years in Oxford, and I think being poor made it worse. On one occasion during my first year I borrowed money from Lewis' gardener to entertain some American guests.

But I only bring this in to explain why my work on Lewis' papers could not be hurried. It was during the years at Wadham College, 1965-1967, that I edited Lewis' *Studies in Medieval and Renaissance Literature* (1966), and *Of Other Worlds* (1966) and *Christian Reflections* (1967). These volumes contained some of the papers Warnie gave me before he left The Kilns, as well as uncollected pieces Lewis had published in various periodicals and forgot about. I like everything Lewis wrote—but I expect I share with you a particular interest in his Christian apologetics.

From the time I began editing Lewis I have tried to keep in mind that it is his work—not mine—and that I should not include in the preface or notes anything that contradicts Lewis' own writings. This was hardly a difficulty for me because there are, I expect, few thoughts in my mind that did not come from Lewis. It was something of a surprise to find that I am often criticized for my lack of analysis. Perhaps I am at fault, but it does not worry me. In a letter to the great William Blake scholar, Kathleen Raine, Lewis spelled out what I have long regarded as my model in editing Lewis: "Plenty of fact," he said, "reasoning as brief and clear as English sunshine, and no personal comment" (*The Collected Letters of C. S. Lewis: Volume III, Narnia, Cambridge and Joy 1950-1963*, letter of 7 November 1963, 1477).

A good many commentators have complained that Lewis' work is "dated." Owen Barfield and I discussed this many times, and he did more than anyone to help me see that those who have written about what Lewis "should have said" have wanted to replace Lewis' works with vogue words that invariably have briefer "shelf lives" than what he originally wrote. I would not replace a single word in any of Lewis' books. What interests me far more is that Lewis goes on and on and on being read and picking up new converts. Owen had seen so many of his friends' works go out of print when they died that he often remarked about Lewis' growing popularity, "How much longer will it last?"

It is inevitable that language and much else will change. To use the title Lewis chose for the Introduction to his *English Literature in the Sixteenth Century* (1954)—there will be "New Learning and New Ignorance." I am going to tell you why I have so much faith in Lewis' writings retaining their relevance. I do this by putting together passages from two great Christians who did not know one another but overlapped.

The first is Lewis who, in his essay on "Dogma and the Universe" answered the question, "How can an unchanging system survive the continual increase of knowledge?" His answer was that

> ... Wherever there is real progress in knowledge, there is some knowledge that is not superseded. Indeed, the very possibility of progress demands that there should be an unchanging element.... I take it we should all agree to find this sort of unchanging element in the simple rules of mathematics. I would add to these the primary principles of morality. And I would also add the fundamental doctrines of Christianity. To put it in rather more technical language, I claim that the positive historical statements made by Christianity have the power, elsewhere found chiefly in formal principles, of receiving, without intrinsic change, the increasing complexity of meaning which increasing knowledge puts into them. (45)

The second is Pope John XXIII who, when he opened the Second Vatican Council in 1962, said:

> The deposit of faith itself and the truths contained in our venerable doctrine are one thing, and the manner in which they are annunciated is another, provided that the same fundamental sense and meaning is maintained. (*Acta Apostolicae Sedae* 54, 791-792)

That, I think, says it all. The Deposit of Faith—that is, the body of saving truth entrusted by Christ to the Apostles and handed on by them (e.g. 1 Tim 6:20; 2 Tim 1:12-13)—is one thing—the way of presenting it, whether by apologetics, fairy tales, romances—is another—but however it is presented it must retain the "same sense and meaning" contained in the Gospel. That is never "dated"! Or, as Lewis said in *The Four Loves*, "All that is not eternal is eternally out of date" (156). I always had this in mind when editing anything by C. S. Lewis.

During my three years at Jesus College—1976-1971—I managed to keep together several of the geniuses of Lewis. Those years saw the publication of three new books by Lewis, *Narrative Poems* (1969), *Selected Literary Essays* (1969), and the one which I worked hardest on: *God in the Dock: Essays on Theology and Ethics* (1970). This last was published by Eerdmans of Grand Rapids, and I think I must have still had plenty of American determination. I was appalled when the publishers sent me a contract offering Lewis a royalty of 10%--that is what you give authors for their first book. Owen Barfield stared open-mouthed which I struck through 10% and wrote 15%. To me Lewis was not on trial—but going on from the high position he had when he died. To my surprise, the publishers agreed and paid 15%!

Let me say before going any further that I always knew that anything I wrote in my prefaces pales into insignificance beside the writings of Lewis. On 7 June 1977 this was etched on my mind. I had a visit From Charles Colson, the founder of Prison Fellowship. Before we went to the Bird and Baby for lunch Colson began praising *God in the Dock*. "You must read it!" he said. "*Promise* me you will read it!" I did not have the heart to mention that I had edited the book, for Charles Colson—rightly—was interested in what Lewis said.

You must not imagine me acting alone in this editing. Lewis' many friends offered their help and encouragement every step of the way. Books were copyrighted for a period of fifty years at that time, and because Barfield and Harwood, the original Trustees of the Lewis Estate, knew they were not likely to survive another half century, they appointed me an additional Trustee in 1967. We worked as a team, and with the encouragement of Lewis' many other friends, Tolkien, of course, but also Hugh Dyson, Nevill Coghill, Humphrey Havard, Commander Dundas-Grant, Austin and Katharine Farrer, Roger Lancelyn Green and others.

When I gave Professor Tolkien a copy of Lewis' *God in the Dock*, he said "You know, Jack Lewis is the only friend I have who has published more *after* his death than before!" "The same," I said, "will happen to you." "Oh, no it won't!" he said. "Christopher will find that I've left very little, and in any event, he won't know what to do with it." I can not imagine anyone being proved so wrong. Christopher Tolkien has done his father immensely proud. Indeed, what Tolkien said about Lewis' writings has proved far truer of his own: J. R. R. Tolkien has published far more since he died than before.

By the time I was in my last year as Chaplain of Jesus College the Lewis Estate had turned a corner, and I knew Lewis had been wrong about the sales of his books, and that I had been right. I will probably never fully understand what happened, but a huge change in the readership of Lewis' books was taking place. Those liberal denominations that abandoned Lewis in the 1960's were abandoning him still, but he was being read in great numbers by Catholics, and even more by Evangelicals everywhere. In other words, Lewis was popular with those who believed in the supernatural—in such miracles as the Resurrection of Christ.

Owen Barfield put me in charge of translations, and I was deeply touched to find that Polish translators—under the heel of Communism—were keen to translate Lewis' works. As they had almost no money I charged them the smallest amount possible—half a cent per book. I learned later that the moving force behind the Polish translations was the future Pope—John Paul II. But the Estate could easily afford to be generous to Poland for there was an enormous and growing interest in Lewis almost everywhere, especially in the States.

Warnie had continued to imagine he was very poor when he went to live in his little house near the Kilns, and one day I found him really afraid of "going off to the Poor House"—which institutions had long disappeared from England. "What would Tolkien say," he asked me, "if he were standing outside and they came and took me off to the Poor House?" I discovered that every time he received royalties from his brother's books he invested the money. Thus, when he got a bill for taxes, he did not have enough to pay. "But you still *have* the money," I argued. "But it's invested!" he replied. I mentioned the problem to Owen Barfield, and after this he withheld enough money from the royalties to pay the taxes, and gave the rest to Warnie.

The best thing to happen during this period was that in 1967 Warnie had enough of living extremely frugally in the little house. We both of us nearly froze to death. Our only heat was from little electric heaters and Warnie would only allow us to have one electric bar burning in whatever room we were in. We switched off the electric bar in the sitting-room when we went to the dining-room, and vice versa. The result was that neither room ever got really warm. I remember a poster that you saw everywhere at that time showing a glamorous woman leaning on a radiator advertising central heating and saying, "It's not a *sin* to be warm."

Warnie apparently agreed with this because he moved back to The Kilns in 1967, with his housekeeper and her husband there to look after him. The great bulwark of his life—Jack—had disappeared, and Warnie lost his ability to sustain any interest long enough to write another book. I tried pushing him, but several times he pulled me up short saying, "Remember, you're not Jack. You can't *make* me do anything." But what a nice man! I would give almost anything—always excepting my Cat—for another hour of his company. He was sometimes very like his brother, as sharp and entertaining. I know a number of people who enjoyed his company more than that of Jack, finding him more relaxing. The brothers, for all they had in common, were as different as chalk and cheese, but both so fine that if you were going to spend the rest of your life on a desert island with one of them—I am not sure which brother would be the wiser choice for you. Best of all would be to share the desert island with both of them.

I should mention that before I finished my final term at Jesus College in 1971 the Trustees of the Estate—Barfield and Harwood—talked to Warnie and I was promised a salary I could live on if in return I devoted myself full-time to the business of the Lewis Estate. And so a great burden was lifted from my mind.

We had been through so much together that I was shattered when Warnie died in April 1973—a few months before Tolkien died in September of that same year. Austin and Katharine Farrer had died in 1968 and 1972, and something of my deep love for them went into the biographies I wrote of them for Volume III of Lewis' *Collected Letters*. I still had Owen Barfield and a few others, but the great pillars that made up the world of the Inklings were disappearing. The best-natured of all Lewis' friends, Roger Lancelyn Green, was still a young man, and in 1969 he and I had started work on our biography of C. S. Lewis. Warnie had gone over all the chapters except the last. There were also what one might call "The Inkling children," many of whom became good friends. No one during my forty-five years in Oxford has been as kind to me as the children of J. R. R. Tolkien.

Meanwhile Warnie's death meant that Owen and I had to pay death duties for the second time on C. S. Lewis' Estate. But this time the government did not stick out its hand and say, "Pay me what you owe!" This was because it could not decide what we owed. They knew more about writers than I imagined. They told us that the sales of an author's books usually went down and down to almost nothing three years after he died, but that something "very different" had happened with those of C. S. Lewis. As a result, they could not decide what to charge in inheritance tax. We were responsible for passing the royalties on to those who had inherited them, but we dared not because we were personally responsible for the death duties. After, finally, getting our lawyer to force them to a decision, the Government came up with the figure of approximately £100,000. That sum represented 40% of what they estimated the Lewis copyrights to be worth—a much larger amount than the £20,000 paid when Lewis died.

What this meant for me was not more money in my pocket, but the realization that we had turned a corner. Lewis was becoming very popular again—in fact, more popular than he had been in his own lifetime. By this time I knew much of it had to do with such successful ventures as the New York C. S. Lewis Society, and their bulletin, *CSL*, which reached nearly everywhere. The Society was founded in 1969, and in the summer of 1969 I had a visit from one of its founding members, a man who should have been baptized "The Great Jim Como." Dr. Como and his fellow New Yorkers, as well of course as Professor Clyde Kilby of Wheaton College, were doing more than anyone to make Lewis better known in the United States, and their influence is more appropriately the subject of a book, not a mention in this paper.

In 1975 one of Lewis' oldest friends and Trustee, Cecil Harwood, died. This same year the Lewis Estate went through a major change. One of the most exacting of the Trustees' jobs concerned copyright. It had become hideously complicated, especially in the United States. Anyway, as both beneficiaries of Lewis' will lived abroad, and were unfairly forced to pay English income tax, they approached us about setting up of a C. S. Lewis Company. We saw the sense in this, and we made over our rights as Trustees to this new Company. Owen was nearly eighty and he enjoyed the chance to retire. I was asked to stay on as the Editor of Lewis, and because I had worked for almost nothing the first ten years, they promised me a pension when I retired. And so was born C. S. Lewis Pte Ltd., or the C. S. Lewis Company.

At the same time, Lewis' publisher, Jock Gibb, retired as Manager of Geoffrey Bles Ltd. Bles had been bought by Collins Publishers in 1953, and they had always published the paperbacks of Lewis' books. But Jock Gibb's retirement and the winding up of Geoffrey Bles Ltd. meant we were free to choose another publisher. I had never met Sir William Collins of Collins Publishers and I wondered if he would be as reasonable as Jock Gibb? As it turned out, the one I dealt with turned out to be a "she," not a "he"—in fact the other half of Collins Publishers.

Lady Collins—wife of Sir William Collins—was the pre-eminent builder of the Fontana religious list—and she had published Lewis' *Screwtape Letters* as one of her Fontana paperbacks in 1955. I had just started work on the most ambitious work I had yet undertaken, *They Stand Together: The Letters of C. S. Lewis to Arthur Greeves*, and Barfield and Harwood deputized me to discuss the matter with Lady Collins in April 1974. No one could have prepared me for such a meeting. I was shown into Lady Collins' office which was a beautiful eighteenth-century room, with a carved fireplace, the furniture covered in green velvet. Sitting in a chair with a Chihuahua on her lap was Lady Collins smoking a Russian cigarette. As Lewis would say, "My world was unmade." No woman had so completely overwhelmed me. Tea was served, from—of course—a Georgian silver teapot. Lady Collins was beautiful, svelte, calm, dignified, shrewd. For me this was almost the equivalent of Ransom meeting the Green Lady on Perelandra.

If she had told me to leap out of the window I would have gladly done so. But she was as interested in Lewis as I was, and we talked about what should happen about his books. When it came to the new one—*They Stand Together*—I stuck to my plan and said, "We will allow you to publish this new book on one condition—you bring back *two* of Lewis' books that have gone out of print." She looked up from playing with her dog and said: "*Which* two, and *which* would you like to begin with?" "*The Abolition of Man* must come first," I said. "All right," she said, "as long as you write the blurb to go on the cover." Lady Collins, a devout Roman Catholic, was as good as her word. It was with Lady Collins that I worked on *The Dark Tower, They Stand Together, Of This and Other Worlds*—which is dedicated to her—and several others. When Lady Collins retired in 1986 at the age of 85 I felt lost. We made a good team, and if anyone writes a history of C. S. Lewis and his publishers, a chapter should be devoted to that great lady.

But I must hurry along. Over time I became something of a "fixture" for Collins Publishers. I was asked to edit a day-by-day book of Lewis, and the result was *The Business of Heaven* (1984). As it turned out the older I got the more was expected of me. But let us be clear about one thing. If someone were able to write a full and true account of what has happened to the books of C. S. Lewis since he died in 1963 I might not warrant more than a footnote. I am certain it is a very complicated story, most of it probably unknowable. However it has come about, whenever I am very tired I say to myself: "Remember, this is what you *wanted* to happen. Don't complain."

In the late 1980's Owen Barfield and I decided I should edit the diary Lewis kept from 1922 to 1927. Our charming friend, Professor G. B. Tennyson of UCLA, was visiting from the States and brought to our attention the fact that, beginning with a couple of books in 1988, Lewis' life was taking on elements of a soap opera—with good characters and very bad characters. This happened, he thought, when a famous writer begins to attract people who are not really interested in a writer's works, but think instead of "characters"—some they like, some they hate violently. It, in turn, gives rise to what might be called "soap opera scholarship."

This was beginning to happen with C. S. Lewis and his old friend Mrs. Janie Moore. Owen Barfield had known Mrs. Moore well, and he was keen to correct the general picture of her, as "a kind of baleful stepmother and inexorable taskmistress" (Forward, *All My Road Before Me: The Diary of C. S. Lewis 1922-1927* x) that appeared in a recent work on Lewis. To correct this impression, Owen agreed to write a Foreword to the Diary. After deciding which portions of the diary to include, the publishers having made it clear they would not publish it all, I found myself tortured about what I should say about Lewis and Mrs. Moore in my Introduction. I had been the confidant of many of Lewis' friends over the years, and this was an instance in which I was not sure how much it was morally right to reveal. Since we met in 1969 I depended upon Jim Como to lead me through editorial thickets, and without a visit to New York to talk with him I am not sure I would ever have completed the Introduction to the Diary.

Our new publisher, Collins, meanwhile had an eye on what other publishers were bringing out about C. S. Lewis. After Colin Duriez published his *Handbook to C. S. Lewis* (1992) I had a visit from a member of HarperCollins, as the firm had now become, suggesting a "C. S. Lewis Handbook." "There is already one," I replied. "Yes," he said, "but not one by *you*." What HarperCollins wanted from me was a 137-page handbook mainly devoted to Narnia and Lewis' marriage. I spent four years on what they called *C. S. Lewis: A Companion & Guide* (1996), and I do not know whether to bow my head in shame, or to laugh, at how wide of the mark my "handbook" turned out to be. Why is it so long? Professor Tennyson was right. Lewis' life and writings were in some quarters taking on the quality of a soap opera, and after witnessing the liberty taken by the screenwriter of the film, *Shadowlands*, it seemed to me that that the real C. S. Lewis was being replaced by a mythological one. As a result, I thought I saw how a factual account of Lewis' life and his works might serve as a kind of *cordon sanitaire* – a quarantine barrier between the myth and the reality.

I mentioned writing short biographies of Austin and Katharine Farrer. It was partly as a result of collaborating with Roger Lancelyn Green on a biography of Lewis, but more than anything my study of Boswell and Johnson, that I came to see that those who have the most important influence on a famous person are not usually themselves famous. I wanted to provide memorials for those who, as George Eliot said in *Middlemarch*, have "lived faithfully a hidden life, and rest in unvisited tombs" (896). And so it was that the first part of the *Companion* to be written was the "Who's Who" section.

I was very tired by the time the *Companion* was finished, but after a break I returned to a plan I had discussed with the publishers years before, that of editing *The Collected Letters of C. S. Lewis*. I had been collecting Lewis' letters for the Bodleian Library since 1968, and Wheaton College had been collecting since 1964, and the two libraries supplied one another with copies of their holdings. New letters will probably be showing up for a long time yet, but we assumed that most of those which survive had been found. Volumes of letters, even those of famous people, do not sell well, and the publishers on both sides of the Atlantic made it clear they would only accept three volumes. As so often, I began discussing the division of the letters with Jim Como, and I began work on Volume I in December 1996. I am very, very far from thinking that the letters have been edited as well as they could be, or should be: I claim only that I did the best I could.

As with the *Companion & Guide*, it seemed important to provide biographies of Lewis' correspondents. I thought a footnote-biography would do for those to whom Lewis wrote a single letter, but surely more ought to be said about those to whom he wrote often and who had no memorial? The time given to writing the biographies occupied almost as much time as editing the letters.

Neither Jack nor Warnie could ever discover when their teacher, W. T. Kirkpatrick—"The Great Knock"—was born, and finding that date became something of a crusade with me. After a search of five years Mr. Kirkpatrick's birth-date appeared in Volume I of the *Collected Letters*. The other two volumes presented other challenges. While writing a biography of Cecil Harwood's wife—Daphne—for Volume II, I asked her children if they knew the date of their mother's birth. They said Mrs. Harwood had written the date of her birth—1898—in the family Bible. This, however, did not square with her age when she died in 1950. The discovery of a birth certificate revealed that the lady had knocked ten years off her age. I hope I am forgiven for that revelation. Finally, in Volume III, I was given the chance to erect memorials for most of the remaining Inklings and Lewis' close friends, George Sayer, John Lawlor, Colin Hardie, Nan Dunbar and others.

And dare I admit it—there was exasperation too. After seven years editing those letters I found myself arguing in my mind with Jack Lewis. "How could you *do* this to me!?" I asked him. "Jack, I bet I've spent more time editing your letters than you did writing them!" "*That*," he seemed to reply, "is why I chose you as my secretary. It's part of the deal." But ladies and gentlemen, do not bother to get Charles Colson back over here to remind me that it is the words of C. S. Lewis—not those of this editor—that will be read and read for many years to come.

WORKS CITED

Acta Apostolicae Sedis 54. 1962. *Inside the Vatican* Aug.-Sept. 2007.

Barfield, Owen. Forward. *All My Road Before Me: The Diary of C. S. Lewis 1922-1927.* Ed. Walter Hooper. London: HarperCollins, 1991. ix-xiii.

Eliot, George. *Middlemarch.* Ed. W. J. Harvey. Harmondsworth: Penguin Books, 1966.

Hooper, Walter. *C. S. Lewis: A Companion and Guide.* New York: HarperSanFrancisco, 1996.

Hooper, Walter, ed. *The Collected Letters of C. S. Lewis: Volume III, Narnia, Cambridge and Joy 1950-1963.* San Francisco: HarperSanFrancisco, 2007.

—. *The Dark Tower and Other Stories.* London: Collins, 1977.

Lewis, C. S. *The Allegory of Love: A Study in Medieval Tradition.* Oxford: Clarendon Press, 1936.

—. "Dogma and the Universe." *God in the Dock: Essays on Theology and Ethics.* Ed. Walter Hooper. Grand Rapids: Eerdmans, 1970. 38-47.

—. *The Four Loves.* London: Geoffrey Bles, 1960.

—. *Surprised by Joy: The Shape of My Early Life.* 1955. London: Fount Paperback, 1998.

Kilby, Clyde S. and Marjorie Lamp Mead, eds. *Brothers and Friends: The Diaries of Major Warren Hamilton Lewis.* San Francisco: Harper & Row, 1982.

Robinson, J. A. T. *Honest to God.* London: SCM Press, 1963.

❖ Part 1 ❖

C.S. LEWIS AS SOCIAL CRITIC:
PHILOSOPHY
PSYCHOLOGY
SCIENCE
&
ETHICS

It would be quite false . . . to suppose that the Christian view of suffering is incompatible with the strongest emphasis on our duty to leave the world, even in the temporal sense, 'better' than we found it.

The Problem of Pain

Chapter One

Culture and Public Philosophy: Another C. S. Lewis
(Being Finally an Exhortation)

James Como

Please consider with me some achievements of the medieval monastery. From Thomas. E. Woods, Jr., in *How the Catholic Church Built Western Civilization* (Regnery, 2005, *passim*), we learn that Henry Goodell, president of the Massachusetts Agricultural College, held that, " . . . the work of these grand monks during a period of fifteen hundred years . . . saved agriculture when no one else could save it. . . . They labored with their own hands, drained morasses, and cleared away forests. By them [the land] was rendered a fruitful country." Gregoire, Moulin, and Oursel, authors of *The Monastic Realm* (Rizzoli, 1985), go further: "[The monks] were the skillful and unpaid technical advisors of the third world of their times. . . . There is no activity . . . in which the monks did not display . . . a fertile spirit of research." The regnant view was expressed best nearly one hundred years ago (1909) by Flick, in *The Rise of the Medieval Church*, explaining that the monasteries ". . . converted the wilderness into cultivated country. . . ." That is (from *cultus*) they beheld a field, "a sodded place fit for tilling and providing for growth" – thus making a *culture*.

I posit these assessments for a personal and, I admit, quirky reason: whenever meeting in conference on the subject of C. S. Lewis I delight in imagining my fellow conferees as medieval monks and nuns and our venue as a monastery. Consider: Are we not surrounded by a world largely bereft of manners and morality? Do we not seek to till that landscape so as to replenish it and thus grow the old faith anew? Do we not seek links to other such enclaves? Moreover, is not Lewis rather like our Father Abbot Jack who, providing purpose and direction, above all cultivates that indispensable fruit which is Hope, thereby motivating us to even greater cultivation? That Lewis we know best – the enduring apostle of Hope; the lay theologian, fantasist, and Narnian; the Christian *Romantic* (in Lewis' own lexicon) and apologist; and, of course, the literary steward, to whom a dwindled few pay any attention these days – *that* Lewis is the father abbot whom we commonly spirit from monastery to monastery, now and again dispatching him into the larger world (the West End, Broadway, PBS, Hollywood) for what good he may do.

But there is another Lewis, an un-romantic chap who, unlike the monks within the monasteries, has directly engaged his massively ruined and ruinous landscape. This Lewis is the Public Philosopher who acknowledges few temporal demarcations and submits to no school; who strikes opportunistically, even improbably, especially journalistically; and whose voice – here, as always, direct and proximate – differs from the familiar and inviting Narnian's. By no means is this other persona unrecognizable: as is the case with most deft and supple writers, Lewis' voices interpenetrate each other. Like the Renaissance ("so-called," I hasten to add, in deference to the master) with its chronological neighbors, there is no bold line of demarcation separating one persona from another.

Rather, my argument is, first, that the tone of this public philosopher's voice *concentrates* certain features which in the popular Lewis' voice are more temperate and diffuse than in the former and are thus less noticeable – in fact, more tolerable – than in the philosopher's. (I will designate those features presently.) Second, this concentration of tonal features in the public philosopher accompanies *a)* distinctive subjects, *b)* disparate (and often surprising) views on those subjects, and *c)* is tuned to readers more closely fitted to those subjects than are conventional Lewis readers. Third, this *concentration* of features, subjects, views and audience gives rise to a literary persona somewhat less . . . *comforting* . . . than that of the much better-known – we might say, the iconic – Lewis.

But the plot thickens. As a public philosopher Lewis presents two broad aspects, that of a Prophetic Public Philosopher and that of a Social one. I will deal with both, for both evince that concentration of tonal features I have alluded to. These features are rhetorical and logical severity, a daunting perspective and cultural capaciousness (unbound by time, space or school), a lack of sentimentality that can be downright chilling, and an unrelenting intellectual seriousness undistracted by the the trendy or the iron-clad "ism."

However, just as Lewis' Christianity and his popular defense of it cost him both the support and the serious attention of the intellectual elite of his day (e.g. Empson, Cooke, Orwell, Russell – their name is legion), I suggest – this being the final prong of my four-prong argument – that owing to that discomfiting quality I have alluded to this other Lewis persona has dampened, not only popular attention (preponderantly) to the public philosopher but our own scholarly attention as well. Certainly scholars among us have labored mightily towards an understanding of the prophetic species of the public philosopher – David Mills, Victor Reppert, Michael D. Aeschliman, Gilbert Meilander, William Luther White, and James Patrick (*The Magdalen Metaphysicals* being my personal favorite) – and they have succeeded, to an extent. But they are few, and the public philosopher – especially the Social Public Philosopher – remains ignored by mainstream public intellectuals (see the third preface to *C. S. Lewis at the 'Breakfast Table,'* now titled *Remembering C. S. Lewis*) and by the reading public, including Lewis' own. Might, then, part of the blame be ours?

In short, as Lewis has enacted *his* Great Knock (the legendary, relentlessly logical and beloved pre-Oxford tutor W. T. Kirkpatrick), we have largely neglected an aspect of our own Knock – oh, not the apologist and transcendent religious thinker, nor the seminal scholar, and certainly not the Christian romantic and fantasist who, frankly, takes up far too much of the available popular oxygen, but the public philosopher, especially he of the social variety.

Now, unlike us, in our neo-monastery, public philosophers (or "public intellectuals") are free to walk about the culture, to pick their spots; properly speaking, they are more *preaching friars* than monks. That is, our neo-friar is within the culture, not removed from it. Public philosophers come from the university, the law, journalism or the think tank, though on occasion they freelance the intellect. Often they seek to modify a cultural agenda or radically to change it: they often speak adversarially. In doing so they are confident that ideas – ideas are the raw material of this figure – are the seeds of cultural change. Who are they? A varied group, to be sure. From the eighteenth-century (when journalism, not coincidentally, came into its own) to now they have been people such as Addison and Steele, Swift, Dryden, Pope, and Dr. Johnson; the Adamses, Paine, the *Federalist* writers Madison, Hamilton and Jay; Tocqueville; William F. Buckley, Norman Podhoretz, Richard Rorty, Peter Singer, the Kristols, Stanley Fish, Thomas Sowell, the Himmelfarbs, and Jean Kirkpatrick. Many of Lewis' own period are in this well-worn tradition as well: Cooke, Orwell, Belloc, Chesterton, Mencken, Dewey, Russell, Wells, Muggeridge, Shaw, Hook, and the prototype himself, Walter Lippmann, who first publicly philosophized on the nature and importance of public opinion and the role of the public intellectual in its formation (*Public Opinion*, 1922).

What *was* the cultural milieu like during Lewis' time, roughly the middle third of the twentieth century? Nearly his entire life was lived during one of the worst declines in human history. Did I say *one* of the worst? Let me not be cautious for caution's sake: the twentieth century offers mostly ruins and constitutes a net moral and cultural loss. So I ask: could that – that cauldron of infernal depredation – be to some small measure the result of cultural idolatry? After all, which of our modern, twentieth-century cultures was most elevated if not the German? Hitler could quote Schopenhauer from memory. In *The Fall of Berlin, 1945* Antony Beevor tells us that on the night of April 12, 1945, as the Red Army began its final assault on Berlin, the philharmonic was performing Beethoven's Violin Concerto, Gruckner's Eighth Symphony, and the finale of Wagner's Gotterdammerung. "After the performance," he goes on, "the Nazi Party had organized Hitler Youth members to stand in uniform with baskets of cyanide capsules." Wolf Lepenies's *The Seduction of Culture in German History* describes an intellectual attitude that can be observed throughout German history: the overrating of culture. Surely Lewis' wonderful application of the phrase "enemy-occupied territory" to Western culture must come to mind.

To be sure we have witnessed cultural idolatry before. But it seems the differences of degree that marked the twentieth century have added up to a difference in kind. Now when freedom is equated with license *the equation is celebrated*. For example, just how do we "ism"? Let me count the ways: relativism, subjectivism, nihilism; narcissism, scientism, solipsism (*Self* magazine!); Madonna praised, not as singer or dancer, but as self-inventor (every man his own creator!); emotivism and sentimentalism; and the belief that technologism + scientism = "progress." These may be no more than twitches, instances of a sort of cultural Tourets; but they take their massive toll, and we pass them on. After all, that is what "education" does; it transmits. In short, John Dewey (such a good man, too) has won. The function of education, he argued, is to *challenge* the received notions of Western civilization, such as Judeo-Christian religious belief, since religion is socially dangerous, seeking (as it does) to mold conduct in light of norms beyond temporal society. For Dewey, reports Jude B. Dougherty in *John Dewey and the Decline of American Education*, "The function of education is to challenge, not perpetuate, the inherited."

Has Lewis's Great Divorce *ever* been greater? How has man *not* been *abolished*? Baby Boomers are still babies, and they are booming. Certainly our catalogue of depravities is prodigious, and they do predate the twentieth-century. No, our problem is not novelty but *proliferation*: mass adolescence

+ mass technology = a massively misshapened landscape. But I hear myself – I am in the middle of a Jeremiad! So I ask: is there nothing to redeem the century? So I look, and I find . . . the advent of movies, the maturation of baseball, and the ready availability of ibuprofen, for those of us delusional enough to think we can still play the second instead of merely watching the first.

But they are the depredations of the century, not its saving graces, that bring us to Lewis – and Lewis to us, for he is a Providential man if ever there was one.

Owing to the enduring vitality of two staggeringly visionary works, the prophetic Lewis is, as I have avowed, much better known than his social counterpart. He looks ahead (though the prophetic philosopher is not to be confounded with a prophet). And what Lewis saw he said unsparingly in *The Abolition of Man* and in *That Hideous Strength*. Putting aside *Miracles* (as is our wont, alas), in which Lewis writes more or less classically as a philosopher in response to David Hume's philosophical rejection of miracles, the prophetic philosopher is the Lewis most people usually know if they know Lewis as a philosopher in the first place.

In that light, and for our shared recollection, I review this Lewis' features: an aspect of Chesterton may come to mind. In addition to that unalloyed seriousness I have mentioned, the prophetic philosopher is 1/ broadly moral, 2/ keenly, even intuitively, attentive to culturally subterranean assumptions, 3/ intellectually fresh, penetrating, and analytical, 4/ anticipatory, and 5/ typically admonitory. He offers dispositive statements on natural law and human nature, and on the working of these in the realm of practical events (ethics) and on aspects of the broader culture (education). He anticipates (though not in detail, of course; prophetic philosophers leave matter, method and dates to the pure prophet): cloning, legalized and epidemic abortion, legalized euthanasia, genetic engineering, and the rampant redefinition of fundamental, axiomatic premises (e.g. 'family'). He reminds us that values are premises not conclusions; introduces new, telling concepts, such as the Innovator and the Conditioner; and instructs us respecting what, exactly, is at stake in the debate – freedom and dignity – and the consequence of their disappearance not so far into the future, the abolition of man.

That is the Prophetic Philosopher, well-(if-not-widely-) known, thanks to the scholars I have mentioned earlier. In contrast is the Social Philosopher, who is neither. I turn to him now, but with an apology both to him and to you for the brevity of my treatment – a Cook's Tour, but not therefore unrepresentative of the whole landscape. Perhaps there is here a prospective dissertation- or book-writer looking for an apt subject?

Rather than looking ahead, the *social* public philosopher is a diagnostician, looking around and, in Lewis' case, often by first looking back. Alas, our attention to this Lewis does not match his to the culture. Too infrequently, for example, do we read or cite, let alone examine carefully, such essays and sermons as "Modern Man and His Categories of Thought," "Is History Bunk?", "On the Reading of Old Books," "Life in the Atomic Age" and "Is English Doomed?" (all conveniently collected in Lesley Walmsley [ed.], *Essay Collection: Literature, Philosophy and Short Stories*, HarperCollins, 2000).

This neglect includes *The Pilgrim's Regress* and is particularly anomalous, even unpardonable. In this, the first book Lewis wrote as a Christian, we have nearly all of Lewis and his hard features at once: the romantic examines *Sehnsucht*, the apologist defends the claim of its Christian etiology, the parabolist allegorizes its application, and the philosopher (under both species) lays waste to its opponents both direct and oblique, temporal and spiritual, physical, psychological and intellectual. Lewis would come to describe it as being of "an uncharitable temper"; I describe it as severe, unsentimental, serious, realistic, capacious . . . I describe it as The Lewis Template. Here is how Jane Spence Southron described it in the *New York Times Book Review* (December 8, 1935):

> A modern man's intricate journey . . . and the highly complex mental processes that distinguish him from creatures of a different order are resolved, here, into the utmost simplicity. . . . He is . . . an intellectual of our own day, who is not content to take anything in life at its face value and who makes use of the stored-up knowledge of the past and the possibilities of practical adventures in living to help him in his explorations. . . . The language, throughout, is plain, straightforward and leanly significant.

With the exception of some of the Augustans – particularly Dr. Johnson and Swift – no public philosopher comes close to achieving the perspective – the cultural scope and intellectual reach – that Lewis achieves in this one book.

As for the essays and relevant sermons, take, for example, "Learning in Wartime," preached at the Church of St. Mary the Virgin on December 22, 1939:

> The war creates no absolutely new situation: it simply aggravates the permanent human situation so that we can no longer ignore it. Human life has always been lived on the edge of a precipice. Human culture has always had to exist under the shadow under of something infinitely more important than itself. . . . Life has never been normal. . . . I reject at once an idea . . . that cultural activities are in their own right spiritual and meritorious. (Walmsley 580-583)

This insistence on a *long* perspective – an insistence which subverts unspoken, and often unexamined, assumptions respecting our exceptionalism – is typical of Lewis, of course, and it is severe: it practices no attenuation of thought, offers no rhetorical mitigation.

And he just does not let up. Five years after that dismissal of Matthew Arnold's cultural idolatry would come a classic double jab, the first at Deweyism (though Lewis may not have known of John Dewey) and the second at F. R. Leavis. In "The Parthenon and the Optative" (Notes on the Way, *Time and Tide*, XXV, March 11, 1944) we read:

> The one [the 'optative', standing for the tough study of a difficult language] begins with hard, dry things like grammar, and dates, and prosody . . . the other [the Parthenon [discussion of the Greek temple], begins in 'Appreciation' and ends in gush. . . . [It] fails most disastrously when it most succeeds. It teaches a man to feel vaguely cultured while he remains in fact a dunce. It makes him think he is enjoying poems he can't construe. It qualifies him to review books he does not understand, and to be intellectual without intellect. It plays havoc with the very distinction between truth and error. . . . Mr. A [just down from reading English with Dr Leavis at Cambridge] pours out his personality – in pure non-factual Appreciation to his form. (Walmsley 444-446)

Most pieces in "Notes on the Way" are brief, journalistic, and semi-occasional; thoughtful, usually non-religious and written quite accessibly. Lewis is cognizant of venue and audience. I suppose these pieces did not have a wide "adversary" circulation. Neither do they seem to have circulated widely among us.

More typical of Lewis-as-public-philosopher are "The Necessity of Chivalry," "Bulverism," "Democratic Education," and "Priestesses in the Church" (I omit "Delinquents in the Snow" as the work of an aggrieved, and soon to be grieving, man): all unsparingly diagnostic – and all, by the way, substantially unrefuted (as opposed to sneered at). One of my personal favorites, though, is "Sex in Literature" (*Sunday Telegraph*, 87, September 30,

1962). I recall my surprise followed by delight when first I read it. If you do not know it, I wonder if you will share either the delight or the surprise:

> It is a bad thing that the results of trials should depend on the personal moral philosophy of a particular jury rather than on what has been proved in court. . . . When the prevalent morality of a nation comes to differ unduly from that presupposed in its laws, the laws must sooner or later change and conform to it. This is the case with "obscene" literature: masturbation, perversion, fornication and adultery were great evils; now the intelligentsia are not sure, but even if the acts are evils, they do not think the law should be meddling. My own view . . . is that they are evils, but that the law should be concerned with none of them except adultery . . . because it offends the Hobbesian principle 'that men perform their covenants.' . . . The lesser of the evils now before us is to abandon all moral censorship. We have either sunk beneath or risen above it. If we do, there will be reams of filth. But we need not read it. Nor, probably, will the fashion last forever. (Walmsley 479-481)

That happens to be a rare instance of Lewis causing me to believe that he is sometimes naïve and that, in fact, I know better. But instead of ourselves as typical readers of this essay, we should think of other public philosophers. What can they make of this, coming, as it does, from the dogmatic, theology-soaked, popularizing fantasist? Why, they say nothing. And scarcely do we.

Two essays that appeared in remote, if not quite esoteric, venues *have* gotten our attention. In "Vivisection," a pamphlet first published by the New England Anti-vivisection Society in 1947 then by the National Anti-vivisection Society in 1948, Lewis tells us, " . . . the victory of vivisection marks a great advance in the triumph of ruthless, nonmoral utilitarianism over the old world of ethical law. . . " (Walmsley 696). He did not use the locution "Old Western," as he does so prominently elsewhere, but he might just as well have; having looked around, he concludes by looking back, invoking the concept of a natural moral order. In "The Humanitarian Theory of Punishment," published in Australia (*20th Century: An Australian Quarterly Review*, 1949) because he could not publish it elsewhere, we note Lewis' characteristic subversion of contemporary unexamined assumptions (about the nature of justice and human accountability), cultivating instead Old Western assumptions respecting both human nature and the role of the state:

> The Humanitarian theory removes from Punishment the concept of Desert. But the concept of Desert is the only connecting link between

punishment and justice. It is only as deserved or undeserved that a sentence can be just or unjust. . . . Thus when we cease to consider what the criminal deserves and consider only what will cure him or deter others, we have tacitly removed him from the sphere of justice altogether; instead of a person, a subject of rights, we now have a mere object, a patient, a 'case'. (Walmsley 699)

Those are two pieces which, though not entirely obscure to us, were certainly so at the time of their publication and have remained so to the world-at-large. No matter their standing, they are classic Lewis in their severity and especially in their unsentimentality.

Going where the argument leads when given certain premises, as well as stating them, are the tasks of philosophers, public or otherwise, and constitute a pronounced Lewis strength. The question is whether or not anyone beyond the monastery pays attention. For his part Lewis does not always make it easy; in addition to the usual tasks, he brings not only his signature severity (characteristics of effective abbots and preaching friars, by the way) but some confoundedness too. He can be full of surprises. Five essays epitomize this Lewis, and all appeared prominently. Noteworthy is this refreshing, and perhaps unsettling, fact: Lewis rarely has a "side," as we now conceive sides. The "Old Western Man" of his famous inaugural lecture at Cambridge does not necessarily equal Conservative.

Does Lewis have a *moral* objection to obscenity? Not if we read him in "Prudery and Philology" (*Spectator*, January 21, 1955):

> It is the words, not the things, that are obscene. That is, they are words long consecrated (or desecrated) to insult, derision, and buffoonery. You cannot use them without bringing in the whole atmosphere of the slum, the barrack-room and the public school. . . . When authors rail too much . . . against public taste, do they perhaps betray some insufficiency? (Walmsley 516-517)

Well then, because of his class and upbringing, is he a bigoted elitist, a man fearful of "the revolt of the masses"? Not if we read him in "Private Bates" (*Spectator*, December 29, 1944):

> We must get rid of our arrogant assumption that it is the masses who can be led by the nose. As far as I can make out, the shoe is on the other foot. The only people who are really the dupes of their favourite newspapers are the intelligentsia. It is they who read leading articles: the poor read the sporting news, which is mostly true. (Walmsley 606)

So then, having deposited this body of faith in "the common man," Lewis might, we would expect, defend democracy on their behalf. But he does not – not on their behalf. And his reasoning is quite simple: he regards a zeal for equality as nothing more than a superstition. He tells us as much in "Equality" (*Spectator*, August 27, 1943):

> I am a democrat because I believe in the Fall of Man. . . . I don't deserve a share in governing a hen-roost, much less a nation. Nor do most people. . . . This introduces a view of equality rather different from that in which we have been trained. I do not think that equality is one of those things (like wisdom or happiness) which are good simply in themselves and for their own sakes. I think it is in the same class as medicine, which is good because we are ill. . . . When equality is treated not as a medicine or a safety-gadget but as an ideal we begin to breed that stunted and envious sort of mind which hates all superiority. (Walmsley 666-667)

Of course, we have always known how seriously Lewis takes the Fall of Man. His political application of the belief, however, is unforgiving (so to speak), another example of his logical severity. In "Willing Slaves of the Welfare State" (*The Observer*, July 20, 1958, No. 2 in the series "Is Progress Possible? [a reply to C.P. Snow's "Man in Society."]) he makes clear the basis of his objection to all collectivist paradigms:

> Now I care far more how humanity lives than how long. Progress, for me, means increasing goodness and happiness of individual lives. For the species, as for each man, mere longevity seems to me a contemptible idea. . . . It seems childish not to recognise that actual government is and always must be oligarchical. Our effective masters must be more than one and fewer than all. But the oligarchs begin to regard us in a new way. . . . Let us not be deceived by phrases about 'Man taking charge of his own destiny'. All that can really happen is that some men will take charge of the destiny of the others. They will be simply men; none perfect; some greedy, cruel and dishonest. The more completely we are planned the more powerful they will be. Have we discovered some new reason why, this time, powers should not corrupt as it has done before? (Walmsley 746-751)

Whether in the thirties (Auden's "low, dishonest decade"), forties, or fifties, such unrelenting, rhetorically unadorned, and inexorably counter-dominant public thinking would have made Lewis unpalatable to the regnant verbal class – but far too cogent to permit of refutation.

One aspect of Lewis' career is not merely largely, but near-universally, ignored (though Walter Hooper is about to remedy that – and soon, we hope). For all of his professional life Lewis was, if not exactly a prolific, then certainly a trenchant and durable, book reviewer. And in his reviews we see the same severity of thinking, along with his untempered willingness to lay it out. The difference, perhaps, between his book reviews and the essays noted above is their greater economy-of-expression. "Hardly possible," one might say; yet true. Here is a sampling, and though I've taken some elliptical liberties, there are none that accelerate Lewis' style or deceptively abbreviate his thinking. Do note that these four range over four decades.

On December 6, 1928, he reviewed W. P. Ker's *Form and Style in Poetry* for *Book News and Reviews*: "There is . . . a cooling [sic] card here and there for those who believe too intemperately in the Renaissance." Well, we certainly will hear more of that in years to come! Six years later, in the midst of the decade made low and dishonest by its ruling left-wing intelligentsia, he reviewed T. R. Hen's *Longinus and English Criticism* for the *Oxford Magazine* (December 6, 1934): "It is rather an attempt to relate his [i.e. Longinus's] teaching to the 'advanced' criticism of the Cambridge Left Wing – the diagrammatic, psychological and 'practical' school." The next review is of a book which he thought variously flawed but could not help liking, indeed, virtually adopting. In June of 1940 he reviewed de Rougement's *Passion and Society* for *Theology*. His last sentence is actually a quotation from Rougement, though it is unquoted, and, I believe, Lewis would lift it wholesale and insert it into *The Screwtape Letters* (I do recall his citing it with admiration in a letter): "M. de Rougement . . . maintains with eloquence the incompatibility between the Christian conception of marriage and the modern notion according to which every marriage must have 'falling in love' as its efficient, and worldly 'happiness' as its final, cause. . . . But all of us need to learn, almost daily, that Eros ceases to be a demon only when he ceases to be a god (321)."

Not long before his death he was no less penetrating than he had been forty years earlier. Note his impatience with prudery, his anger over avoidable ignorance, his analytical acuity, and his impatience with certain modern methodologies in this review of David Loth's *The Erotic in Literature* for *The Observer Weekend Review* of March 4, 1962.

> He gives a pretty full and very damaging history of the law's confused and largely futile attempts to control, or even to define, pornography. He also casts serious doubts on common assumptions as to what will or will not corrupt the young reader. . . . They [who answer questionnaires] betray their abnormality by the very act of answering. . . . Anything

which mentions copulation – for whatever purpose, in whatever tone – is for him 'pornography' – a hymn from a Sumerian fertility rite, the story of Judah and Tamar, Sophocles's "Electra." It ought to be made impossible for the repressive party to include the scatological under the pornographic or to call a book immoral because it offends their taste. It should be equally impossible for the other party to make a remark that 'sex is innocent'. If *sex* means the biological fact, it is no more innocent or guilty than a turnip. If it is meant that human sexual behavior is all and all equally, innocent, we want to be told why. No one claims a similar liberty for all economic or political behavior. . . . When the morality embodied in the law departs too widely, either for better or worse, from that really current in a society, the law must sooner or later either sink or rise into conformity. Till it does, confusion and inconsistency are inevitable. . . . The author treats *erotica* as a singular and *orgiastic* as the adjective of orgasm.

The last line here is the last line of Lewis' review: except during actual combat, it seems Lewis did not take prisoners.

And so we have Lewis the Social Public Philosopher, he who laid waste to chronocentrism and its snobbery, not merely seeing through trends and movements but restoring some perspective for those of us who know so much less cultural history than he; the man who could write, "I believe I just proved that the Renaissance never happened and that, if it did, it didn't matter!" In short, our favorite fantasist was fundamentally that serious realist, both philosophically and rhetorically, and realism can hurt. Indeed, when expressed severely and unsentimentally it surely does become God's megaphone to a fallen world. In eschewing "isms," and by seeing instead the quiddity of things and apprehending their currency, Lewis became a providential time traveler, seeing the ruins, certainly, but seeing beyond them as well. Skeptical of received opinion and trendy abstraction, he is not merely unsentimental but anti-sentimental. This is a father abbot to be reckoned with, a friar to be heeded.

So I will attempt to reckon. The public philosopher – especially he of the social aspect – seems somehow . . . different. Capacious in his perspective, severe in his thinking, unrelenting in his combativeness, and rhetorically uninsulated, this unflinching realist is, as I have suggested earlier, not entirely unfamiliar to us. He is the "ruthless dialectician who insists that reason not stop short of its goal: truth," as Richard Cunningham so cogently puts it (and much else) in his ground-breaking *C. S. Lewis: Defender of the Faith*. He knocks as greatly as ever did his master. But we are unaccustomed to such concentrated doses of these qualities, to the subjects they vivify and the views they convey, and even to the audiences they address: somehow not us. What sort of persona, then, gives rise to such a voice? It is not the voice of that familiar, benevolent persona who has comforted us, often as though shoulder-to-shoulder, even cozily, and so abidingly. Not exactly. This persona is *sophisticated*. And he is . . . off-putting.

One of the tricky meanings of that tricky word is *mixed* – not necessarily with impurity or inauthenticity, but mixed by experience (the OED tells me), in fact worldly-wise, "subtle, discriminating, refined, *cultured*." Certainly Lewis's humors were mixed, but so was that magnificent and magnificently furnished, nuanced, supple, and dexterously militant intellect. This Lewis may no longer be *of* that culture, but he certainly was, once; and the public philosopher is certainly *in* it. Not a snob, though he was once, and priggishly so; and not condescending, though he once was a master of condescension, this Lewis is nevertheless not the romantic Narnian, and there is certainly nothing *mere* about him. We recall that near the end of his life this Lewis taught us how to read and judge literature. That lesson from *An Experiment in Criticism* is simple: read in "the same spirit as the author writ." Are we up to the challenge when reading the public philosopher? After all, much is at stake: Lewis also insists that the proper way to judge a book is by what good readers say about it. I am suggesting not only that we read this Other Lewis but that we read him "in the same spirit as the author writ."

Why so, and urgently? Because in the twenty-first century *insula such as ours – such as this very seminary, and this very conference – are, in fact, counter-dominant neo-monasteries*. Remember? " . . . [T]he work of these grand monks . . . saved agriculture when no one else could save it. . . . They labored [and] drained morasses. . . . By them [the land] was rendered a fruitful country." "[The monks] were the skillful and unpaid technical advisors of . . . of their times. . . . There is no activity . . . . in which the monks did not display . . . a fertile spirit of research." The monasteries ". . . converted the wilderness into cultivated country. . . ." That is they beheld a waste and made a *culture*. And why not? Our own severity, long perspective, and seriousness – our own conveyance, not only of Lewis as our father abbot-romantic apologist but as our preaching friar-public philosopher, indeed *our very own sophistication* – will engage a waste that needs him . . . and us, and this very Center [L. Russ Bush Center for Faith and Culture at Southeastern Baptist Theological Seminary, Wake Forest, NC], as Prof. Bruce Little's review of its mission made pellucidly clear. Lewis will always remain our apostle of Hope, the much-studied and popular Lewis. But he must again be *our public philosopher who "happens to be a Christian"*: an *emissary* to the wider culture and as sophisticated, speaking its unsentimental language. *That* Lewis simply must have his oxygen, which is for us to deliver.

And the culture may be waiting. In 2002 Jurgen Habermas, he of Cultural Criticism and De-constructionism and as Leftist an atheist as we have ever had, seems dis-positively to have refuted the facile Dewey, suggesting (*Religion and Rationality: Essays on Reason, God, and Modernity*, ed. Eduardo Mendieta, MIT) that the culture in fact should "perpetuate the inherited":

> [F]or the normative self-understanding of modernity, Christianity has functioned as more than just a precursor or a catalyst. . . . the ideals of freedom and a collective life in solidarity, the autonomous conduct of life and emancipation, the individual morality of conscience, human rights, and democracy, is the direct legacy of the Judaic ethic of justice and the Christian ethic of love. . . . The search for reasons that aspire to general acceptance need not lead to an unfair exclusion of religion from public life, and secular society, for its part, need not cut itself off from the important resources of spiritual explanations. . . .

Lewis agrees, of course, and typically has provided a context for the insight – his signature long perspective. It is from *Punch* (July 9, 1958). In it we witness Lewis' reach, disinterested devotion to truth, and his penetrating diagnostic power. The essay is "Revival or Decay?":

> Is there a homogeneous 'West'? I doubt it. Everything that can go on is going on all round us. Religions buzz about us like bees. A serious sex – quite different from the cheery lechery endemic in our species – is one of them. Traces of embryonic religions occur in science fiction. Meanwhile, as always, the Christian way too is followed. But nowadays, when it is not followed, it need not be feigned. That fact covers a good deal of what is called the decay of religion. Apart from that, is the present so very different from other ages or 'the West' from anywhere else? (Walmsley 740-741)

The doctor, as they say, is in, and I remind myself that, as with "learning in Wartime," Lewis did *not* write that in the twenty-first century; that he did not write that *yesterday*.

Our avatar of the abbot, friar, emissary, and apostle of hope remained true to his "rule," selecting and occupying a "tillable *cultus* suitable for growth," notwithstanding opposition, ridicule and neglect. Intellectually and spiritually, and publicly so, he was a brave man – he certainly is a hero of mine – who fought the good fight, ran the race, and kept the faith, and did so "to the ruddy end." But this we already knew.

And we – we have swamps to drain.

WORKS CITED

Beevor, Antony. *The Fall of Berlin 1945*. New York: Penguin, 2003.

Cunningham, Richard. *C. S. Lewis: Defender of the Faith*. Louisville: Westminster John Knox, 1967.

Dougherty, Jude. B. Rev. of *John Dewey and the Decline of American Education*, by Henry T. Edmonson III. *The Review of Metaphysics* 59.4 (2006): 883-334.

Flick, Alexander Clarence. *The Rise of the Medieval Church*. New York: Burt Franklin, 1909.

Goodell, Henry. "The Influence of the Monks in Agriculture." *How the Catholic Church Built Western Civilization*. Ed. Thomas E. Woods, Jr. Washington: Regnery Publishing, 2005.

Gregoire, Reginald, Leo Moulin, and Raymond Oursel. *The Monastic Realm*. New York: Rizzoli, 1985.

Habermas, Jurgen. "A Time of Transition." *Religion and Rationality: Essays on Reason, God, and Modernity*. Cambridge: MIT Press, 2002.

Lepensie, Wolf. *The Seduction of Culture in German History*. Princeton: Princeton UP, 2006.

Lewis, C. S. *The Collected Letters of C. S. Lewis, Vol. II: Books, Broadcasts and War, 1931-1949*. Ed. Walter Hooper. London: HarperCollins, 2004.

—. "Equality." in *C. S. Lewis: Essay Collection and Other Short Pieces*. Ed. Lesley Walmsley. London: HarperCollins, 2000. 666-668.

—. "The Humanitarian Theory of Punishment." in *C. S. Lewis: Essay Collection and Other Short Pieces*. Ed. Lesley Walmsley. London: HarperCollins, 2000. 698-709.

—. "Learning in War-Time" in *C. S. Lewis: Essay Collection and Other Short Pieces*. Ed. Lesley Walmsley. London: HarperCollins, 2000. 579-586.

—. "The Parthenon and the Optative." in *C. S. Lewis: Essay Collection and Other Short Pieces*. Ed. Lesley Walmsley. London: HarperCollins, 2000. 44-446.

—. "Private Bates." in *C. S. Lewis: Essay Collection and Other Short Pieces*. Ed. Lesley Walmsley. London: HarperCollins, 2000. 604-606.

—. "Prudery and Philology." in *C. S. Lewis: Essay Collection and Other Short Pieces*. Ed. Lesley Walmsley. London: HarperCollins, 2000. 515-518.

—. "Revival or Decay?" in *C. S. Lewis: Essay Collection and Other Short Pieces*. Ed. Lesley Walmsley. London: HarperCollins, 2000. 738-741.

—. "Sex in Literature." in *C. S. Lewis: Essay Collection and Other Short Pieces*. Ed. Lesley Walmsley. London: HarperCollins, 2000. 479-481.

—. "Vivisection." in *C. S. Lewis: Essay Collection and Other Short Pieces*. Ed. Lesley Walmsley. London: HarperCollins, 2000. 693-697.

—. "Willing Slaves of the Welfare State." in *C. S. Lewis: Essay Collection and Other Short Pieces*. Ed. Lesley Walmsley. London: HarperCollins, 2000. 746-751.

Southron, Jane Spence. *New York Times Book Review*. December 8, 1935.

Chapter Two

The Hangman's Duty:
C. S. Lewis on Christian Citizenship in Wartime

Justin D. Barnard

In a 1939 letter, C. S. Lewis states that it is "absurd to give to the private citizen the *same* right and duty of deciding the justice of a given war which rests on governments" ("Just War" 325). Lewis's argument for this claim is partly based on an implicit assumption about the level of epistemic certainty proper to moral response. In this essay, I make that assumption explicit and discuss its application to the issue of war and Christian citizenship. Specifically, I show how Lewis' assumption provides a structure enabling more effective dialogue about how private Christian citizens ought to respond in times of war.

In the spring of 1939, C. S. Lewis published a brief letter in the journal *Theology*, in which he offered a critical response to a series of notes entitled, "The Christian and the Next War" by E. L. Mascall (1905-93), a Professor of Historical Theology at King's College, London. In this somewhat disconnected set of thoughts, Mascall discusses what he calls the "concrete question" for Christian citizens during times of war. He queries, "If there is a war tomorrow, what am I to do?" (Mascall, "Next War" 53). In the process of offering his reflections on this question, Mascall outlines six conditions for a just war. These, along with other considerations that Mascall offers, are provided as a resource for individual Christian citizens to fulfill what Mascall takes to be their principal task when it comes to passing judgment on the justice of war. Mascall writes, "We have to decide each case for ourselves *as Christians*" (57).

Among the observations that Lewis makes in his letter of response about Mascall's conditions for just war is that "equally sincere people can differ to any extent and argue forever as to whether a proposed war fulfills

[Mascall's proposed] conditions or not" ("Just War" 325). Consequently, Lewis turns his attention to the "practical" issue of "authority" (325). The practical issue, according to Lewis, is this. In circumstances in which a nation-state is embroiled in debate about whether the conditions for a just war, whatever those may be, have been met, *who* is vested with the authority to make such a determination as well as the power to act in accordance with it? In responding to this question, Lewis begins with a cultural observation. "Modern discussions", Lewis writes, "tend to assume without argument that the answer is 'The private conscience of the individual,' and that any other answer is immoral and totalitarian" (325-6).

Lewis argues that this impulse on the part of ordinary citizens (or politicians *qua* ordinary citizens) to imagine that they possess both the duty and the authority to make precise, authoritative determinations about the justice of a given war is wrongheaded. He defends this claim with an analogy. If we assume that orthodox Christian theology is not, in principle, incompatible with capital punishment, then it is possible for a Christian to serve lawfully and honorably as an executioner. At the same time, Lewis notes, the moral license to serve in such a capacity does not imply a freedom for the Christian executioner to put to death whomever she wills. Specifically, she must not put to death a prisoner that she *knows* to be innocent. However, the executioner's obligation to refrain from knowingly executing the innocent does not, according to Lewis, entail a corresponding duty on the executioner's part to investigate the charges being brought against the prisoner with the same degree of rigor as those involved in the proceedings of criminal court. Lewis writes:

> I conclude that the hangman has done his duty if he has done his share of the general duty, resting upon all citizens alike, to ensure, so far as in him lies, that we have an honest judicial system; if, in spite of this, and unknowingly, he hangs an innocent man, then a sin has been committed, but not by him. ("Just War" 326)

Obviously, there is much to say about Lewis' comments here. For starters, at least some would take issue with his assumption that capital punishment is compatible with a Christian ethic. Others might object to his analysis of the moral guilt borne by the executioner in unknowingly putting to death an innocent man. Still others might take offense at the abrupt tone and unfeeling language in which the entire argument is cast. Such worries notwithstanding, Lewis' principal (albeit conditional) philosophical point seems correct. In executing his function *as a hangman*, the hangman bears neither the same duty nor the same authority to make determinations about the guilt or innocence of his subjects as those who participate in the judicial process itself. Rather, he has a prima facie obligation to exercise his responsibilities as an executioner in keeping with an implicit trust in the judicial process. To be sure, the prima facie obligation to trust the judicial process does not rise to the level of blind obedience. Lewis notes as much in making it clear that the prima facie obligation is overridden in cases in which the executioner *knows* that a prisoner is innocent. Still, the fact that there is such an exception to the prima facie obligation and that such exceptions do occasionally occur, does not entail that the executioner is thereby charged with the responsibilities of judge and jury.

Lewis goes on to suggest that the situation of the executioner is parallel to that of an ordinary citizen with respect to the latter's duty and authority to make determinations about the justice of a war. Lewis explains:

> This does not mean that private persons must obey governments commanding them to do what they know is sin; but perhaps it does mean (I write this with some reluctance) that the ultimate decision as to what the situation at a given moment is in the highly complex field of international affairs is one which must be delegated. ("Just War" 326)

In connection with the analogy of the executioner, Lewis' comments suggest that with respect to decisions about war, ordinary citizens have a prima facie obligation both to trust in the determinations made by their leaders and to act in accordance with that trust. At the same time, Lewis clearly recognizes the possibility that the prima facie obligation may be overridden in recognizing that no private citizen, especially a Christian, is obliged to do what she knows to be sinful out of sheer obedience or blind trust in government.

Still, Lewis explicitly expresses his own reservation about this position, though he does not elaborate on the reasons for his hesitancy. Moreover, as is well-known, both from this particular letter and from Lewis' other works, Lewis himself did not regard the intentional taking of human life as intrinsically wicked. Thus, he does not here countenance the possibility that to act out of accord with the norms of Christian pacifism is to act sinfully.

Both Lewis' expressed reservations and his deliberate refusal to deal with the pacifist position in this context leave his conclusion about the obligations of ordinary citizens in times of war somewhat tenuous. If ordinary citizens do have a prima facie obligation to trust in the determinations of their governments with respect to the justice of a military conflict, then such an obligation must be grounded in something more than the mere fact of the complexity of international affairs. Unfortunately, Lewis does not use this particular letter as an occasion to explain the rationale behind his intuition for this obligation. However, Lewis tends to display a remarkably high degree of philosophical consistency in his work. Thus, it should not surprise us to discover the grounds for this obligation elsewhere in the Lewis corpus.

In the remainder of the essay, I intend to offer a partly speculative interpretation of what I imagine that Lewis' grounds for this obligation may have been. However, the speculative nature of my interpretation of Lewis is not merely an exercise in historical, psychological curiosity. For the rationale for this prima facie obligation ultimately provides a structure for effective dialogue about the moral response of ordinary Christian citizens in times of war.

In 1941, Lewis delivered a paper to an Oxford pacifist society entitled, "Why I Am Not a Pacifist". In this essay, Lewis makes his case against pacifism on the basis of several aspects of moral judgment: facts, intuition, reason, and historical authority. Lewis frames his entire discussion in light of a general Aristotelian claim. In his *Nicomachean Ethics*, Aristotle writes:

> It is the mark of an educated mind to expect that amount of exactness in each kind which the nature of the particular subject admits. It is equally unreasonable to accept merely probable conclusions from a mathematician and to demand strict demonstrations from an orator. (9)

Presumably the nature of mathematics is such that "strict demonstrations" are the reasonable "amount of exactness" that we should expect in mathematical truths. Thus, for Aristotle, the nature of the object of our inquiry determines the degree of epistemic certainty we should expect about conclusions regarding those objects. Similarly, in "Why I Am Not a Pacifist", Lewis himself distinguishes between "moral" and "mathematical certainty". In an Aristotelian vein, Lewis describes moral certainty as "that degree of certainty proper to moral decisions" ("Pacifist" 59). He subsequently proceeds to argue against pacifism – aiming for a conclusion that admits of moral rather than mathematical certainty. The details of Lewis' case against pacifism need not detain us here. However, the distinction between moral and mathematical certainty is worth exploring independently of the uses to which Lewis puts it.

Specifying a sharp distinction between these two kinds of epistemic certainty is perhaps intrinsically impossible. Epistemic certainty is a phenomenological feature of the subject's epistemological situation. Still, anyone who has deliberated about both complex moral and simple arithmetical problems will grasp the basic difference. The degree of certainty that accompanies my conclusion that the sum of five and seven is twelve is phenomenologically stronger than the degree of certainty that accompanies my conclusion that non-abortifacient forms of artificial contraception are morally permissible in Christian marriage. Thus, the distinction is useful despite its obvious lack of analytical precision.

My suggestion here is that, for Lewis, this distinction supports a philosophically unobjectionable – but significant – unstated principle of action that motivates both Lewis' arguments in "Why I Am Not a Pacifist" and in his published response to Mascall. Moreover, once that principle is made explicit, we are better situated to understand the grounds for both Lewis' conviction about the prima facie obligation of ordinary citizens to trust governing authorities in matters related to the justice of war and his simultaneous hesitance about this very conclusion. The principle that I have in mind is a practical epistemological one – one that I shall refer to as the principle of epistemic moral certainty. According to the principle of epistemic moral certainty, in circumstances calling for a moral response, one should always act on that information together with those moral principles about which one is the most clear or about which one has the greatest degree of epistemic certainty.

As an epistemic principle, the principle of epistemic moral certainty is intrinsically relative in two ways. First, whether any given set of data and moral principles is the most clear is relative to the subject engaged in the moral deliberation. Quite simply, what is most clear to you may not be most clear to me. This is because, as we noted with the distinction between moral and mathematical certainty, epistemic certainty is, in general, always relative to the epistemic agent. In other words, how certain one is of any particular conclusion during moral deliberation depends upon the *apparent* strengths and weaknesses of the relevant premises in competing arguments. Second, the degree of certainty that an epistemic agent possesses about competing sets of information and moral principles is relative to the information and moral principles which a subject has within her epistemic grasp. One's relative degree of epistemic certainty about some information or moral principles must be measured against one's relative degree of epistemic certainty about other information and moral principles. One important consequence of this feature of the inherent relativity of this principle is that one's level of epistemic moral certainty can change. Indeed, there may be cases where once new information is gathered or once a new argument is heard in defense of a new set of moral principles, what seemed most certain during prior moral deliberation no longer seems as certain as the new set of information or principles. Thus, this principle leaves room for what we might think of as epistemic moral growth.

As a practical principle, the principle of epistemic moral certainty is about action. It presupposes that when an ordinary human being is engaging in moral deliberation, it is impossible to achieve complete or perfect epistemic certainty about what course of action is morally best. This assumption seems supported by two aspects of human nature that Christians accept; we are both finite and fallen. Because we are finite, it is impossible for us to grasp all of the considerations (i.e., information and moral principles) that are potentially relevant to making the ideal moral decision in any given circumstance. Because we are fallen, it is impossible for us to be certain that our grasp of what is the best course of action in moral deliberation has not been corrupted by sin. Thus, if we supposed that we should not act apart from perfect moral certainty, then we would never act. Since I take it that the failure to act is itself a form of action, the reality is that we must act. And since we must act, this principle requires that we must act on that which is the clearest to us in the circumstances calling for action.

As previously noted, the principle of epistemic moral certainty strikes me as philosophically unobjectionable. However, at least one observation is worth noting in its favor. Our intuitive judgments about moral culpability are what support this principle. In general, there is strong intuitive support for the idea that people who *knowingly* do wrong bear a greater degree of moral responsibility than people who do wrong in ignorance. This is not to say, however, that one cannot be culpable for a wrong committed in ignorance. It is simply that it is far worse to commit a wrong knowingly than it is to commit a wrong in ignorance. If this intuition is right, then it provides at least some support for the principle of epistemic moral certainty. For what motivates it is precisely the idea that in a situation calling for a moral response, it would be worse, morally speaking, to act wrongly in light of information and moral principles that seemed very clear to the agent than to act wrongly in light of information and moral principles that did not seem as clear.

As previously noted, the principle of epistemic moral certainty figures importantly in Lewis' motivation for his conclusion about the obligation of ordinary citizens to trust governing authorities in making determinations about the justice of war. However, seeing this connection requires some degree of speculation about the manner in which Lewis may have tacitly employed it. Nevertheless, I maintain that doing so is warranted insofar as it explains both the strength with which his convictions are expressed in response to Mascall and his qualms about the same.

My speculation is that in the process of reasoning about the obligations of ordinary citizens to respond in times of war, Lewis tacitly employed the principle of epistemic moral certainty in a relatively straightforward way. For this principle supports the following line of reasoning.

> 1. As a Christian and an earthly citizen, my prima facie moral obligation to obey governing authorities is very clear. [from Scripture]
>
> 2. So, if it is not at least as clear or more clear to me that obeying the governing authorities would violate some moral obligation that I have as a heavenly citizen (a citizen of the kingdom of God), then I should obey the governing authorities. [from 1 and the principle of epistemic moral certainty]
>
> 3. It is not as clear to me that trusting in the determinations of the governing authorities about the justice of a war and acting in accordance with that trust violates some moral obligation that I have as a heavenly citizen as it is that I should fulfill my prima facie obligation to obey governing authorities.
>
> 4. Therefore, if, as an ordinary Christian citizen, the governing authorities require my support for a military conflict, I have a prima facie obligation to obey. [from 2 and 3]

As I have pointed out, Lewis did not explicitly disclose his reasoning for the prima facie obligation that he thought ordinary citizens had to trust in the determinations of governing authorities about the justice of war. Thus, aside from a passing reference to the complexity of international affairs, we are left with supposing either that Lewis was merely asserting an ungrounded preference or that he was relying on a plausible, yet implicit, line of reasoning. Regrettably, many current discussions in the public square among ordinary citizens about the justice of armed conflict eventually deteriorate to the point where both parties view the other as merely asserting ungrounded preferences. Undoubtedly, the brevity of Lewis' letter in response to Mascall would have contributed to at least some original readers viewing Lewis as doing nothing more than this. However, if my speculation is correct, Lewis' position was framed by a larger theoretical framework. That framework includes the principle of epistemic moral certainty, along with my speculation that Lewis tacitly applied it along the lines suggested above.

The support for my speculation derives from its ability to explain both the strength with which Lewis expressed the obligation to trust governmental determinations about the justice of war and his reticence about the same. That my speculative line of thought achieves both explanatory aims is evident in the reasoning itself. Both the conclusion and the reasoning that supports it have a strong presumption in favor of the ordinary citizen's obligation to obey governing authorities. This cuts strongly against the radical individualism upon which Lewis clearly frowns in his passing remark about modernity, autonomy, and the "private conscience of the individual". At the same time, the conclusion of the reasoning is ultimately conditional. One does not have an absolute obligation to obey governing authorities. Moreover, the principle of epistemic moral certainty – a principle on which the proposed line of reasoning relies – accounts for the conditional nature of the conclusion in a fairly precise and personal way. Specifically, the conclusion that I am obliged to obey my government if it requires my support in war is subject to change relative to information or moral principles about which I may subsequently achieve greater epistemic certainty. This explains Lewis' own reluctance in concluding "that the ultimate decision as to what the situation at a given moment is in the highly complex field of international affairs is one which must be delegated" to governing authorities ("Just War" 326). In expressing this reluctance, Lewis implicitly recognizes the possibility that his own epistemic certainty about pertinent information or moral principles might reach a point at which the prima facie obligation to trust governing authorities about the justice of a given war is overridden.

Even if my speculation about the rationale for Lewis' position is correct, at least one question remains. Why frame the discussion so heavily in favor in the apparently small virtue of dutifully fulfilling one's legal obligations with respect to governing authorities? Lewis' answer to this question is made explicit in his response to Mascall, and it is arguably consistent with New Testament teaching (see I Peter 2:13-17). Quite simply, respect for governing authorities is essential to Christian witness. Lewis writes:

> Decisions by the private conscience of each Christian in the light of Mr. Mascall's six rules would divide Christians from each other and result in no clear Christian witness to the pagan world around us. But a clear Christian witness might be attained in a different way. If all

Christians consented to bear arms at the command of the magistrate, and if all, after that, refused to obey anti-Christian orders, should we not get a clear issue? A man is much more certain that he ought not to murder prisoners or bomb civilians than he ever can be about the justice of a war. It is perhaps here that 'conscientious objection' ought to begin. I feel certain that one Christian airman shot for refusing to bomb enemy civilians would be a more effective martyr . . . than a hundred Christians in jail for refusing to join the army. ("Just War" 326-7)

Of course, what Lewis expresses here about effective Christian witness in war flies directly in the face of the tradition of Christian pacifism. For according to the latter, effective Christian witness is partly a matter of refusing to comply with any governmental orders that would require the intentional taking of human life. Obviously, a rationally compelling case against Christian pacifism is far beyond the scope of this essay – perhaps it is beyond the scope of any essay. Moreover, even though Lewis argued directly against pacifism himself, one might legitimately remain within his rational rights in finding Lewis' case less than compelling. Yet apart from a rationally compelling case against Christian pacifism, one might be tempted to wonder whether the Lewisian line of reasoning developed in this essay has any merit.

Let me suggest, by way of conclusion, that the value of Lewis' reasoning for the idea that ordinary citizens have a prima facie obligation to trust in the determinations of governing authorities about the justice of war and to act in accordance with that trust lies in its capacity to focus discussions about Christian citizenship, war, and our moral response. Even if Lewis is wrong about pacifism, his reasoning frames the dialogue in a helpful way. For, if in our roles as ordinary citizens, we discuss the nature of Christian citizenship, war, and our moral response through the framework presented here, the typical excruciatingly complex threads of argument come to a point. Either Christian pacifism is true or we have a prima facie obligation to trust, to support, and to obey determinations made by governing authorities about the justice of a given military conflict. Moreover, the mere logical possibility that Christian pacifism is true is irrelevant in the Lewisian framework. This is because in circumstances calling for moral response, one must act in accordance with those moral principles about which one has the greatest degree of epistemic certainty. Thus, since, for the Christian, the obligation to obey governing authorities is very clear, the case for Christian pacifism must, for the individual citizen in question, possess a *significantly* high degree of epistemic certainty if it is to override the prima facie obligation in question. Aside from this, there is, as Lewis' response to Mascall makes quite clear, not a great deal for ordinary Christian citizens to discuss in times of war.

Undoubtedly, the line of thought that I have described, endorsed, and attributed to Lewis, will strike some as the creation of an overly simplistic moral universe. Those whose moral palates are more refined will perhaps prefer the more nuanced flavors expressed in Mascall's reply to Lewis. Mascall writes:

> I do not deny the right and duty of the individual to trust his government if he believes he has reason to do so; I do urge, however, that he must consider whether it *is* trustworthy and not blindly obey it simply because it is the government. And this duty will obviously bind in proportion to the intelligence and opportunity of enlightenment of the individual; the professional student of international affairs must use more diligence than the man who is illiterate. ("Just War" 457)

Mascall's cautionary note will certainly appeal to academics, myself included, for whom the cultivation of intellectual virtue is a matter of deep vocational significance. Still, Lewis' reasoning about moral response on the part of ordinary Christian citizens in times of war seems to situate intellectual virtue properly. The cultivation of intellectual virtues should never come at the expense of the cultivation of the moral virtues of trust and obedience. For what does it profit a man if he gains the whole world of an intellectually sophisticated, informed, private conscience, yet loses the soul of a moral community in action?

WORKS CITED

Aristotle. *Nicomachean Ethics*. Trans. H. Rackham. Cambridge: Harvard UP, 1994.

Lewis, C. S. "The Conditions For A Just War." *God in the Dock*. Ed. Walter Hooper. Grand Rapids, MI: Eerdmans, 1970. 325-7.

—. "Why I Am Not a Pacifist." *The Weight of Glory and Other Addresses*. Ed. Walter Hooper. New York: Simon & Schuster, 1996. 53-71.

Mascall, E. L. "The Christian and the Next War." *Theology*. 38 (1939): 53-8.

—. "The Conditions for a Just War." *Theology*. 38 (1939): 457-8.

Chapter Three

Can Science Be Saved?
C. S. Lewis on Science, Magic, and Ethics

Michael P. Muth

Science is a mode of thought and practice that, over the past several centuries, has come to be treated as our culture's principal arbiter of truth, the discipline to which society turns for certainty and knowledge. It has thus come to have increasing social power and authority. This authority, which shows no signs of weakening as we enter the 21st century, is built on the claim that science generates knowledge that is identifiable as such because it provides us with means for doing things in the world, i.e., of manipulating the world in increasingly powerful and useful ways. Thus the expectations and designs of the earliest modern scientists – that science will provide the new, post-medieval, post-superstitious, post-Aristotelian world with the material means for the "advancement" of human society – are as strong now as they were in the early modern period, perhaps even more so as science continues to generate more (and more efficient and powerful) technologies.

Science is thus accepted as a basic form of human rational practice, the principal bulwark of modern society's claim to advancement over earlier periods. So important is science to society today that to express suspicions about science's place in or effects on society puts the questioner in serious peril of being branded as anti-intellectual, a reversion back to that medieval, superstitious, Aristotelian (and thus ignorant) past. To question science is to question reason itself and all the social benefits that scientific reason has created. C. S. Lewis, however, expresses precisely such suspicions about science, worrying that science is a danger to human beings and society. And Lewis, I wish to argue, is right to be suspicious. Science, as a practice committed to increasing human power over nature and without a set of values internal to it that can limit and guide it, is a tool for power that begs to be used by those who seek power over others. Science is thus not a merely neutral practice, but is itself a "fallen" practice, with a natural bent toward what Augustine calls *amor dominandi* – the love of power and dominance (598).

My claim that Lewis is suspicious of science itself (and that he is rightly so) is opposed by many Lewis commentators, who are generally very careful to argue that Lewis does not commit the sin of questioning science but rather rejects only "scientism." Michael Aeschliman for example defends Lewis' rational orthodoxy: "In *The Abolition of Man* C. S. Lewis noted that nothing he could say would keep some people from saying that he was anti-science, a charge he was nevertheless eager to refute" (16). Henry Schaefer, in "C. S. Lewis on Science and Scientism," also claims that Lewis' *The Abolition of Man* and *The Space Trilogy* are not attacks on science *per se* but rather on "scientism." Though Lewis defines scientism as a theory about humanity's moral end, specifically as "the belief that the supreme moral end is the perpetuation of our own species, and that this is to be pursued even if, in the process of being fitted for survival, our species has to be stripped of all those things for which we value it – of pity, of happiness, and of freedom" (Reply 71-72), Schaefer takes Lewis to be rejecting scientism as a methodological theory, borrowing a definition from a version of Webster's dictionary: "a thesis that the methods of the natural sciences should be used in all areas of investigation including philosophy, the humanities, and the social sciences; a belief that only such methods can fruitfully be used in the pursuit of knowledge" (122). Lewis does critique this sort of methodological position, which he believes supports the claim about our moral end, and many who comment on Lewis's views on science rightly point out Lewis's rejection of such epistemological or ontological reductionism. For these writers, Lewis is not guilty of blasphemy against science, but wants only to keep it in its proper place.

Two passages from Lewis' writings are key to this defense of his rational and scientific orthodoxy. The first is Lewis' response to J. B. S. Haldane's criticisms of his *Space Trilogy*. In his "A Reply to Professor Haldane" Lewis addresses Haldane's claim that he (Lewis) "traduces scientists," claiming that, though one text (*Out of the Silent Planet*) may do so, *That Hideous Strength*, which Haldane singles out as the locus of Lewis' attack, is not actually an attack on scientists, but on "scientism" (71). If anyone should be offended by *That Hideous Strength*, Lewis says, it shouldn't be scientists but civil servants and some philosophers (73). His real attack in the novel, he continues, was against "a certain view about values," i.e., the "scientism" mentioned earlier

(73). It is worth noting here that in this "Reply" Lewis only explicitly denies that he was attacking *scientists*. He does not, however, similarly deny that he was critiquing *science*.

The second important passage from Lewis addresses the charge that *The Abolition of Man* is an "attack on science" (it is the text referenced by Aeschliman above):

> Nothing I can say will prevent some people from describing this lecture as an attack on science. I deny the charge, of course: and real Natural Philosophers (there are some now alive) will perceive that in defending value I defend *inter alia* the value of knowledge, which must die like every other when its roots in the *Tao* are cut. (75)

If anything could clear Lewis of the charge of being "anti-science," this passage certainly would seem to do so, since Lewis explicitly denies attacking science in a book that otherwise appears to express deep suspicion of science. But Lewis immediately continues this passage with: "But I can go further than that. I even suggest that from Science herself the cure might come" (75). We need to note several things about this entire passage. First, Lewis clearly implies that he thinks something is in fact *wrong* with science, since otherwise it would need no cure: "Those who are well have no need of a physician, but those who are sick" (Luke 5:31 RSV). Second, his suggestion that "from Science herself the cure might come" is only gestured at in the rest of the text and his gestured reply would imply, if we try to flesh out what he means, a radical rethinking of science that would, for instance, end science's objectivity. Third, note the peculiar shift from talking of "science" to talking of "natural philosophy," a rather antiquated (even quaint) term no longer used by scientists themselves, and the claim that his defense of value in *The Abolition of Man* is also a defense of the value of knowledge. The implication is that "natural philosophy" is about knowledge. But in the rest of *The Abolition of Man* (as well as several other texts) Lewis denies that this is true of science – knowledge, he argues, is not, and has not been since its inception, the primary goal of science. It is this true goal that grounds Lewis' anxieties about science. But if knowledge is not the goal of science, what is?

Popular history has come to imagine that science began as an intellectual search for knowledge through adherence to a new empirical rationality expressed in a new methodology – hypothesis and experimentation. This popular history assumes that this new science was opposed to earlier superstitions, especially magic, the idea that human beings could, through words and gestures, manipulate the natural "sympathies and antipathies" of the universe to make it do what the magician wants. In both *The Abolition of Man* and *English Literature in the Sixteenth Century*, Lewis, however, attacks this popular history of science and its supposed war on magic. Modern science and magic, Lewis argues, were both creations of the early modern period, "born of the same impulse:"

> The serious magical endeavour and the serious scientific endeavour are twins: the one was sickly and died, the other strong and throve. But they were twins. They were born of the same impulse. I allow that some (certainly not all) of the early scientists were actuated by a pure love of knowledge. But if we consider the temper of that age as a whole we can discern the impulse of which I speak. (*Abolition* 76-77)

This age, Lewis claims, was particularly concerned with issues of *power*, and the shared impulse that unites science and magic is their common pursuit of power over nature:

> There is something which unites magic and applied science while separating both from the 'wisdom' of earlier ages. For the wise man of old the central problem had been how to conform the soul to reality, and the solution had been knowledge, self-discipline, and virtue. For magic and applied science alike the problem is how to subdue reality to the wishes of men: the solution is a technique; and both, in the practice of this technique, are ready to do things hitherto regarded as disgusting and impious – such as digging up and mutilating the dead. (77)

"Man's conquest of Nature" (53), then, is the shared goal – the power to manipulate and control nature to suit our ends, whoever "we" might happen to be, and regardless of the tasks necessary in order to gain that power. The magician is willing to flirt with spiritual beings that are at best neutral, perhaps hostile, to humanity and God. The scientist is willing to desecrate graves or other "superstitious" prohibitions in order to gain the knowledge that leads to power.

The sort of magic Lewis has in mind here is not "mere witchcraft – traditional, perhaps Satanistic, rites practiced by the poor, the ignorant, or the perverted" (*Sixteenth* 7) nor the rather "fairie"-like magic of medieval literature, whereby "Merlin does this or that 'by his subtilty,' Bercilak resumes his severed head" (8). Lewis is writing about the "high magic" that one finds in the works of such thinkers as Giovanni Pico della Mirandola, Marsilio Ficino, Heinrich Cornelius Agrippa, Paracelsus, and John Dee (8). These new devotees of magic claimed that they were reaching back before the middle ages (which they reject as ignorant) to the ancient Greek and Roman world to find the sources for this magical knowledge and technique. Thus the magic Lewis connects to science is something characteristic of the modern age, part of a rejection of the medieval and a renewed fascination with the ancient and classical. It is a bookish magic that calls on neutral spirits (the aerial spirits or daemons) – not the evil ones (that is goety or *goetia*, black magic) – or manipulates natural sympathies that connect disparate parts of the universe in order to affect the course of things in the world. The goal is to use words, gestures, and rituals to gain power over these spirits and sympathetic relations so that they can be manipulated to bring about desired effects in the state of the universe.

And just as these magicians sought to control the forces of nature through their bookish spells, so the modern scientists also sought (and seek) to master nature, though through a different technique. Once the myopia of our historical eyes has been cured and we no longer believe that science and high magic were opposed, we can recognize that:

> ...the new *magia*, far from being an anomaly in that age, falls into its place among the other dreams of power which then haunted the European mind. Most obviously it falls into place beside the thought of Bacon. His endeavour is no doubt contrasted in our minds with that of the magicians: but contrasted only in the light of the event, only because we know that science succeeded and magic failed. That event was then still uncertain. Stripping off our knowledge of it, we see at once that Bacon and the magicians have the closest possible affinity. Both seek knowledge for the sake of power (in Bacon's words, as a 'spouse for fruit' not a 'curtesan for pleasure'), both move in a grandiose dream of days when Man shall have been raised to the performance of 'all things possible'. (*Sixteenth* 13-14)

Only our bad history, which imagines science to be opposed to magic, has hidden from us the fact that the goal of science and the goal of magic are one and the same – control and power over nature. The new science is to replace the old useless one, not as a system of "mere knowledge," but as a means for control. Thus Francis Bacon begins *The Great Instauration* with this statement on the purpose of the new science:

> That the state of knowledge is not prosperous nor greatly advancing, and that a way must be opened for the human understanding entirely different from any hitherto known, and other helps provided, in order that the mind may exercise over the nature of things the authority which properly belongs to it. (7)

Authority and power, then, is the goal of this new science, a goal that can only be achieved when we understand how nature works. Hence knowledge is important, but is not in and of itself the goal of science:

> For the matter in hand is no mere felicity of speculation, but the real business and fortunes of the human race, and all power of operation. For man is but the servant and interpreter of nature: what he does and what he knows is only what he has observed of nature's order in fact or in thought; beyond this he knows nothing and can do nothing. For the chain of causes cannot by any force be loosed or broken, nor can nature be commanded except by being obeyed. And so those twin objects, human knowledge and human power, do really meet in one; and it is from ignorance of causes that operation fails. (28-29)

So we must understand the way the world works, not for mere knowledge (as a "curtesan for pleasure"), but rather so we can use the knowledge to gain mastery over the world (as a "spouse for fruit").

Bacon's goal for the new science, his "dream of power," was not peculiar to him, but in fact characteristic of early scientists. For example, Rene Descartes echoes the same goal in his *Discourse on Method*:

> For they have satisfied me that it is possible to reach knowledge that will be of much utility on this life; and that instead of the speculative philosophy now taught in the schools we can find a practical one, by which, knowing the nature and behavior of fire, water, air, stars, the heavens, and all other bodies which surround us, as well as we now understand the different skills of our workers, we can employ these entities for all the purposes for which they are suited, and so make ourselves masters and possessors of nature. (40)

So our new knowledge is not in itself the goal, but rather it is for the purpose of making us masters of nature. Thus the purposes we put natural entities to are our own purposes, the purposes determined by human beings and human societies. The scientist steps into the role of supreme authority, since she is the one with the knowledge that makes possible our manipulations of the world. Descartes immediately makes it clear that technology is an important part of this goal, when he claims in the very next sentence that:

> This would not only be desirable in bringing about the invention of an infinity of devices to enable us to enjoy the fruits of agriculture and all the wealth of the earth without labor, but even more so in conserving health, the principal good and basis of all other goods in this life. (40)

We can see this commitment to practical outcomes for the new science from its earliest days when we consider that many early scientists were involved in creating technologies for wealthy patrons, especially princes and parliaments. Sciences such as ballistics and optics – two sciences that were quickly brought to a state of sophistication – and the related technologies of warfare were especially popular and lucrative. The telescope, it is worth remembering, was originally a military device intended to aid gunnery, before Galileo turned it to astronomical uses.

So we find at the beginning of modern science the claim that knowledge is important only for the achievement of power over nature, and especially for the creation of technologies that aid us in manipulating nature for our benefit. Knowledge is thus not the goal of science, but the tool. When Lewis says in *Abolition* that "in defending value I defend *inter alia* the value of knowledge" (75) this does not defend science from suspicions that it is a danger to human existence, because knowledge is not the goal of science. This, I think, explains Lewis' shift from "scientist" to "natural philosopher" in this passage from *Abolition*, since a natural philosopher, as a philosopher (literally "one who loves wisdom"), pursues a discipline that does have knowledge as its goal. "Real natural philosophers" would value knowledge principally for its own sake and only secondarily for any practical use. But, supposing that what I, following Lewis, have argued is true of science—that science seeks knowledge only as a means for power—how is science a danger? Surely this power is good for humanity – after all, it relieves us of disease and toil, just as Descartes had hoped. So what is the problem, why Lewis's suspicions?

Because science is a practice aimed at giving human beings power over "Nature," the problem turns out to be twofold. First, science affects how we envision Nature, including human nature, and therefore how we are related to Nature. To the scientist, the things of Nature appear as complex machines to be manipulated so that their inner workings can be discovered and understood and thus further manipulated, not for any purposes or goals innate to the things of Nature, but to achieve the outcomes human beings desire. Thus emptied of innate goals and ends – i.e., any God-given *teloi* – Nature, including human nature, becomes the raw material for whatever goals or ends "we" (whoever "we" are) wish to accomplish. But science, and this is the second problem, does not possess the resources within itself to provide the values that a practice requires for its direction and limits, and science's goal, power over Nature, is largely directionless – power for whom, to what or whose ends? Thus science is a practice that inevitably turns outside of itself for its ultimate direction and so comes to serve whoever happens to have political or economic control.

Let's take up the first point, the transformation of Nature into raw material. This view is clearly encouraged by Bacon and Descartes (and is for that matter pursued by many contemporary scientists) who, like the magicians, envision the new science as a powerful means for manipulating the world. Even the method of the new science encourages this revisioning. The hypothetical method in and of itself is an innocent form of rationality, one that has roots in Plato and further back in early Greek geometers. But the hypothetical method of science, Lewis notes, adds new elements that have profound effects on our conceptions of nature:

> What was fruitful in the thought of the new scientists was the bold use of mathematics in the construction of hypotheses, tested not by observation simply but by controlled observation of phenomena that could be precisely measured. On the practical side it was this that delivered Nature into our hands. And on our thoughts and emotions… it was destined to have profound effects. By reducing nature to her mathematical elements it substituted a mechanical for a genial or animistic conception of the universe. The world was emptied, first of her indwelling spirits, then of her occult sympathies and antipathies, finally of her colours, smells, and tastes. (*Sixteenth* 3)

The scientific method is thus not a methodology of mere observation. It demands the active manipulation of nature through experimentation ("controlled observation of phenomena"), so that we find science's very method requiring control and power over Nature, treating Nature as raw material. Further, science "reduces" Nature to "mathematical elements," numbers to fit *our* calculations. Science thus rejects earlier visions of Nature, both the Nature of the ancient world (and its renaissance imitators) with its "indwelling spirits" and "occult sympathies and antipathies," as well as the teleological and creaturely Nature of the middle ages, which envisioned a universe created and given innate goals and purposes by a loving Creator God. Science's reductionism removes from nature the ends, goals, or *teloi* that ancient and medieval thought saw as intrinsic to creatures, so that human ends can replace creaturely ends. The things of the world, no longer seeking their own God-given ends, become mere objects of human use.

The danger here is that science sets human beings up as tyrants over nature, free to use God's creation for any purposes human beings desire without regard to the Creator of these creatures. Science, in fact, subverts the whole concept of creation – Nature just *is*, a blank slate with no values or goals of its own, a brute fact present to us across a cold, dark abyss of purposelessness. From this perspective, whatever resemblance Nature bears to us is a result of our own anthropomorphic fantasies; any supposed purposes in Nature are merely projections of our own desires. As for a Creator, it seems unlikely any rational, loving, purposeful Being would create a universe so devoid of reason, love, and purpose. And perhaps most importantly the objectification and mechanization of Nature is to include *all* of Nature, even "rational" beings, i.e., human beings themselves. Descartes and others attempted to exempt human beings from the mechanization of Nature, claiming that, because they are rational, human beings are essentially spiritual beings and thus not subject to the same deterministic laws as physical beings. But Hobbes (and later Darwin, Freud, Dawkins, and Dennett) saw clearly the full implications of the new science – there is no justification for excluding human beings from the rest of mechanized Nature. Human beings too are mere machines; the goals and purposes the claim to have are merely the epiphenomena of the accidents of genetic history and the forces of natural selection. Once this Hobbesian step is taken and human beings are envisioned as machines, human beings are in a position to be tyrants over themselves, just as they are over the rest of Nature – or really, as Lewis argues, for one group of human beings to be tyrants over other groups (*Abolition* 58-59, 67, 72-73). It is from all this that we must be saved from science, or perhaps, as Lewis would put it, science itself must be saved. But what could save science? What would prevent this scientific drive to tyranny?

Science is one of many practices that human beings engage in together – such as family life, philosophy, politics (as the search for the common good), Christianity, Judaism, etc. – in order to pursue certain goods that are achievable only in and through those particular practices. Every practice requires both direction and limits that make it possible for us to work together to achieve the goods we seek – direction involves some sort of goal or *telos* that gives shape and structure to the practice, giving the activities of the practice their coherence and meaning; limits involve such values and virtues as justice, respect, humility, honesty, and courage, that structure our relations to one another, so we can pursue the practice's *telos* together and successfully. For many practices, the direction and limits are internal or provided by some larger "metapractice" to which the subordinated practices are coordinated. For instance, for Christians, following Christ is the guiding practice and other practices – family life, career, etc. – should be shaped and guided by it. But what of science? Are the ends and values that science requires in order to be practiced internal to it? In *The Abolition of Man*, Lewis suggests as much, speculating that "from science herself the cure might come" (76), i.e., the goals and values science needs to keep it from degenerating into a form of tyranny could be found within the practice itself. But if the cure must be a set of values and a goal, giving direction and limitations to the practice, science, I argue, does not have enough internal resources to provide these.

My students will sometimes refer to science as "the disinterested search for the truth," which of course is not the case, since if scientists truly had no interests, they would have no reason to search for anything, much less the truth. Science does have its own internal values – it values objectivity, rigor, public scrutiny, and (as we have seen) power, and certainly like other practices science requires justice, honesty, and courage in order to function at all. But are these values enough to save science, to give it direction and head off the threat of tyranny? I don't think so. Mere power over nature is not a sufficiently articulated goal. We are left with the questions: power for what, power to do what, power in whose hands? Within itself science has no further goal, not even, as we have seen, knowledge. From its earliest days, science has handed itself over to the direction and use of other social practices and forces, especially economic and political ones. We have already considered how early scientists enthusiastically involved themselves in pursuing sciences important for military uses and in creating military technology. Nineteenth- and twentieth-century scientists continued this trend: for slaveholders and, later, fascists, scientists created racial theories; for the Nazi regime, they devised V-2 rockets, jet engines, and experiments on concentration camp inmates (to further medical knowledge, though of course for military purposes); for the US government, scientists (including some of the most prominent theoretical scientists of the day, the ones who are supposed to be the most immune to external influences) invented atomic and nuclear weapons; for corporations, scientists create numerous lucrative technologies, from television to Viagra. Science is thus no stranger to being led by the goals and desires of others outside the practice itself.

In his suggestion that "from Science herself the cure might come," Lewis states that:

> It might be going too far to say that the modern scientific movement was tainted from birth; but I think it would be true to say that it was born in an unhealthy neighborhood and at an inauspicious hour. Its triumphs may have been too rapid and purchased at too high a price; reconsideration, and something like repentance, may be required. (78)

Lewis's reconsideration or reimagining of science is not well spelled out – he himself says, "I hardly know what I am asking for" (79). But his reconsideration seems to involve a rejection of any form of objectivity that "explains away" the "objects" of study by reducing them to raw material: "The regenerate science which I have in mind would not do even to minerals and vegetables what modern science threatens to do to man himself" (79). At this point Lewis turns to the work of Martin Buber and suggests that science must not lose sight of the I-Thou relation – though how it could do this and remain recognizably science I am not sure. In any case this regenerate science would require a serious change in methodology.

Perhaps, in the end, repentance is the more fruitful suggestion. As Lewis draws *The Abolition of Man* to a close, he states that, if science cannot provide the limits and direction needed to arrest science's tyrannical tendency, "then someone else must arrest it" (80). In the past as the present, politicians and demagogues have given science direction, as have merchants and corporations. The results of these alliances have been mixed at best, disastrous at worst. Lewis is pointing to a different way – to repentance and humility, to the recognition of science's (and scientists') limits and failures. But repentance and humility require something or Someone before whom one is humble and to whom one repents, and so also belief in that something or Someone, as well as a mind and heart that recognizes the propensity to sin in each person and in the practices and institutions we create and pursue.

An obvious objection to what I, working from Lewis' suspicions, have argued here is that many scientists are in fact committed to a religious faith – Christian, Jewish, Hindu, etc. – and see no conflict between the two; they do not harbor Lewis's (and my) fears about science. And I must admit that few scientists are budding Hitlers. (I must mention, however, that in the last chapter of *Darwin's Dangerous Idea*, Daniel Dennett takes an unsettlingly totalitarian line, suggesting that someone will need to "cage or disarm" religious believers when they step over some moral line: "The message is clear: those who will not accommodate, who will not temper, who insist on keeping only the purest and wildest strain of their heritage alive, we will be obliged, reluctantly, to cage or disarm..." (516). Who the "we" are who are to do the caging is unclear, but the fascistic overtones of "caging" those who refuse to accommodate to some scientific orthodoxy are, from what I have argued here, not surprising, except in Dennett's honesty in expressing them.) Though most scientists exercise small-scale tyranny over their labs and experiments, they are not tempted to conquer the world – the National Science Foundation is not the National Institute for Co-ordinated

Experiments (the N.I.C.E. – see *That Hideous Strength*). But the values and goals that give their scientific studies and activities direction and limits do not, I claim (and I think Lewis would agree with me), come from within science itself. They come instead from other non-scientific commitments, commitments to what Lewis calls the *Tao*, such as a scientist's commitment to a liberal political society. Especially, however, the faith commitments of religious scientists provide the needed goals and limits and keep any subterranean dreams of scientific tyranny in check. Because many scientists are committed to God (or to the Tao in some way), they readily direct their scientific practice away from tyrannical ends and toward more humane ones, and often do not see the tensions that I have tried to make clear here. These goals and values guide and motivate most scientists.

My fear, however, is that science might turn out to be a parasite – i.e., it uses values from outside itself (such as those provided by religious commitments of many scientists) to sustain itself, but then, because it mechanizes nature, driving out all goals and values from it, it ends up attacking the very values that make science as a practice possible. Jacques Monod states this parasitism explicitly: "It is perfectly true that science attacks values. Not directly, since science is no judge of them and must ignore them; but it subverts every one of the mythical or philosophical ontogenies upon which the animist tradition, from the Australian aborigines to the dialectical materialists, has based morality, values, duties, rights, prohibitions" (160). This parasitic tendency helps explain the recent spate of texts by scientists attacking religion and religious faith. Dawkins, Dennett, and Hitchens all attack religion in the name of values they learned from religion, especially the Judeo-Christian tradition – peace, love, respect, humility, concern for the poor and weak, etc. By attacking the religions that give these values a grounding, they attack the values themselves – the possibility that we can somehow ground these values in the vagaries of natural selection is highly doubtful.

If there is hope for science's salvation, and of humanity's salvation from science, it will come, I believe, from those scientists who are willing to commit themselves to God and to God's purposes. It will not come from within science itself, which does not possess the moral and spiritual resources necessary for its own direction and purpose. Politics and business also have proven incapable of guiding science into non-tyrannical directions. If science is to have a hope of becoming a practice helpful to human flourishing, it must then be turned to divine ends. But this is a process that cannot be effected by anyone other than scientists. Governments can perhaps create laws that demand that scientists not step over certain socially acceptable lines, but they cannot dictate a goal (when political power has done so, the results often have been less than pleasant, witnessed in the Soviet Union and Nazi Germany). The Church, on the other hand, can provide a goal, though she must be careful not to dictate what hypotheses will be countenanced and which will not. In the end, the responsibility rests on all our shoulders—on scientists to understand science's limits in regard to morality and value, and on moral and spiritual leaders in society to warn clearly when science oversteps its boundaries.

WORKS CITED

Aeschliman, Michael. "C. S. Lewis on Mere Science." *First Things* 86 (October 1998): 16-18.

Augustine. *Concerning the City of God against the Pagans*. Trans. Henry Bettenson. London: Penguin, 1984.

Bacon, Francis. *The New Organon and other Related Writings*. Indianapolis: Bobbs-Merrill, 1960.

Dawkins, Richard. *The God Delusion*. New York: First Mariner Books, 2006.

Dennett, Daniel. *Breaking the Spell: Religion as a Natural Phenomenon*. New York: Penguin, 2006.

—. *Darwin's Dangerous Idea*. New York: Simon and Schuster, 1995.

Descartes, Rene. *Discourse on Method*. Trans. Laurence LaFleur. New York: The Liberal Arts Press, 1956.

Hitchens, Christopher. *God is not Great: How Religion Poisons Everything*. New York: Twelve, 2007.

Lewis, C. S. *The Abolition of Man*. San Francisco: HarperCollins, 2001.

—. *English Literature in the Sixteenth Century excluding Drama*. Oxford: Clarendon, 1954.

—. *On Stories and Other Essays on Literature*. New York: Harcourt Brace Jovanovich, 1982.

—. "A Reply to Professor Haldane," in *On Stories and Other Essays on Literature*. 75.

Monod, Jaques. *Chance and Necessity*. Trans. Austrin Wainhouse. London: Fontana, 1974.

Schaefer, Henry F. "C. S. Lewis on Science and Scientism." *Science and Christianity: Conflict or Coherence?* Ed. Henry F. Schaefer III. Watkinsville, GA: The Apollos Trust, 2003: 121-136.

Chapter Four

"The Colour of Things in Dark Places":
C. S. Lewis and the "New Science" of Psychology

Byron Brown

One winter afternoon in 1930, C. S. Lewis felt a sudden thrill of joy while taking his daily walk. It was no ordinary sense of satisfaction. Writing to Arthur Greeves that evening, he described it as an "intense feeling of delight" that "sort of stopped me in my walk and spun me around." He had accepted the reality of God several months earlier, and these flashes of euphoria were coming more and more frequently. Their origins, he assumed, were spiritual, a kind of reward for his efforts to exercise more self-control. At the same time, the pleasure was suspiciously visceral. "Indeed," he confided to Greeves, "the sweetness was so great, & seemed so to affect the whole body as well as the mind, that it gave me pause—it was so very like sex."

For Lewis, this joy was not merely a pleasure to savor; it was a puzzle to solve. The stakes were high: at issue was the very nature of spiritual experience. Two explanations were at Lewis' disposal. As he continued his letter that evening, he saw both clearly:

> One knows what a psychoanalyst would say—it is sublimated lust . . . which fancy gives one to compensate for external chastity. Yet after all, why should that be the right way of looking at it? If he can say that *It* is sublimated sex, why is it not open to me to say that sex is undeveloped *It*? as Plato would have said. And if as Plato thought, the material world is a copy or mirror of the spiritual, then the central feature of the material life (= sex), must be a copy of something in the Spirit. . . . (*They Stand Together* 338)

For Lewis, the emotions of that afternoon were personally significant. In less than two years, these moments of spiritual elevation would help complete his conversion to the Christian faith he rejected as a thirteen-year-old. For us, his meditation upon them is the important thing.

On that afternoon's walk, Lewis weighed two paradigms for understanding his experience. He knew both well. One was the Freudian psychology that he had found fascinating if not fully persuasive ever since he had returned to Oxford in 1919. Its perspective was "scientific"; it assumed that human feelings are inseparable from biological events. Freud's aim, as he had stated it in 1895, was "to furnish us with a psychology that shall be a natural science," one that will "represent psychical processes as quantitatively determined states of specifiable material particles" (qtd. in Evans 38). Like the strings of a violin, the emotions cannot vibrate until they are plucked. And the finger that plucks them is, ultimately, a chemical agent, a biological secretion, an electrical impulse passing along a nerve. The other paradigm was Platonic transcendentalism, which gave priority to spirit. Spirit, alone is real, which is to say permanent; everything physical merely reflects something immaterial. Both explanations could not be right.

The thirty-one-year-old Lewis was well versed in psychological explanations of spiritual life. As a young intellectual, he felt their weight of scientific authority. The human mind had been an object of empirical study since 1875, when Wilhelm Wundt established the first laboratory dedicated to that purpose at the University of Leipzig. By the time Lewis enrolled in Oxford, psychology had come to offer a "new foundation" for understanding the humanities and social sciences (Shamdasani "Approaching Babel"). Sigmund Freud laid the first stone of that foundation in 1900 when he suggested that story of Oedipus appeals to its readers on a psychological level (Hartocollis 315). In less than a decade, psychologists like C. G. Jung, Alphonse Maeder, and Franz Riklin were routinely referring to myths as the dreams of society (Shamdasani *Jung* 138). Soon, conventional wisdom held that literature, art, and religion similarly reveal the complex workings of the inner life. Furthermore, as these new psychologists employed a vocabulary of "soul," "spirit," and "psyche" to describe subconscious mental contents, they promised a scientific explanation of spiritual experience that satisfied the increasingly secular spirit of the age.

An avowed atheist when he returned to Oxford in 1919, Lewis was fascinated by these new theories. The reasons are not hard to find. Throughout his life, Lewis had acutely felt a sense of inner division. As he recalled in *Surprised by Joy*, "The two hemispheres of my mind stood in sharpest contrast. On the one side a many-islanded sea of poetry and myth; on the other, a glib and shallow 'rationalism'" (170). As an undergraduate, he continued to possess a fundamentally religious sensibility, a tendency that did not escape his friends' notice. Leo Baker, an early friend, had predicted that the "chimney stack" of Lewis' rationalism would eventually "turn into a spire" (*All My Road* 94). At the same time, Lewis was doggedly pursuing the "New Look" of unsentimental realism, holding to a philosophy of "Stoical Monism" (*Surprised by Joy* 201-05). This philosophy gave him "a great sense of peace," but it could not account for the lusts and longings that continued to surge against the walls of rational materialism he had constructed. For him, as for many of his generation, psychoanalysis promised to open a rational portal to that other side.

The diary Lewis began keeping in April 1922 testifies to his interest in the new "science" of psychoanalysis. That June he read Freud's *Introductory Lectures on Psychoanalysis* (June 3), Havelock Ellis' *The World of Dreams* (June 4), and William James' *On the Varieties of Religious Experience* (June 11). On July 3 he read H. Crichton Miller's *The New Psychology and the Teacher*. The following day, he secured a copy of C. G. Jung's *Collected Essays on Analytical Psychology* for Arthur Greeves. Later that month, he recorded reading W. H. R Rivers' *Instinct and the Unconscious* (July 10), R. H. Hingley's *Psycho-Analysis* (July 14), and Havelock Ellis' *Studies in the Psychology of Sex* (July 26). On July 30 he discussed the anima at length with Leo Baker (*All My Road* 77). During this period, Lewis records many of his dreams as well as offers psychoanalytical interpretations of his friends' dreams. And this interest persisted for several years. In April 1923, Lewis proposed writing a thesis on the metaphysics of modern psychology, a project he eventually abandoned (*All My Road* 230). It also influenced his creative work during this period, especially *Dymer*, a long poem on the dangers of wish fulfillment. Begun in 1922 and published in 1926, it was influenced, Lewis wrote in 1950, by "the new psychology [that] was just beginning to make itself felt in the circles I most frequented at Oxford" (*Narrative Poems* 4).

Lewis tells the story of these years in *The Pilgrim's Regress*, the allegorical account of his conversion that he wrote in August 1932. Book Three, entitled "Through Darkest Zeitgeistheim," will reward our careful attention. It is interesting because it fictionalizes the flash of insight Lewis experienced that winter afternoon in 1930. It is important because it reveals the crucial role that coming to terms with psychoanalysis played his spiritual journey. But it is indispensable to us as we enter a new millennium. What is has to offer, though, it not what we might suspect.

Its value does not primarily lie in Lewis' critique of Freudian psychoanalysis. Since Lewis wrote, Freud's own profession has tried his model of the mind and found it wanting (Cohen). Professional psychologists are best qualified to weigh its merits. We must trust them to judge their own.

Nor is it valuable because it debunks empirical studies of the mind. It is true that psychology has yet to become a unified science with universally accepted methods and falsifiable claims. As Sigmund Koch, editor of a monumental history of the discipline that the American Psychological Association commissioned in 1959, has observed, psychology has been riddled with "heterodoxy and conflict" since its beginning (Koch Foreword 29). Indeed, some psychologists still wonder if their field is the science it aspires to be. In 1999, Koch gloomily concluded, "The . . . history of psychology can be seen as a ritualistic endeavor to emulate the forms of science in order to sustain the delusion that it *is* a science" (Koch "The Image of Man" 313). However, to acknowledge the limits of psychology is not to dismiss the very real knowledge that has come to us through empirical studies of the mind. It is only to acknowledge that psychoanalysts' dream of a coherent, unified science of the mind has proven elusive.

Instead, Lewis' critique of Darkest Zeitgeistheim matters because it reminds us that the pursuit of God begins with the exercise of reason. Like Lewis, we live in an age of faith. Unfortunately, that faith, in our day as in his, is tragically misplaced. Perhaps even more than Lewis, we live in a world where flurries of untested theory swirl across our campuses and through the media. They drift unchallenged into the popular imagination. Ideologues slip on lab coats and present questionable claims and tenuous connections as empirically established truths that should not be subject to the astringent tests of dialectic. In this environment we, like Lewis, are engaged in a deadly serious version of PacMan, the popular video game of the 1980s that featured electronic ghosts and the hero in endless eat-or-be eaten interaction. To survive, PacMan had either to devour his opponents or to be devoured by them. On that January afternoon in 1930, Freudian psychoanalysis threatened to swallow up Lewis' religious experience in a materialist explanation of spiritual realities. Lewis had to incorporate the genuinely scientific insights associated with Freudian psychotherapy into a theistic worldview or else give up the game. Only one could—and can—win. As we wrestle with philosophical and ideological challenges to Christian faith that present themselves as unassailable "science," we can only admire—and hope to emulate—Lewis' spirited battle for reason in an age of misplaced faith. In short, John's passage through Darkest Zeitgeistheim is important because it dramatizes the triumph of reason over blind faith in conventional wisdom. This is a lesson that modern believers must learn. The only other way is to answer one blind faith with another.

Our episode begins as Sigismund Enlightenment imprisons John, Lewis's spiritual seeker, in a cave that is overshadowed by the mountainous Spirit of the Age. Under the Spirit's terrible gaze, living beings become transparent. John watches in horror as a fellow prisoner dissolves into a collage of glands, nerves, blood vessels and organs:

> A woman was seated near him, but he did not know it was a woman, because, through the face, he saw the skull and through that the brains and the passages of the nose, and the larynx, and the saliva moving in the glands and the blood in the veins: and lower down the lungs panting like sponges, and the liver and the intestines like a coil of snakes. (60-61)

In this modern version of Plato's cave, the giant's reductive eye misses the complex reality of living human identity. What he sees is true, but his bizarrely limited perception yields figures that, if anything, are less substantial than Platonic shadows. Lewis, though, is not merely satirizing the act of taking a narrowly biologically view of your neighbor or co-worker. It is similarly mad to view a friend or acquaintance only as a nexus of subconscious contents. The head note he added to the second edition explains his intent: "He [John] sees all humanity as bundles of complexes" (*The Pilgrim's Regress* 61). If I focus solely on the subconscious contents of my mind, Lewis would say, the moods I feel during a brisk fall walk may appear intolerable, just as if I focused solely on the workings of my organs. If I look only at my biological functions, I might assume that my sense of spiritual well-being arises from my stomach as it grunts and writhes in contented digestion. If I look only at the content of my subconscious, I may assume that joy is sublimated infantile sexuality delighting itself in a garden rather than a parent's body. Viewed in isolation, both the human body and the human mind appear unseemly at best, disgusting at worst.

Trapped in this prison of misperception, John nearly despairs. But when his jailer claims that the milk he brings is merely one of several animal "secretions" and that his captives might as well drink one as another, John questions this monumental confusion of categories. Milk, he protests, is intended for food; it is materially different from secretions that eliminate waste. For this dangerous exercise of common sense, Sigismund drags him into the dock to be tried by the Spirit of the Age. There Reason, a "sun bright virgin clad in steel," comes to his defense. She poses three riddles that the Spirit of conventional wisdom cannot ignore and that he cannot answer. In Lewis' allegory, her questions liberate John and set him back on the path to find the Landlord. We could do worse than consider them ourselves.

Reason's first riddle forces the Spirit of the Age to acknowledge two things about the nature of meaning. First, it challenges him to admit that his vision of humanity is "half created" as well as "half perceived." Here is her question: "What is the colour of things in dark places, of fish in the depth of the sea, or of entrails in the body of man?" (64). Color, of course, is merely reflected light. It cannot exist in the absence of light. The obvious, if cryptic, answer is, "If they are in the dark, then they have no color." The giant does not respond. To do so would be to acknowledge a devastating truth. If organs and psychological complexes naturally exist in the darkness of the body and the subconscious, then they naturally have no color. Any "color" they appear to have is artificial, merely reflection of the unnatural light that has been used to illuminate them.

Moreover, her question reminds John that meaning is contextual. "If you take an organ out of a man's body," Reason later tells John, "—or a longing out the dark part of a man's mind—and give to the one the shape and colour, and to the other the self-consciousness, which they never have in reality, would you expect them to be *other* than monstrous?" (71; emphasis mine). If you remove anything from the system to which it belongs, Lewis' riddle reminds us, you cannot hope to see it for what it is. Severed and displayed in museum cabinets, human lips and nostrils would be hideous indeed. Viewed in living human faces, they may and do appear beautiful. The only truth that matters, Lewis argues, is the one that lies in the whole.

A meaningful whole, however, exceeds the sum of its parts. According to the quasi-scientific Spirit of the Age, the reality of living things lies in the physical components that make them up. From one point of view, that is unquestionably true. The Internet is composed of wires, diodes, and silicon wafers linked by fiber optic cables. From another, the Internet that matters is a living archive of conversations, images, news, and blogs. For Lewis, the "reality" of any system—whether it be physical or psychological—lies not in the parts that make it up individually considered, but in the whole to which each contributes. Here is Reason's explanation:

> . . . in the real world, our inwards are invisible. They are not coloured shapes at all; they are feelings. The warmth in your limbs at this moment, the sweetness of your breath as you draw it in, the comfort in your belly because we breakfasted well, and your hunger for the next meal—these are the reality: all the sponges and tubes that you saw in the dungeon are the lie. (70)

Only a madman walks through his front door and sees wires, wood, drywall and caulking rather than his home. A man who looks at his wife and sees only hairs, skin, mascara and slightly yellowed tooth enamel no doubt sees something horrible, but he has not seen his wife.

We must acknowledge that Lewis' skepticism is not indiscriminate. In "Psycho-Analysis and Literary Criticism," Lewis grants the premise of infantile sexuality, namely,

> (1) That infantile sexual experience of the sort described by Freud does occur in all human beings; (2) That latent thought on such subjects does utilize the images [fathers, mothers, journeys, small animals, gardens] I have mentioned; and (3) . . . that wherever such images occur in dream, imagination, or literature, the latent thought which Freud mentions is unconsciously present. (127)

Lewis concedes a lot. If a poet uses images that originate in his latent sexual impulses, then they must contribute in some way to his poem's meaning. Our question is, "how?" Freud would argue that they must appeal, subconsciously, to the same impulses in his readers. Lewis would not completely disagree. But he insists, as should we, that while latent sexuality may contribute to its meaning, it does not constitute the totality of its meaning. The context is key.

We might think of it this way. Whatever force a suppressed psychological complex has in a literary work, it has as a hidden part of a higher, more comprehensive whole. As part of the living poem that vibrates in the speaker's voice and echoes in its hearer's consciousness, this hidden complex takes on a new "color," a new quality. The disgusting color it seems to have when viewed in artificial isolation is transformed by the new spectrum of light shining upon it in this new context. Chefs have learned this lesson in the kitchen. In barrel or bottle, a drop of fish sauce merely smells like fermented flesh. In a Caesar salad or casserole, it mingles with a dozen other flavors to create a totally different culinary effect.

We may think of it another way. Words, Lewis tells us in *Studies in Words*, may have multiple meanings. These meanings depend on the word's context. If I am describing my best friend, *kind* may mean *gentle* or *gracious*. If I am comparing two styles of jazz, it may refer to *type* or *category*. Context, Lewis tells us, has an "insulating power" (11) that allows the same word to have multiple meanings. The half-formed childish longing that Freud calls "Oedipal" may have one meaning in its author's subconscious. What might repel us in that context may have a very different meaning, and a different effect, in a poem.

But I believe the question of context will take us further. As Lewis explains in "Transposition," some meanings are "higher," that is to say, more complex, than others. A poem may translate an impulse from a biological to a spiritual register. What is merely a muddy, half-formed, childish impulse in the subconscious may become a clear and luminous idea in *Paradise Lost*. The more complex meaning is not biological but spiritual; its true meaning is determined by its highest, most manifold realization, not its inchoate origins. No sane person would say that a human hand is "really" just the flipper of a month-old fetus. Nor the "real" marigold, a half-germinated seed.

I shall address Reason's next two riddles more briefly. The second I will paraphrase as follows: "Is it better to have a bridge to your castle that both you and your enemy can use—or to have no bridge at all?" The "castle," of course, is one's claim, one's conclusion. The "bridge" is the argument one uses to get to that end. This riddle reminds us that Reason's sword is double-edged and cuts both ways. This, of course, is the insight Lewis had in January of 1930 when he realized that, if the spiritual elevation he called *It* could be sublimated sexual desire, then sexual desire could simply be a biological echo of *It*. Lewis and his circle were fond of turning arguments "the other way round," and that is precisely what Reason invites John to do when she explains the meaning of her riddle. If belief in a "Landlord" fulfills a wish, she tells him, then so may the denial that there is a Landlord. Once John finally understands the fundamental law of reason, he laughs so hard at the "vastness and impudence and simplicity of the fraud that had been practiced upon him" that the broken chains of that still cling to him shatter and fall from his arms (72). This law of reason, the principle of reciprocity, has not lost its liberating power. The student who reads Richard Dawkins' *The God Delusion* and asks if its author suffers from an Atheist Delusion has learned its lesson. The goal is not to create students adept at making glib reversals. It is to create thinkers who consider every logical option, who will thrust as well as parry in the dialectical skirmishes we must fight. Lewis' second riddle reminds us that "science," for all its confident assertions and complex methodologies, has an older, simpler, and more powerful sister, Reason, whose interrogations she must ultimately bear, whether she will or not.

Reason's third riddle and final riddle reveals the limits as well as power of ratiocination. It takes the form of an apparently simple question: "By what rule do you tell a copy from an original?" (64). As John later confesses to Reason, his longing for the Island and his lust for "brown girls" felt very much alike. Worse yet, his glimpses of the spiritual Island all too often ended in carnal union. This riddle, like the first, directly addresses the problem posed by Freudian psychology. If spiritual and sexual longings appear together, then how do you know that they are not simply different manifestations of the same thing? For John—and Lewis—the question was, "How do we distinguish between "It" and sexual libido? For us, it may take the form of, "How do we distinguish between genuine faith and a "father complex" or between spiritual compassion and a "mother complex"?

Like Reason's second riddle, her third one broadens John's horizon of judgment by challenging him to see that psychology's claims are not necessarily logical conclusions. They may be nothing more than beginning assumptions. She reminds him that when two things possess more similarities than chance can explain, then he must consider at least three possibilities:

A is a copy of B;

B is a copy of A; or

Both A and B are copies of C.

John had been oppressed in the giant's prison because he had accepted the one option presented to him rather than considered all of the possible options. "Sexual libido is the origin of spiritual longing," this option stated, "because physical things are real and spiritual ones are not." The moment that this assumption is put into words, though, other logical options become evident. In *The Science of God*, Gerald Schroeder employs the third option as an argument for the existence of God. Pointing out the repetitions of the "exponential spiral" through the universe, from the Nautilus seashell to the distribution of stars in spiral galaxies to the relationship of what he calls "earth time" and "genesis time," he suggests that if the same pattern is echoed in both time and space, then they must share a common origin that lies outside either (60-71). We may not be persuaded by Schroeder's evidence, but Lewis' Reason would no doubt approve the breadth of his vision, his willingness to consider options that lie outside the boundaries of conventional wisdom.

Before the two part company, Reason assures John that she is a better guide to the mind than is psychoanalysis. "I can bring things out of the dark part of your mind," she tells him, and into the light part of it" (67). The things she draws out are ideas, assumptions, and concepts whose proper existence lies in the light of consciousness. This illumination ripens them into the intellectually sustaining fruit of self-knowledge and sound judgment. Psychoanalysis, on the other hand, projects its dim, distorted light into hidden recesses of the mind that were never meant to be illumined. The sickly glow of its beams creates horrifying phantasms that, like the shadows Ransom sees in the caverns of Perelandra, only serve to terrify and enervate whoever sees them.

At the same time, Reason cautions John that she cannot be his final guide. Inspired by the spirit of Socratic dialogue, she cautions him, "I can only tell you what you already know" (67). The power to demolish nonsense and to deflate pretensions is valuable indeed. But it can lead no further than a healthy skepticism. In his critique of modern theology—which Lewis distrusted almost as much as psychoanalysis—he affirmed that value:

> . . . agnosticism is, in a sense, what I am preaching. I do not wish to reduce the skeptical elements in your minds. I am only suggesting that it need not be reserved exclusively for the New Testament and the Creeds. Try doubting something else. ("Modern Theology and Biblical Criticism" 164)

Ultimately, reason's greatest power—perhaps its only power—is to deliver us from false claims and partial perceptions. Like the virgin warrior of *The Pilgrim's Regress*, it can liberate us from the Spirit of the Age, but it cannot guide us all the way to the Landlord. Truth must be discovered elsewhere. Philosophy teases with hints of that truth. Theology offers only a sketchy outline. For Lewis as for most of his readers, the best way into that emotionally, intellectually, and spiritually satisfying realm lies in accounts of the soul's experience that only imagination can express.

WORKS CITED

Cohen, Patricia. "Freud is Widely Taught at Universities, except in the Psychology Department." *New York Times* 25 Nov. 2007, late ed. (East Coast), sec. 4: 6.

Evans, C. Stephen. *The Person: A Look at the Human Sciences*. Vancouver: Regents College P, 1994.

Hartocollis, Peter. "Origins and Evolution of the Oedipus Complex as Conceptualized by Freud." *The Psychoanalytic Review* 92 (2005): 315-334.

Koch, Sigmund. Foreword. *A Century of Psychology as Science*. Ed. Sigmund Koch and David E. Leary. New York: McGraw, 1985. 7-35.

—. "The Image of Man in Encounter Groups." *Psychology in Human Context: Dissidence and Reconstruction*. Ed. David Finkelman and Frank Kessel. Chicago: U of Chicago P, 1999. 312-328.

Lewis, C. S. *All My Road before Me: The Diary of C. S. Lewis, 1922-1927*. Ed. Walter Hooper. 1991. San Diego: Harvest-Harcourt, 1992.

—. Introduction. *Dymer. Narrative Poems*. Ed. Walter Hooper. New York: Harcourt, 1969.

—. "Modern Theology and Biblical Criticism." 1959. *Christian Reflections*. Ed. Walter Hooper. 1967. Grand Rapids: Eerdmans, 1980. 152-66.

—. *The Pilgrim's Regress: An Allegorical Apology for Christianity, Reason, and Romanticism*. Rev. ed. London: Bles, 1943.

—. "Psycho-Analysis and Literary Criticism." *They Asked for a Paper*. London: Bles, 1962. 120-38.

—. *Studies in Words*. 2nd ed. Cambridge: Cambridge UP, 1967.

—. *Surprised by Joy*. San Diego: Harvest-Harcourt, 1955.

—. *They Stand Together: The Letters of C. S. Lewis to Arthur Greeves (1914-1963)*. Ed. Walter Hooper. New York: Macmillan, 1979.

—. "Transposition." *They Asked for a Paper*. London: Bles, 1962. 166-82.

Schroeder, Gerald. *The Science of God*. 1997. New York: Broadway-Bantam, 1998.

Shamdasani, Sonu. "Approaching Babel: Psychology as a 'New Science' in 1905." Perimeter Institute for Theoretical Physics. Waterloo, Canada. 4 Oct. 2005. *Perimeter Institute Media*. <http://pirsa.org/05100009>.

—. *Jung and the Making of Modern Psychology: The Dream of a Science.* Cambridge: Cambridge UP, 2003.

❖ Part 2 ❖

REASONED TRUTH

&

TRUTH TOO DEEP FOR REASON

> My task was therefore simply that of a translator – one turning Christian doctrine, or what he believed to be such, into the vernacular, into a language that unscholarly people would attend to and could understand.
>
> *Rejoinder to Dr. Pittenger*

Chapter Five

Compulsion and Liberation:
God's Sovereignty and Human Responsibility in the Writings of C.S. Lewis

Brad Mercer

In 1946, Professor J.B.S. Haldane wrote an article in which he directed scathing criticism at some of the characters in C.S. Lewis' science fiction trilogy. He said, as Lewis records in his "Reply to Professor Haldane," that they act "like slugs in an experimental cage who get a cabbage if they turn right and an electric shock if they turn left" (74). To which Lewis responded, "Although I believe in an omnipotent God I do not consider that His omnipotence could in itself create the least obligation to obey Him." He goes on to imply that seventeenth century Calvinists worshipped God as a rather "diabolical" deity (Lewis, "Reply" 74-83).

These statements, however, differ markedly from the ones Lewis offers in his interview with Sherwood Wirt several months before his death. "Do you feel that you made a decision at the time of your conversion?" Wirt asks. Lewis replies, "I was the object rather than the subject in this affair. *I was decided upon* [emphasis mine]." During the course of the conversation, Wirt remarks to Lewis that he appears in *Surprised by Joy* to say that he was "compelled" by God to become a Christian. Lewis answers saying that the most profoundly compelled actions are also the freest actions. "It is a paradox. . . . I expressed it in *Surprised by Joy* by saying that I chose, yet it really did not seem possible to do the opposite" ("Cross-Examination" 261). These are just two examples of many that can be marshaled to illustrate the ongoing tension between God's sovereignty and human responsibility in Lewis' writings.

In order to at least begin to come to terms with Lewis' views on this issue, we must first address his manner of communication. How does he communicate Christian truth? Second, we must address the matter (the substance or essence) of what he communicates. Third, and finally, we must take into account Lewis' great concern to emphasize Mere Christianity.

The Manner of Communication

Lewis is profoundly influenced by the Augustinian medieval worldview which helped shape both Roman Catholicism and Protestantism (Meilaender 235), but he never claims expertise in any theological realm. He consistently presents himself as a teachable layman attempting to communicate basic Christian truth. He sees himself not as a preacher, but as an evangelist and an apologist. Although he regards evangelism with a mixture of "awe and even fear" (Vanauken 134), it is "the real business of life" (Lewis, "Christianity and Culture" 14).

Lewis pursues his evangelistic goals through methods best described as "translating" ("Apologetics" 93, 98) and "smuggling" (*Letters* 322). For Lewis, the content of Christianity must be communicated in an accurate and understandable way. It must never be couched in specialized language or in what Michael Aeschliman calls "linguistic inflation" (5). Says Lewis, "Our business today is to present that which is timeless (the same yesterday, today, and forever) in the particular language of our own age." "Any fool," Lewis writes, "can write learned language. The vernacular is the real test. If you can't turn your faith into it, then either you don't understand it or you don't believe it." This is Christianity for "storekeepers, lawyers, realtors, morticians, policemen and artisans" ("Rejoinder" 183).

When he realizes that reviewers did not recognize the subtle Christian imagery in his first science fiction novel, *Out of the Silent Planet*, he argues that "any amount of theology can now be smuggled into people's minds under cover of romance [romantic, imaginative literature] without their knowing it" (*Letters* 322). Of course, this ability to "steal past those watchful dragons" (Lewis, *On Stories* 47) has made Lewis famous.

On the one hand Lewis works to remove intellectual barriers to Christianity, and on the other he strives to engage the imagination and heart with a vision for what Christianity looks like in action. He conveys what Christians believe and how they behave to thousands of listeners through fifteen-minute radio addresses. He debates atheists at the Oxford Socratic Club and argues in his books for the reality of a fixed moral law that transcends all local cultures. He writes whimsical children's tales that both entertain and instruct, and he re-writes ancient myths overlaying them with Christian imagery. He offers practical advice on everything from how to pray to how to experience genuine affection, friendship, and romantic love, to how to face the inevitable reality of suffering. He instructs his readers on how to read the Bible, how to work, and even how to tithe.

These themes are important for what they reveal about his purpose. Much of the content of Lewis' writings focuses on human responsibility, accountability, and obedience. Social and ethical themes form the heart of Lewis' theological vision (Meilaender 2). Through a variety of literary genres, he seeks to convince, challenge, move, and motivate his readers to look to Jesus Christ for salvation and live lives of love, obedience, and faithfulness to Him and their fellow creatures.

The Matter of What is Communicated

Christian theologians and philosophers have traditionally attempted to reconcile God's omnipotence and omniscience with human freedom by the using the paradigms of Compatibilism and Libertarianism.

Compatibilism, or soft determinism, is the view often held by theologians and philosophers in Augustinian and Calvinistic theological traditions. Martin Luther, John Calvin, Jonathan Edwards and C.H. Spurgeon defend this view. Compatibilism attempts to address the sovereignty-responsibility tension by asserting that human ability to make choices is "compatible" with theistic determinism. For the compatibilist, God is absolutely sovereign. Martin Luther emphasizes that God "foresees, purposes, and does all things according to His own immutable, eternal, and infallible will." This truth is nothing less than a "bombshell" that destroys the libertarian view of free will (80).

The compatibilist also affirms that humanity makes choices in accord with desires. Although human beings do not possess the absolute power of contrary choice, they do make voluntary choices. Calvin does not hesitate to attribute freedom, in the compatibilist sense, to humanity. He writes:

> If anyone, then, can use this word [free] without understanding it in a bad sense, I shall not trouble him on this account. But I hold that because it cannot be retained without great peril, it will, on the contrary, be a great boon for the church if it be abolished. I prefer not to use it myself, and I should like others, if they seek my advice, to avoid it. (266)

Philosopher and theologian John Frame argues that "even if every act we perform is caused by something outside ourselves (such as natural causes or God), we are still free, for we can still act according to our character and desires." Men and women are "free" to do what they want to do, but their decisions flow from their inner motives, desires, and character, or what Frame calls, "heart-act consistency" (136). Unregenerate human beings are "free" to act according to their strongest desires, but by nature they are morally incapable of pleasing God. This moral inability does not eliminate moral responsibility (Frame 137). Human accountability before God is not based upon libertarian freedom. It is based upon the fact that "God made us, owns us, and has a right to evaluate our conduct" (Frame 140).

Socinians, traditional Arminians, open theists, process thinkers, and many modern evangelical theologians and Christian philosophers espouse libertarian freedom. Libertarians argue that the human will has the inherent ability to choose between two or more alternatives: people's choices begin and end with themselves. There is nothing in heaven or on earth that compels a person to make certain decisions or that causes a person to act in a certain way. Human beings possess "the power of contrary choice" (Wright 44) or "the liberty of indifference" (Helm 67). For the Libertarian, God is sovereign but self-limiting. He exercises providential control over all of his creation and creatures by responding to their free choices and taking them into account when he works out his plan.

Recently, a group of theologians, Bible scholars, and philosophers referring to themselves as free will, or open theists, has argued that a consistent view of libertarian freedom entails the admission that God's knowledge of future events is not exhaustive. If God has exhaustive knowledge of future events, the future is already in some sense determined. Clark Pinnock, in his essay on "Systematic Theology," maintains that "Total knowledge of the future would imply a fixity of events. . . . It also would imply that human freedom is an illusion" (121).

This would mean that human beings have no choices or responsibility. This is unacceptable to open theists. Thus, Pinnock is careful to point out that because human beings have the power of contrary choice, God cannot exhaustively know future free human choices before these choices are made ("Theology" 123). God chooses to delegate power to the humanity he creates, and as a consequence makes himself "vulnerable" to their free decisions (Pinnock, "Theology" 115). Pinnock affirms that God is omnipotent, but he argues that he possesses the "quality of power" that enables him to adapt and respond to unforeseen "surprises" ("Theology" 113).

As Scott R. Burson and Jerry L. Walls point out in *C.S. Lewis and Francis Shaeffer*, libertarians argue that in order for human beings to be held responsible for their actions, they must be free to make first cause, contrary choices (67-8). They assert that God does not pre-determine human choices only to hold people accountable for those choices. In their view, this would be unbiblical and nonsensical. It violates the law of non-contradiction and makes God the author of sin (Burson and Walls 91-3).

What about C.S. Lewis? Where does he fit? Does he fit at all? Is it fair to Lewis to evaluate him using these traditional paradigms?

Lewis the Compatibilist

When recounting his own conversion in *Surprised by Joy*, Lewis portrays himself as being tracked down by the relentless hound of heaven, but at the same time, offered "a moment of wholly free choice" (224). It is not unusual for compatibilists to use Lewis' oft-quoted statement that "The hardness of God is kinder than the softness of men, and His compulsion is our liberation" to reinforce their positions (*Joy* 229). Compatibilist Anthony Hoekema uses this quotation to articulate the Calvinist's view of "Irresistible Grace" (105). In Lewis' interview with Sherwood Wirt, he argues that God closes in on him and he is "decided upon," but "the most deeply compelled action is also the freest action." He pictures God as absolutely sovereign in his salvation, and yet his own freedom as vitally important: "It is a paradox" ("Cross-Examination" 261).

In *Perelandra*, Ransom recognizes that future acts are fixed and unalterable, yet at the same time humanity is free: "You might say, if you liked, that the power of choice had been simply set aside and an inflexible destiny substituted for it. On the other hand, you might say that he had been delivered from the rhetoric of his passions and had emerged into unassailable freedom" (149). Lewis appears to be saying that predestination and freedom are parallel truths. For Ransom, predestination and freedom are "identical" (*Perelandra* 149).

In *The Lion, the Witch, and the* Wardrobe, Aslan, the Christ-figure of Narnia, initiates and secures Edmund's salvation by his atoning death on the stone table (130-63). Edmund is completely passive in the process. Aslan sovereignly breathes new life into the stone creatures outside the castle of the White Witch (*Lion* 164-74). He gives new life to Eustace after he had become a dragon, but Eustace must choose to ask him for this new life. In *The Magician's Nephew*, when Narnia is created, Aslan chooses which animals will speak and which will remain dumb" (115-18). In *the Last Battle*, he judges some of his creatures as fit for heaven and others for damnation (153). In *the Horse and His Boy*, Aslan providentially guides and protects Shasta, and he waits patiently for Shasta to turn from his pride and selfishness and trust in him (157). In the *Silver Chair*, Aslan declares to Jill that he is the only way of salvation, and people cannot call upon him until he first calls them (24-5).

In *Till We Have Faces*, Orual finds herself helplessly under the knife of the cosmic surgeon (266). The god of the Grey Mountain clearly has a plan for Orual, and he continually intervenes in her life. He will not leave her alone until his desired result is accomplished. He providentially drives her to her knees. She sees herself for the sinner that she is, turns from that sin, and relies on the grace of the god. The god will have her whether she wants to be had or not. But, at the same time, she must choose him. For Orual, compulsion *is* liberation.

When Lewis illustrates the creator-creature relationship, he often uses the playwright-actor or author-character model. He argues that the events in a play happen as a result of other events in the play, but they also happen because the playwright writes them into the play. Lewis asks in *Miracles*, "Did Ophelia die because Shakespeare for poetic reasons wanted her to die at that moment—or because the branch broke?" He answers, "For both reasons" (179). John Frame and Wayne Grudem suggest the author-character model as one of the best ways to illustrate compatibilism (Frame 156-59; Grudem 321-22). I. Howard Marshall, in his essay on "Predestination in the New Testament," points out that Lewis does not articulate the author-character model precisely the same way that Frame and Grudem do, but libertarians often dismiss this model because of its affinities with determinism (132-33, 139).

Lewis the Libertarian

Although Lewis at times appears to espouse some form of compatibilism, many of his statements on the subject of sovereignty-responsibility are unequivocally libertarian.

When Lewis addresses the problem of evil, he uses the free will defense. Lewis adapts what Paul Helm calls the "risky view" of God's providence (39). As Lewis says in *The Problem of Pain*, human beings, made in God's image, are free to love and obey him or to reject him (51). God is sovereign and good, but he takes a risk in creating human beings with the power of absolute contrary choice. To Lewis, human beings are not "automata" or "toy soldiers" (*Mere Christianity* 53, 159). God is willing to limit the exercise of his own power and pay this "intolerable compliment" to humanity so that he might enjoy a genuine, loving, give-and-take relationship with them (Lewis, *Pain* 84) He humbles himself and "chooses to need" his creatures (Lewis, *Pain* 50). He makes himself vulnerable to the real possibility that they will reject him, but this is a chance worth taking. As Lewis writes in *Mere Christianity*, "Try to exclude the possibility of suffering which the order of nature and the existence of free wills involve, and you find that you have excluded life itself" (34). For Lewis, libertarian freedom is a necessary condition of human personality and accountability.

Human beings choose to reject God and bring evil into the world, but God takes these free, sinful choices into account and uses them to advance his ultimate good purposes. He responds by bringing about, what Lewis calls, a "complex kind of good" (*Pain* 84). In the relationship between God and humanity, God's actions are still "consequent upon, conditioned by, elicited by, our behaviour" (Lewis, *Malcolm* 50). He is never surprised by human rebellion because he sees all of time as a single moment. He reacts and responds to the ongoing free choices of his creatures. Using the give-and-take of the dance metaphor, Lewis says:

> The world is a dance in which good, descending from God, is disturbed by evil arising from the creatures, and the resulting conflict is resolved by God's own assumption of the suffering nature which evil produces. The doctrine of the free fall asserts that the evil which thus makes the fuel or raw material for the second and more complex kind of good is not God's contribution but man's. (*Malcolm* 50)

God never compels any person to trust in him. Each individual must freely choose to accept or reject Jesus Christ. Lewis sees that God "is holding back to give us that chance. . . . We must take it or leave it" (*Mere Christianity* 66). Unfortunately, some are "successful rebels to the end" (Lewis, *Pain* 127).

In *The Four Loves*, Lewis emphasizes that the natural loves, affection, friendship, and romantic love, will never be what they are designed to be until they are transformed by the supernatural love of God. How can we forget Lewis' poetic depiction in an epitaph describing good love gone bad?

> Erected by her sorrowing brothers
> In memory of Martha Clay.
> Here lies one who lived for others;
> Now she is at peace. And so are they. (*Poems* 134)

However, Lewis is confident that human beings are not "unaided" in their salvation, but their "slow and painful approach" must be their own (*Loves* 19). People must conform their actions to God's revealed will. Lewis describes God as omnipotent and sovereign, but this is a sovereignty that never compels. God requires human "consent." The final choice rests with man (*Loves* 16).

In "On Special Providences," Appendix B of *Miracles*, Lewis emphasizes that God determines all that will happen by taking human free choices into account and weaving those choices with other events in the natural world into a unified, seamless whole (174-81). He says, "before all worlds His providential and creative act (for they are all one) takes into account all the situations produced by the free acts of His creatures" (*Malcolm* 50). Here, Lewis' views resemble the traditional Arminan views. God is immanently involved in the lives of his creatures, but his providence takes into account situations brought about by their free choices (Lewis, *Malcolm* 50).

Screwtape, of Lewis' *Screwtape Letters*, makes his anger with Wormwood known when he notes, "your patient has become a Christian." This situation is dire but not without hope: "hundreds of these adult converts have been reclaimed after a brief sojourn in the Enemy's camp and are now with us" (11). In *Mere Christianity*, Lewis states that human beings can "cease" to be Christians (178). People freely choose to become converts to Christ, and they freely choose to no longer be converts to Christ. They make these decisions "on their own" (Lewis, *Screwtape* 13).

In spite of Lewis' affinities for traditional Arminian theology, he is not an Open Theist. He would deny Pinnock's argument in "From Augustine of Arminius: A Pilgrimage in Theology" that "Decisions not yet made do not exist anywhere to be known even by God" (25). Lewis' commitment to a Boethian-Augustinian view of time and God's exhaustive knowledge of future events rules out this view. In *Mere Christianity*, he makes it very clear that "Every one who believes in God at all believes that He knows what you and I are going to do tomorrow" (84). In *The Problem of Pain*, he criticizes the "ridiculous idea that the Fall took God by surprise and upset His plan" (84). God is never surprised.

Lewis' Anglo-Catholic conception of grace lends itself to a liberation paradigm more than a compatibilist paradigm. Because he makes no distinction between justification and sanctification and advocates a view of infused righteousness, what emerges is a transformational model of salvation. Man, through a series of first cause, contrary choices, is always advancing toward heaven or hell but never fully assured that he is in right relationship with God (Burson and Walls 58-62). The infusion of grace brings about the spiritual and moral renewal of sanctification, but this grace can eventually be lost through poor moral choices. Perhaps R.K. McGregor Wright gets it right when he intriguingly labels Lewis an "Evangelical Arminian Anglo-Catholic" (237).

The Emphasis on Mere Christianity

Sometimes Lewis sounds like a compatibilist; sometimes he sounds like libertarian. His statement in *Mere Christianity* gets to the heart of his position:

> You see, we are now trying to understand, and to separate into watertight compartments, what exactly God does and what man does when God and man are working together. And, of course, we begin by thinking it is like two men working together, so that you could say, 'He did this bit and I did that.' But this way of thinking breaks down. God is not like that. He is inside you as well as outside: even if we could understand who did what, I do not think human language could properly express it. (132)

Overall, Lewis is closer to the traditional Arminian, libertarian position, but his own conclusion that human language is inadequate to articulate the mystery of sovereignty-responsibility echoes arguments made by compatibilists. As much as adherents to either of one these views would like to enlist Lewis as a theological ally, he simply does not consistently fit into either category.

D.A. Carson, in *Divine Sovereignty and Human Responsibility*, attributes the ongoing sovereignty-responsibility tension to "an unbridgeable ontological gap" between a transcendent-immanent God and humanity (211). He argues that the biblical writers never attempt to alleviate this tension. In the Bible, God's sovereignty and humanity responsibility are parallel truths. Fair interaction with the biblical data will always leave the issues "restless in our hands" (Carson 220). Attempts to resolve this tension inevitably distort the biblical balance (Carson 221). Lewis would agree.

Lewis contends that the "Calvinist question" of predestination and free will can never be answered with complete clarity. When an individual repents and places faith in Christ, who takes the initiative in this process? It is hard to say. "After all," writes Lewis, "when we are most free, it is only with a freedom God has given us: and when our will is most influenced by Grace, it is still our will" (*Letters* 427). Lewis' conclusions here sound a great deal like those of his friend, Anglican theologian Austin Farrer. In *Faith and Speculation*, Farrer writes, "Both the divine and the human actions remain real and therefore free in the union between them; not knowing the modality of the divine action we cannot pose the problem of their mutual relation" (66).

Lewis argues that practically speaking, many of the questions about how God's sovereignty relates to human responsibility are "meaningless." They never come up in "any concrete case" (*Letters* 427). A Christian who reflects back upon his conversion might be tempted to make his particular experience universal. But he must not assume that his actions and God's actions in his conversion operate in the same way for all Christians. Ultimate reality is self-consistent, but on a human level exactly how God's sovereignty and human freedom operate in every convert cannot be known. As Carson maintains, "For us mortals there are no rational solutions to the sovereignty-responsibility tension . . . neatly packaged harmonisations are impossible" (218). Lewis concludes that rather than deny or weaken sovereignty or responsibility, "it is better to hold two inconsistent views than ignore one side of the evidence" (*Letters* 433).

What does this mean for the daily life of a Christian? Lewis offers a hybrid of Calvinism and Arminianism that is consistent with his portrayal of himself as a "mere Christian": "I find the best plan is to take the Calvinist view of my own virtues and other people's vices: and the other view of my own vices and other people's virtues" (*Letters* 433). He suggests that if a person finds the mystery of God's sovereignty and human responsibility beyond comprehension, "there is nothing to be *worried* about," just credit your own virtues and other people's vices to God's sovereignty and your own vices and other people's virtues to human responsibility (*Letters* 433).

While he asserts that human faculties are not adequate to draw generalizations about God's omnipotence and human freedom from individual experience, Lewis maintains that the Scriptural evidence for sovereignty and freedom is too great not to affirm both. He does not leave his conclusions to the sovereignty-responsibility tension in the realm of abstract theological conundrum. He looks to the texts of Scripture: "It is plain from Scripture that in whatever sense the Pauline doctrine is true, it is not true in any sense which *excludes* its (apparent) opposite" (*Letters* 433).

The "Pauline doctrine" here is God's omnipotence, and the "opposite" is human freedom. Lewis says that the Scriptures teach both. The fact that humanity cannot comprehend and communicate the intersection of these two doctrines does not diminish the fact that both are true. The biblical writers never attempt to reconcile God's sovereignty with human responsibility.

Just months before his death, Lewis wrote that Philippians 2:12, 13 teaches "pure Pelagianism" and "pure Augustinianism" (*Malcolm* 49). All Christians must work out their "salvation with fear and trembling" knowing that "it is God who worketh" in them (Lewis, *Malcolm* 49). He asserts that in the life of a Christian, God's actions and human actions are hard to distinguish. God is the omnipotent creator. He is, Lewis says, "absolute being" who speaks into existence "derivative being" (*Malcolm* 49), but he reacts to his creatures with forgiveness and answered prayer. Human beings are responsible for their actions and free to embrace or reject Jesus Christ. These divine and human actions are "two-way traffic" on the same road (*Malcolm* 50). When people attempt to explore God's actions and human actions in sin, salvation, and prayer, they are faced with a metaphysical "Frontier," a "mysterious point of junction and separation" (*Malcolm* 49).

Lewis refuses to be drawn into the reductionism and "easy solutions" so typical of the sovereignty-responsibility debate (*Malcolm* 220). He avoids the pitfalls inherent in trying to force questions and answers into artificial philosophical categories, placing disproportionate emphases on God's transcendence or immanence, or filtering all questions through an unassailable, intuitive sense of freedom and fairness. He does not run from the unresolved tensions intrinsic to the subject, but, like compatibilists, he appeals to mystery and commends a hardy both/and approach. For Lewis, sovereignty-responsibility is not a problem to be solved, but a mystery to be embraced. Based on practical experience and biblical evidence, he concludes that these parallel truths must be accepted regardless of the appearance of contradiction.

In the end, Lewis accepts, without understanding or explaining, God's omnipotence and omniscience and human freedom because Scripture just "sails over the problem" (*Malcolm* 49). Earthly mysteries have heavenly solutions. This is where he is content to leave the sovereignty-responsibility debate. As he emphasizes at the end of *A Grief Observed*, he says, "Heaven will solve our problems, but not, I think, by showing us subtle reconciliations between all our apparently contradictory notions. The notions will all be knocked from under our feet. We shall see that there never was any problem" (83).

Those who might be tempted to reject Lewis' conclusions on the sovereignty-responsibility tension calling them "illogical," "contradictory," "inconsistent," or "ambiguous," would be to wise to heed the words of one of his foremost mentors, G.K. Chesterton: "As long as you have mystery you have health; when you destroy mystery you create morbidity." The ordinary man "has always cared more for truth than for consistency. If he saw two truths that seemed to contradict each other, he would take the two truths and the contradiction along with them" (*Orthodoxy* 29). For Chesterton (and Lewis), "The riddles of God are more satisfying than the solutions of man" ("Introduction").

WORKS CITED

Aeschliman, Michael D. *The Restitution of Man: C.S. Lewis and the Case Against Scientism.* Grand Rapids: Eerdmans, 1998.

Burson, Scott R. and Jerry L. Walls. *C. S. Lewis and Francis Schaeffer: Lessons for a New Century from the Most Influential Apologists of Our Time.* Downers Grove: InterVarsity Press, 1998.

Calvin, John. *Institutes of the Christian Religion.* Ed. John T. McNeill. Trans. Ford Lewis Battles. 2 vols. Philadelphia: Westminster, 1960.

Carson, D.A. *Divine Sovereignty and Human Responsibility: Biblical Perspectives in Tension.* Grand Rapids: Baker Book House, 1994.

Chesterton, G.K. "The Book of Job." *On Lying in Bed and Other Essays.* Ed. Alberto Manguel. Calgary, Alberta: Bayeux Arts, 2000.

—. *Orthodoxy: The Romance of Faith.* New York: Image Books, 1990.

Farrer, Austin. *Faith and Speculation.* London: Black, 1967.

Frame, John M. *The Doctrine of God.* A Theology of Lordship. Phillipsburg, NJ: P&R Publishing, 2002.

Grudem, Wayne. *Systematic Theology: An Introduction to Biblical Doctrine.* Grand Rapids: Zondervan, 1994.

Helm, Paul. *The Providence of God.* Downers Grove, IL: InterVarsity, 1994.

Hoekema, Anthony. *Saved By Grace.* Grand Rapids: Eerdmans, 1989.

Lewis, C.S. "Christian Apologetics." *God in the Dock: Essays on Theology and Ethics.* Ed. Walter Hooper. Grand Rapids: Eerdmans, 1994. 89-103.

—. "Christianity and Culture." *Christian Reflections.* Ed. Walter Hooper. Grand Rapids: Eerdmans, 1967. 12-36.

—. "Cross-Examination." *God in the Dock: Essays on Theology and Ethics.* Ed. Walter Hooper. Grand Rapids: Eerdmans, 1994. 258-267.

—. *The Four Loves.* New York: Harcourt Brace Jovanovich, 1960.

—. *A Grief Observed.* San Francisco: Harper Collins, 1989.

—. *The Horse and His Boy.* New York: Macmillan, 1970.

—. *The Last Battle.* New York: Macmillan, 1970.

—. "The Laws of Nature." *God in the Dock: Essays on Theology and Ethics.* Ed. Walter Hooper. Grand Rapids: Eerdmans, 1994. 76-79.

—. *Letters of C. S. Lewis*. Ed. and with a Memoir by W. H. Lewis. Rev. Ed. Ed. Walter Hooper. San Diego: Harcourt Brace and Co., 1993.

—. *Letters to Malcolm, Chiefly on Prayer: Reflections on the Intimate Dialogue Between God and Man*. San Diego: Harcourt Brace, 1992.

—. *The Lion, the Witch, and the Wardrobe*. New York: Macmillan, 1970.

—. *The Magician's Nephew*. New York: Macmillan, 1970.

—. *Mere Christianity*. New York: Simon and Schuster, 1996.

—. *Miracles*. New York: Macmillan, 1978.

—. *Perelandra*. New York: Scribner, 1996.

—. *Poems*. Ed. Walter Hooper. San Diego: Harcourt Brace and Co., 1992.

—. *The Problem of Pain*. New York: Macmillan, 1962.

—. "Rejoinder to Dr. Pittenger." *God in the Dock: Essays on Theology and Ethics*. Ed. Walter Hooper. Grand Rapids: Eerdmans, 1994. 177-183.

—. "A Reply to Professor Haldane." *Of Other Worlds: Essays and Stories*. Ed. Walter Hooper. New York: Harcourt Brace and Co., 1994. 74-85.

—. *The Screwtape Letters*. New York: Macmillan 1980.

—. *The Silver Chair*. New York: Macmillan, 1970.

—. "Sometimes Fairy Stories May Say Best What's to Be Said." *On Stories*. San Diego: Harcourt Brace and Co., 1982.

—. *Surprised by Joy: The Shape of My Early Life*. New York: Macmillan, 1955.

—. *Till We Have Faces*. San Diego: Harcourt Brace, and Co., 1984.

Luther, Martin. *The Bondage of the Will*. Trans. James I. Packer and O.R. Johnston. Tarrytown: Fleming H. Revell Co., 1957.

Marshall, I. Howard. "Predestination in the New Testament." *Grace Unlimited*. Ed. Clark Pinnock. Eugene, OR: Wipf and Stock, 1999. 127-143.

Meilaender, Gilbert. *The Taste for the Other: The Social and Ethical Thought of C. S. Lewis*. Vancouver: Regent College Publishing, 1978.

McLachlan, H.J. *Socinianism in Seventeenth Century England*. Oxford: Oxford U P, 1951.

Pinnock, Clark. "From Augustine of Arminius: A Pilgrimage in Theology." *The Grace of God and the Will of Man*. Ed. Clark Pinnock. Minneapolis: Bethany House, 1995. 15-30.

Pinnock, Clark. "Systematic Theology." *The Openness of God: A Biblical Challenge to Understanding God*. Eds. Clark Pinnock, et al. Downers Grove: InterVarsity, 1994.

Vanauken, Sheldon. *A Severe Mercy*. San Francisco: Harper Collins, 1980.

Westblade, Donald J. "Divine Election in the Pauline Literature." *Still Sovereign: Contemporary Perspectives on Election, Foreknowledge, and Grace*. Eds. Thomas Schreiner and Bruce Ware. Grand Rapids: Baker Book House, 2003. 63-88.

Wright, R.K. McGregor. *No Place for Sovereignty*. Downers Grove: InterVarsity, 1996.

Chapter Six

Reflections on the Psalms
C. S. Lewis as Biblical Commentator

Gregory M. Anderson

In his only Biblical commentary, C S. Lewis attempts to correct the misunderstanding and neglect of the Psalms. Diana Glyer reminds us that "much of Lewis's critical work is reactive or remedial in nature" (Glyer 38). *Reflections on the Psalms* is a remedial project. He does for the Psalms what he does for Milton in *A Preface to Paradise Lost*. A master of making theology and renaissance literature accessible to popular audiences, Lewis seeks to rehabilitate the Psalms for the reader and worshiper. As we celebrate the fiftieth anniversary of one of the best selling Biblical commentaries of the last century, this paper will examine the reasons for its success.

The major claim I will make is that the book can best be understood from a rhetorical perspective. Lewis claims that both rhetoric and poetry "aim at doing something to an audience" (*A Preface to* Paradise Lost 52). Lewis' audience-based definition of rhetoric and Aristotle's three major artistic proofs—*ethos, pathos,* and *logos* will provide the interpretative framework.

Before the major claim is advanced, three minor claims will be made: (1) that *Reflections on the Psalms* is a more major work than first realized; (2) that Lewis never had a theological failure of nerve that kept him from apologetics after 1947; and (3) that much of the confusion over the book is due to not understanding the genre of biblical commentary.

Three Preliminary Claims

Bibliographical Blunder:
A Very Ambitious "Unambitious Little Work"

Lewis wrote *Reflections on the Psalms* in response to a request made by his good friend Austin Farrer in 1957. Lewis was worried about the health of his wife and was struggling for a topic.

The Psalms provided a splendid topic for a book. Lyle Dorsett describes how the Psalter was built into Lewis' daily life:

> He normally read daily from the Anglican Book of Common Prayer, steeping himself in the Psalms. In fact, following the book's pattern, he read the daily office, and he most likely read through all 150 Psalms each month. During the academic term he also went to morning prayer…As frequently as possible he also liked to set aside time in the late afternoon, preferably around 5:00p.m., when he could read other parts of the Bible and pray. (Dorsett 64)

Farrer's suggestion gave him the chance to write his first commentary based on his devotional as well as intellectual habits.

He worked on it during his long vacation and reported to his friend Arthur Greeves, "I've been writing nothing but academic work except for a very unambitious little work on the Psalms, wh. [ich] is now finished and ought to come out next spring" (Letters III 900).

It is here at this juncture that we have to deal with some bibliographical blunders. According to D. T. Williams, eleven thousand copies of the book were pre-sold. Williams goes on to note that "was for the time an impressive number for a religious paperback" (Williams 238). Actually, the book was a hardback—the paperback edition was not published by Fontana until 1961. Walter Hooper's definitive bibliography gives 2 January 1961 as the paperback printing in the UK and 7 October 1964 as the first U.S. paperback issued by Harvest House Books (Hooper 808).

Edwin Brown further muddies the waters in his recent book In *Pursuit of C.S. Lewis* by claiming to "have never seen a second printing" of the hardcover version (116). There was one. I own one. My copy reads, "First published September 1958 and reprinted December 1958."

Forgive the bibliographical nit-picking but it is critical in the quest for determining the book's popularity and to honor Lewis' incredible respect for textual criticism to get the facts correct.

Reflections on the Psalms was more popular than the most studies of it seem to indicate. Yet, the book never garnered the attention of his other books. The reviews were mixed yet the book caught the eye of the Church of England. Lewis was asked to join the committee of seven that were revising the Psalms that appeared in the *Book of Common Prayer*. George Sayer reports that Lewis "was surprised to find T. S. Eliot, his old 'enemy,' on the same committee and pleased to discover now he rather liked and respected him" (Sayer 240). Lewis, again on the basis of the book, was asked to consult on the New Testament section of *New English Bible*.

To say that *Reflections* was not Lewis' most popular book is not to say that it was not a very successful commentary. It is cited by over one hundred popular and scholarly works on the Old Testament in general and Psalms in particular. A recent look at Amazon's website found it 11,028 in sales of all books, second in sales under Old Testament popular books, and seventeenth in Old Testament reference works (Amazon website.) Not bad for a book that was published fifty years ago.

Biographical Blunder:
The Great Debate Failure or War Work Fulfilled?

This book followed the last of the *Narnia* books and was his first non-fiction religious book since *Miracles* in 1947. This ten-year hiatus has been the source of considerable controversy. Recent biographer Michael White goes as far as to claim: "After February 1948 Lewis never wrote another word of religious commentary. His last books on religious subjects were purely devotional" (White 175). White joins A. N. Wilson's judgment that "Lewis never attempted to write another work of Christian apologetics after *Miracles*" (214-215).

Reflections on the Psalms seems to contradict such assertions. Although Lewis claimed it was not apologetic in nature, it certainly grappled with critical issues of faith. It provides an earlier refutation to the "no more theology" claims than *Letters to Malcolm, Chiefly on Prayer,* which is unabashedly apologetic in nature. Marjorie Lamp Mead, in a brilliant bit of literary detective work, demonstrates that *Malcolm* was a work in progress for almost ten years and the parts of the manuscript were utilized as the chapter nine of *Reflections* (Mead *209-213).*

The myth that Lewis gave up theological writing stems from a famous debate Lewis had with a young philosopher. George Sayer was the first of many who claimed the ten-year hiatus was because of "the humiliation that he thought he had received from an argument with Elisabeth Anscombe" (239). There has been a great debate about a debate. Lewis sparred with Anscombe, a Catholic Oxford philosopher at the Socratic Club on February 2, 1948 over his philosophical defense of miracles. The jury is still out as to who won the debate but many scholars feel Lewis lost confidence in his apologetics if not the debate itself. This is not the place to rehearse the great debate. Donald Williams does it well and in the context of *Reflections on the Psalms* in his recent, "An Apologist's Evening Prayers: Reflecting on C.

S. Lewis' *Reflections on the Psalms."* Victor Reppert's *C.S. Lewis' Dangerous Idea* is a valuable study of the debate as well, with a strong leaning towards Lewis.

What is interesting is that most of Lewis' critics seem to grant that Anscombe, a student and later literary executer of Wittgenstein the victory. Most Lewis partisans give their hero the ballot. But both sides might be making more of the debate than is warranted.

Alan Jacobs claims "theological argument plays a minor role in Lewis' body of work, if it plays a disproportionately large role in the memories of some of his admirers" (Jacobs 237). It just could be that Lewis was ready for other sorts of writing and after the war he was able to get back to his pet projects. My own take on the whole controversy goes back to what Lewis considered his war work. In a work published in 1949 Lewis bemoans the "too numerous addresses I was induced to give during the late war" ("Transposition" 5). Most of his apologetic books and almost all of his sermons are produced during World War Two. J.R.R. Tolkien thought Lewis "took it up in a Pauline spirit, as a reparation...he would do what he could do to convert men or stop them from straying away" (qtd. in Wilson 179).

You do not have to accept my "war work" thesis. The domestic demands of a dying Mrs. Moore, then a new family, his academic writing—including the magisterial *English Literature in the Sixteenth Century Excluding Drama*, a switch from Oxford don to Cambridge professor, as well as the *Narnia* books provide an alternative explanation for a sabbatical from religious writing that had characterized his life from 1939-1947. Perhaps Douglas Gresham says it best: "First, he very busy...looking after my mother.... and second, Jack would not speak unless he had something to say"(Gresham email).

Biblical Studies Blunder: A Genre-Jarring Commentary

Lewis claims in the introduction to the book that "this is not what is called an 'apologetic' work. I am nowhere trying to convince unbelievers that Christianity is true. I address those who already believe it, or those who are ready to 'suspend their disbelief.'" He goes on to add a sentence that has been often quoted, "A man can't be always defending the truth; there has to be a time to feed on it" (7).

It is difficult to "suspend disbelief" that *Reflections* is not a work of apologetics. Lewis carefully marshals ethical, emotional, and exegetical proofs in defense of the Psalms. Is he being disingenuous at best and deceptive at worst this claim? Or is this work a transition back toward the apologetic work that made him so famous in earlier works such as *Mere Christianity* and is evident in his last books of apologetics and devotion, *Letters to Malcolm, Chiefly on Prayer?*

Lewis makes a second disingenuous statement when he states, "This is not a work of scholarship. I am no Hebraist, no higher critic, no ancient historian, and no archeologist. I am writing for the unlearned about things in which I am unlearned myself" (1). In his magisterial *English Literature in the Sixteenth Century* Lewis warned, "an appearance of casualness ('I am no orator as Brutus is') is one of the rhetorician's weapons" (*OHEL* 193). He goes on to note that this is "consciously devised to hold the attention and undermine the resistance of the audience" (193). This is very similar to the studied casualness to the beginning of his great work of apologetics, *Mere Christianity*, where he remarks, "I am not preaching" (6).

Lewis was not unlearned. He did not know Hebrew, but his long-time colleague at Magdalen College, Godfrey Rolles Driver, was Oxford's OT professor. Even after Lewis moved to Cambridge they kept in contact. In a letter written the same year as the book, Lewis lauds Driver as "one of the greatest authorities" and consulted with him (Letters III 845). He might not be an archeologist but he is a critic and an historian. Furthermore, he had a senior common room at Cambridge full of all of the above.

Lewis takes expert knowledge, his own or his fellow scholars, and makes that knowledge understandable to the layperson. He is a translator, as poor Norman Pittenger found out when he challenged Lewis on a point of theology:

> My task is simply that of a *translator*—One turning Christian doctrine...into the vernacular, into language that unscholarly people would attend to and understand. For this purpose, a style more guarded, more *nuanced*, finer shaded, more rich in fruitful ambiguities—in fact a style more like Dr. Pittenger's own—would have been worse than useless. ....If the real theologians had tackled this laborious work of translation, about a hundred years ago, when they began to lose touch with the people (for whom Christ died), there would have been no place for me. ("Rejoinder to Dr. Pittenger" 182)

I will argue that this hybrid book serves as a primer or pre-commentary to the Psalms. John Reumann calls it "a different sort of commentary which combines literary appreciation and devotional meditation" (*C. S. Lewis: The Literary Impact of the Authorized Version* x). Lewis docs not deal with many of the concerns of the traditional commentary. He is able to claim that "in a scholarly work, chronology would be the first thing to settle: in a book like this more need, or can, be said about it"(x). But he does prepare reader to read the Psalms. *Reflections* serves the same function as his *A Preface to Paradise Lost*. Bruce and Michael Edwards include *Reflections* in their treatment of Lewis as "Everyman's Tutor" in "'Everyman's Tutor': C. S. Lewis on Reading and Criticism" who offers the lay reader "an earnest travelogue that prepares them for their own adventures and discoveries inside the text" (Edwards 164).

The fact that it still is valued as a commentary today shows just how valuable his blend of devotional and literary acumen made this a thematic—as opposed to textual commentary—for more than one millennium.

The Rhetoric of the *Reflections*

Lewis was ambivalent about rhetoric. Although when I once advanced this claim James Herrick remarked, "Lewis is ambivalent about rhetoric the way George Patton was ambivalent about Sherman tanks" (NCA Panel). Nevertheless, Lewis complains of rhetorician Saint Augustine's treatment of the Psalms: "Almost, but not quite; the great roaring machine of Latin rhetoric can, at times, deafen the human ear to all other literature" (*They Asked for a Paper* 28). It is debatable how much Lewis liked rhetoric, but he did love poetry. His greatest contribution to rhetoric was linking poetry and rhetoric:

> I do not think that Rhetoric and Poetry are distinguished by manipulation of an audience in the one and, in the other, a pure self expression, regarded as its own end and indifferent to any audience. Both these arts, in my opinion, definitely aim at doing something to an audience. And both do it by using language. (*Preface* 54)

Don King has done a masterful job on the poetic front with his *C.S. Lewis, Poet*. Lewis helps put the two of them in juxtaposition in *A Preface to Paradise Lost*:

> In Rhetoric imagination is present for the sake of passion (and therefore, in the long run, for the sake of action), while in poetry passion is present for the sake of imagination, and therefore, in the long run, for the sake of wisdom or spiritual response—the rightness and richness of a man's total response to the world. Such rightness of course, has a tendency to contribute indirectly to right action. (53)

It is at the intersection of the rhetoric and poetics that Lewis has so much to offer. Lewis is particularly effective in his treatment of the Psalms because he treats them as poems, or more specifically as rhetorical poems—that "aim to do something to an audience...with language." Rhetoric may lead to direct action, whereas poetry leads to action indirectly by way of wisdom and spiritual wholeness. The rhetorical poetics of the Psalms helps explain why they are so persuasive ethically, emotionally, and intellectually.

The most famous definition of rhetoric comes from Aristotle: "Let rhetoric be [defined as] an ability, in each [particular] case, to see the available means of persuasion" (Aristotle 37). Aristotle goes on to list the three "artistic proofs":

> Of the *pisteis* provided through speech there are three species: for some are in character [*ethos*] of the speaker, and some in disposing the listener in some way [*pathos*], and some in the speech itself [*logos*] itself, by showing or seeming to show something" (38). The credibility of the Psalms requires an ethical defense *(ethos)* of their more problematic features—cursing, violence, etc. The audience— ancient and modern-- of the Psalms is touched emotionally *(pathos)* by their poetic rather than sermonic nature. And the interpretation of meaning *(logos)* allows for a focus on the message itself. Aristotle's three proofs provide a framework for understanding the rhetorical artistry of *Reflections on the Psalms*.

Lewis wrote this work after much soul-searching about his methods of defending the faith. He was concerned about credibility, which led to some creative *ethical* arguments. Lewis wrote this work at the happiest time of his life, with his wife Joy in remission from her cancer. This allowed him to appreciate his emotions and to connect with the *emotions* expressed in the Psalms. His major concern was to convey truth and find meaning from the Jewish origin through the early Christian re-interpretation to modern appropriation of the ancient text—*exegesis*. These themes, hinted at in the preliminary controversies, will provide the organizational grid for the exposition of the book itself.

Ethical Proofs

I begin with the characteristics of the Psalter which are at first most repellant. -C. S. Lewis (*Reflections* 6)

I recently attended a small group studying the Psalms. One of the participants expressed discomfort with the Old Testament in general and the Psalms in particular due their violent themes. Last week I was brought to lunch by a professor and a businessman. The topic of conversation was how they struggled with the violence of the Old Testament. There is a tendency for Christians to skip or ignore the bits of the Bible that offend modern or post-modern sensibilities. For this reason Lewis regrets that "they have made the Psalter a closed book to many modern church-goers" (18). There is a tendency of commentaries on the Psalms to ignore the difficulties as well.

Not Lewis. The first three chapters of his book deal with ethical objections the modern reader might have with the Psalms—judgment, cursing and death. He borrows a childhood eating analogy, stating, "It was the sound principle of nursery gastronomy to polish off the nasty things first and leave the tidbits to the end" (7).

The first chapter deals with the "nasty bit" of God's wrath and judgment. To help the reader understand the Jewish conception of justice, he turns to a telling legal analogy:

> The ancient Jews, like ourselves, think of God's judgment in terms of an earthly court of justice. The difference is that the Christian pictures the case to be tried as a criminal case with himself in the dock; the Jew pictures it as a civil case with himself as the plaintiff. The one hopes for acquittal, or rather for pardon; the other hopes for a resounding triumph with   heavy damages. (10)

He builds on this difference in perspective to explain "the fatal confusion between being in the right and being righteous" (18). From a Christian perspective, many of the Psalms appear to be self-righteous but not in the original context of an oppressed people longing for justice.

From judgment he moves to the "cursing Psalms" that seem to display a "spirit of hatred which strikes us in the face like the heat from a furnace mouth" (20). Psalm 137 contains a blessing to those who "snatch up a Babylonian baby and beat its brains out" and even the 23rd Psalm gloats of a feast in the face of one's enemies (21).

Lewis says one way to deal with the imprecatory Psalms is to ignore them. But a better way is to realize that we are "blood-brothers to these ferocious, self-pitying, barbaric men"(24). They remind us that there is evil and we should be indignant. He also warns, "of all bad men religious are the worst" (32).

The third chapter deals with death in the Psalms. Lewis studies the Old Testament and concludes, "there is little or no belief in a future life" (36). He admires their devotion to God without the promise of future reward.

We can quibble how successful Lewis is in facing the problem areas in the Psalms but his way of facing them is certainly more successful than other commentators not facing those problem areas. Lewis makes a strong case for understanding the Psalms on their own level before passing judgment. He hints at the Christian "second meaning" but saves that for the last segment of the book. In the meanwhile, he seeks to establish an ethical defense of the Psalms in the face of modern attacks on ancient credibility. He claims, "Certainly it seems to me that from having had to reach what is really the Voice of God in the cursing Psalms through all the horrible distortions of the human medium, I have gained something I might not have gained from a flawless, ethical exposition" (114).

Emotional Ptoofs

Let us stint all this and speak of mirth.
Walter Scott quote cited by C.S. Lewis (Reflections 44)

The next five chapters deal with matters that are lacking in more traditional treatments of the Psalms. Lewis uses mirth to "show how badly we need something which the Psalms can give us perhaps better than any other book in the world" (44). Lewis, the master apologist, uses arguments from desire to outline major emotional themes—worship, love of God's law, identification with God, nature, and praise.

Fair Beauty of the Lord — Worship

Lewis writes, "the most valuable thing the Psalms do for me is to express that same delight in God which made David dance" (45). Lewis celebrates "Hebraic delight or gusto" (53). Lewis admits that there is "a tragic depth in our worship which Judaism lacked" (52) yet he is envious. He finds in the Psalms an "experience fully God-centred, asking of God no gift more urgently than His presence, the gift of Himself, joyous to the highest degree, as unmistakably real" (52).

Sweeter than Honey

Lewis exegetes Psalm 119 in a way that makes truth beautiful. Lewis the literary scholar and poet is at his best as he explicates Psalm 19. He finds the psalm "the greatest poem in the Psalter and one of the greatest lyrics in the world" (63). The structure of the psalm is "six verses about Nature, five about the Law, and four of personal prayer" (63). Lewis, focusing on the emotional, notes, "the actual words supply no logical connection between the first and second movements" (63). This is a technique of modern poetry but Lewis believes it the psalmist had such a connection in his imagination "between his first theme and his second that he passed from the one to the other without realizing that he had made any transition" (63).

Connivance

Lewis finds Psalm 139:21 "Don't I hate those who hate thee Lord?" a connivance that is "dangerous, almost a fatal game" that leads straight to "Pharisaism" (66). The chapter could fit in the first section with the rest of the ethical issues. Yet the emotional rawness of the connivance Psalms forces us to face our failings. At the same time it is a difficult chapter. Lewis's former student and fellow Inkling John Wain complains that there is "a hard even menacing tone that dogs his weaker writings…for example, the chapter on 'Connivance" (Wain 75).

Nature

Lewis turns out to be "green" before it was popular. To prepare the reader of the Psalms, Lewis notes that "nature poetry" was natural for Jews who were, for the most part, people of the land. He notes that the Psalms are "lyrics not romances," and they give us "far more sensuously the very feel of weather—weather seen with a real countryman's eyes" (77).

Secondly the Jews believed in one God, with God and nature distinct. "By emptying Nature of divinities—or, let us say, of divinities—you may fill her with Deity, for which she is now the bearer of messages" (82-83). This also means that nature is seen not "a mere datum but as an achievement" (83). Lewis goes into a long excursus on monotheism and the precursor to it in Akhenaton, an ancient Egyptian king that is fascinating but beyond the pale of this chapter.

Lewis views Psalms as nature poetry that can provide a basis for a Christian theology of the environment. Such a high view of nature might make even Nobel laureate Al Gore proud.

A Word about Praising

The pleasure that Lewis extracts from the Psalms has inspired writers like John Piper to form a whole movement called "Christian Hedonism" (Piper 15-17). In many ways this is the most brilliant chapter of the commentary. Lewis claims that "it is in the process of being worshipped that God communicates His presence to men. It is not indeed the only way. But for many people at many times the 'fair beauty of the Lord' is revealed chiefly or only while they worship Him together" (93).

He goes on to state: "I think that we delight to praise what we enjoy because the praise not merely expresses but completes the enjoyment; it is its appointed consummation "(95). Lewis warns that heaven will not be like "being in church. For our 'services' both in their conduct and in our power to participate, are merely attempts at worship; never fully successful, often 99.9 per cent failures" (96). Lewis notes that "meanwhile of course we are merely, as Donne says, tuning our instruments" (97).

The emotional tone of these chapters, help us view Psalms as songs and lyric poetry rather than theology. The *pathos* is persuasive.

Exegetical Proofs:

Reflections on the Psalms or "Our Own Silly Faces"

He relates the Psalms to this triple background; to the ancient Judaic religion that produced them, to the age of Christ when they took on new meanings, and to our own daily experience in the modern world.

-C. S. Lewis (*Letters III* 916)

C.S. Lewis warned: "What we see when we think we are looking into the depths of Scripture may sometimes be only the reflection of our own silly faces" (121). Lewis concludes his commentary with three chapters that focus on the place of Christological prophecy or predictions in the Psalms. In the process, he reveals his own views on Scripture that do not fit comfortably in anyone's theological camp. His vocation as a literary critic allows him to make telling observations on the state of biblical criticism.

Second Meanings

Lewis leaves the reading of Psalms "as their poets meant them to be read" and moves to reading them as "they have chiefly been used by Christians" (99). He warns us that "a second or hidden meaning" arouses great distrust to the modern mind. As all biblical exegetes should know, "almost anything can be read into any book if you are determined enough" (99). As a writer of fantasies subjected to reviewers, he quips, "some of the allegories thus imposed on my own books have been so ingenious and interesting that I often wish I had thought of them myself" (99).

Even with the danger of self-deception, Lewis says Christians cannot abandon second meanings in the Old Testament. He writes, "We have a steep hill before us. I will not attempt the cliffs. I must take a roundabout route" (100). Lewis uses the example of a Roman slave in a public bath who said that the water will soon be hot enough. There was an accidental fire that made his words true in more than one sense.

He follows that example with one from Virgil, who medieval Christians thought had some crude prophetic knowledge of the birth of Christ. That is followed by more examples of those who "say that is truer and more important than he knows" (102).

The first is a holy person that predicts life on other planets and later that life is found. The second is a science fiction writer who creates a creature in his fiction that bears amazing similarity to a creature later found. The third is a biologist who creates a hypothetical creature and environment and then finds the creature. The Holy man turned out to be a prophet, the writer's arbitrary fancies were proved true, and the biologist had "something more sensitive than scientific knowledge" (104).

Lewis then goes back to Plato and his "picture of the Righteous One" and Virgil's Adonis as pagan precursors to Christ. "Thus, long before we come to the Psalms or the Bible, there are good reasons for not throwing away all second meanings as rubbish" (108).

Scripture

Lewis is an equal opportunity offender when it comes to his view of the authority of the Bible. Michael Christensen, in the first and most comprehensive study of Lewis's thoughts on inspiration, revelation, and inerrancy, concludes that Lewis saw the Bible "as human literature carrying a divine message" (Christensen 96). Lewis claims, "I have been suspected of being what is called a Fundamentalist. That is because I never regard any narrative as unhistorical simply on the ground it includes the miraculous" (109). But then he distances himself from an infallibility position. He sides with Jerome with said "Moses described Creation 'after the manner of a popular poet' (as we should say mythically)" (109). He mentions that Calvin doubted "whether the story of Job were history or fiction" (109). (Lewis turns out to be wrong about Calvin but he probably meant Luther.)

Lewis finds that "the human qualities of the raw materials show through. Naivety, error, contradiction, even (as in the cursing Psalms) wickedness are not removed" (111). For him the Bible:

> carries the Word of God; and we (under grace, with attention to tradition and to interpreters wiser than ourselves, and with the use of such intelligence and learning we may have) receive the word from it not by using it as an encyclopedia but steeping ourselves in its tone or temper and so learning its overall message. (112)

He finds the Bible "an untidy and leaky vehicle" and respects and pines for "both the Fundamentalist's view of the Bible and the Roman Catholic's view of the church" (112).

He claims that our Lord's teachings, in which there are no mistakes, provide a clue to what could be called an "incarnational" view of the authority of Scripture:

> For we are taught that the Incarnation itself proceeded "not by the conversion of the godhead into flesh, but by taking of (the) manhood into God"; in it human life becomes the vehicle of Divine life. If the Scriptures proceed not by a conversion of God's word into a literature but by taking up of a literature to be the vehicle of God's word. (116)

Lewis makes two major points about Scripture:

1. Scripture is Holy and Inspired.
2. We accept the Old Testament because Jesus Christ accepted it.

Even though he explicates these two principles in a way that will discourage his evangelical fans, the two points fly in the face of the liberal critical consensus as well.

It is almost a commonplace in major universities and mainline theological seminaries that there is no such thing as predictive prophecy in the Old Testament. This critical consensus among Old Testament scholars is summarized by R.W. Moberly:

> On the one hand, the Old Testament does not predict a Messiah, let alone Jesus as that Messiah; if some of Israel's apparently 'larger-than-life' depictions of its king do have wider resonances, then these resonances are with exotic royal ideologies common in the ancient Near East...On the Other hand, Jesus' messianic claims within the gospels can no longer be confidently ascribed to him, for they may be put into his mouth as expressions of the early church. (Moberly 185)

Moberly goes on to ask "is the critical story sufficiently critical?" He finds that most modern critical scholarship is a restatement of the Jewish critique of Christianity. Richard Hays' *Echoes of Scripture in the Letters of Paul* and the work of N.T. Wright have provided sophisticated alternative stories to temper the critical one. Wright summarizes his technical work in his popular *Simply Christian*:

> Presence, Torah, Word, Wisdom and Spirit: five ways of saying the same thing. The God of Israel is the creator and redeemer of Israel and the world, to bring to its climax the great story of exile and restoration, of the divine rescue operation, of the king who brings justice, the Temple that joins heaven and earth, the Torah binds God's people together, and of creation healed and restored. It is not only heaven and earth that are to come together. It is God's future and God's present. (77)

But forty years before all of this, Lewis was already stating the orthodox case with panache. Yet as Lyle Dorsett politely put it, "his love for God's Word did not please all the regiments in the army of the faithful" (62).

Second Meanings in the Psalms

In the final chapter, Lewis brings into play his "triple background; to the ancient Judaic religion that produced them, to the age of Christ when they took on new meanings, and to our own daily experience in the modern world" (*Reflections*, flyleaf). He demonstrates an exegetical technique that does justice to the original reader, the Christian appropriation, and the modern day use of the Psalm. He explicates how "suffer," "king" and "priest" in his treatment of the Christmas Psalms: "For us gentile Christians…are more likely to start from the priestly, sacrificial, and intercessory character of Christ and under-stress the king and conqueror. Psalm 110…corrects this" (124). He has an extended analysis of Psalm 45, another Christmas Psalm "that does not immediately appeal to our own age." He warns that it "restores Christmas to its proper complexity" and to reject it "is to be provincial, to have the self-complacent blindness of the stay-at-home" (130).

He treats Psalm 8 in its Pentecost Sunday modern context, while mentioning the Hebrew scholars and Paul have different interpretations. He bemoans "we stress the Humanity exclusively after the Resurrection; almost as if Christ once became a man and then presently reverted to being simply God" (134). Psalm 8 corrects that. Lewis further muses that the "self-righteousness of the Psalms" make more sense when we realize that "all those assertions were to become true" in Christ's mouth (134). Lewis looks at the cursing Psalms and even transformed the smashed Babylonian babies of Psalm 137 into

The "infantile beginnings of small indulgences" that grow into big sins that should be stopped at the outset (136)—a stretch but you have to admire his effort.

In sum, Lewis provides a fresh and creative look back at Christianity from the Psalms as well as managing to show their second meaning in the more traditional sense of the New Testament completing the Old.

Conclusion

A *Publisher's Weekly* representative was interviewed by Moira Bucciarelli of the Society of Biblical Literature about trends in biblical commentaries. The *Publisher's Weekly* spokesperson complained that commentaries were "either too derivative to be considered noteworthy, or too scholarly for the *hoi polloi* to understand" (SBL website).

The spokesperson noticed "a real turn toward the experiential in Bible-related publishing…. It is based on scholarship, yet, but more importantly in the author's very visceral experiences…. People really resonate with that" (SBL website).

That is just the sort of commentary Lewis wrote. Lewis found the Bible far more interesting than the commentaries on it. He was not one of those who think, to borrow an old truism, that 'the Bible sheds interesting light on the commentaries." He uses an ancient philosopher to make his point. Plato is "much more intelligible than his modern commentator." The simplest student can understand some Plato "but hardly anyone can understand some modern books on Platonism" ("On the Reading of Old Books" 200). Lewis claims "that first-hand knowledge is not only more worth acquiring than second-hand knowledge, but it usually is much easier and more delightful to acquire' (200).

Lewis' goal is to get the modern reader to engage the ancient text for herself. He tries to remove roadblocks in the way and to highlight some themes that will make the Psalms "resonate" on a "visceral" as well as rational level. Lewis uses ethics, emotion, and logic to make the Psalms come alive to himself and then to us.

That brings us back to rhetoric. Lewis practices rhetorical posturing. He poses as an amateur but he is in fact a skilled scholar. The "I am no orator as Brutus is" and "apparent casualness" that he warns about in his *English Literature in the Sixteenth Century* (193) he practices with pinache in his *Reflections on the Psalms*.

Lewis practices rhetorical popularizing. He takes expert knowledge and expresses it in a way that feeds and instructs the popular reader. He does not dumb down to his reader but equips his reader to understand and enjoy the Psalms. He demonstrates that true scholarship can be communicated if one knows one's audience.

Lewis practices rhetorical poetry. He loves to do things with words. He is not as concerned about the difference between rhetoric (persuasion) and poetry (inspiration). He reminds us that the Psalms are rhetorical poems. He encourages us to look at the Psalms, not only as theology, but as poems, or better yet, songs.

Finally, Lewis practices the great rhetorical proofs of *ethos, pathos,* and *logos*. His thematic commentary on them helps the text to touch the reader ethically, emotionally, and intellectually. He firmly faces the moral and ethical issues that so many others avoid. He mines the emotional depths and evocative images of the Psalms to demonstrate that *pathos* is persuasive. He encourages the use of the heart as well as the head. But Lewis never forgets the head. The interpretation of meaning (*logos*) is not lost in the midst of the *ethos* and *pathos*.

The rhetorical artistry of *Reflections on the Psalms* allows us to focus on the artistry of the Psalms themselves. This chapter began as a paper presented at a wonderful C.S. Lewis conference at Southeastern Baptist Seminary. At the beginning of my presentation, I asked how many people had read all one hundred fifty Psalms. Many heads went down and very few hands went up. It was a Christian crowd with many of the audience studying for the ministry. I have had the chance to ask that same question four more times to different groups, and each time to the same dismal response. From this limited survey I surmise that Christians are not reading the Psalms. Lewis has left a legacy not only by writing about the Psalms but by taking a few minutes each day to read them. Five Psalms a day means they can be easily read through in a month. Their themes were worked into his life in a most winsome way. Perhaps we best honor Lewis by practicing what he practiced. May we all experience what Lewis found to be the key to the Pslams, that "it is in the process of being worshipped that God communicates His presence" (*Reflections* 93).

WORKS CITED

Anderson, Gregory M. "The Sermons of C. S. Lewis: The Oxford Don as Preacher." *C. S. Lewis: Life, Works, and Legacy*, Vol 3. Ed. Bruce L. Edwards Westport: Praeger Perspectives, 2007. 75-105.

Aristotle, *On Rhetoric: A Theory of Discourse*, 2nd ed. Trans. G.A. Kennedy. New York: Oxford University Press, 2007.

Bloom, Harold. "Introduction." *C. S. Lewis's The Chronicles of Narnia*. Ed. Harold Bloom. New York: Chelsea House, 2006.

Brown, Edwin. *In Pursuit of C. S. Lewis: Adventures in Collecting His Works*. Bloomington, IN: Author House, 2006.

Christensen, Michael. *C. S. Lewis on Scripture*. Waco, TX: Word Publishing, 1979.

Dorsett, Lyle. *Seeking the Secret Place: The Spiritual Formation of C. S. Lewis*. Grand Rapids: Brazos Press, 2004.

Edwards, Michael I. and Bruce L. Edwards, "'Everyman's Tutor': C. S. Lewis on Reading and Criticism." In *C. S. Lewis: Life, Works, and Legacy*. Ed. Bruce L. Edwards. Westport: Praeger Perspectives, 2007. 163-194.

Glyer, Diana Pavlac. *The Company They Keep: C. S. Lewis and J. R. R Tolkien as Writers in Community*. Kent: Kent State University Press, 2007.

Gresham, Douglas. June 19, 2006 E-Mail to Author.

Hays, Richard. *Echoes of Scripture in the Letters of Paul*. Yale: Yale University Press, 1989.

Herrick, James. "C. S. Lewis, the 20th Century's Great Communicator of the Christian World View." NCA Panel. Chicago, 2007.

Heck, Joel. *Irrigating Deserts: C. S. Lewis on Education*. St. Louis: Concordia Academic Press, 2006.

Hooper, Walter. *C. S. Lewis: Companion and Guide*. London: Harper Collins, 1996.

Jacobs, Alan. *The Narnian: The Life and Imagination of C. S. Lewis*. London: SPCK, 2005.

King, Don. *C. S. Lewis, Poet*. Kent: Kent State University Press, 2001.

Lewis, C. S. *The Collected Letters of C. S. Lewis,* Vol. 3. Ed. Walter Hooper. San Francisco: HarperSanFrancisco, 2007.

—. *English Literature in the Sixteenth Century Excluding Drama.* Oxford: Clarendon, 1954.

—. *God in the Dock.* Grand Rapids: Eerdmans, 1970.

—. *Mere Christianity.* London: Bles, 1952.

—. "On the Reading of Old Books." *In God in the Dock: Essays on Theology and Ethics.* Ed. Walter Hooper. Grand Rapids: Eerdmans, 1996. 200-207.

—. *A Preface to* Paradise Lost. London: Oxford University Press, 1942.

—. *Reflections on the Psalms.* London: Bles, 1958.

—. "Rejoinder to Dr. Pittenger." *In God in the Dock: Essays on Theology and Ethics.* Ed. Walter Hooper. Grand Rapids: Eerdmans, 1996. 177-183.

—. *They Asked for a Paper.* London: Bles, 1962.

—. *Transposition and Other Essays.* London: Bles, 1949.

Mead, Marjorie Lamp. "Letters to Malcolm: C. S. Lewis on Prayer." *C. S. Lewis: Life, Work, and Legacy,* Vol 3. Ed. Bruce Edwards. Westport, CT: Praeger, 2007.

Moberly, R.W. "The Christ of the Old and the New Testament." *The Cambridge Companion to Jesus.* Ed. Marcus Bockmuehl. Cambridge: Cambridge University Press, 2001.

Piper, John. *Desiring God: Meditations of a Christian Hedonist.* Portland: Multnomah Press, 1986.

Reppert, Victor. *C. S. Lewis's Dangerous Idea.* Carol Stream, IL: IVP, 2003.

Reumann, John. "Introduction." C. S. Lewis. *The Literary Impact of the Authorized Version.* Philadelphia: Fortress Press, 1963.

Sayer, George. *Jack: C. S. Lewis and His Times.* San Francisco: Harper and Row, 1988.

Society of Biblical Literature Website. Article.aspx?Artield=83.

Wain, John. "A Great Clerk." *C. S. Lewis at the Breakfast Table and Other Reminiscences.* Ed. James T. Como. London: Collins, 1979.

White, Michael. *C. S. Lewis: The Boy Who Chronicled Narnia.* London: Abacus, 2005.

Williams, D.T. "An Apologist's Evening Prayer: Reflecting on C.S. Lewis's *Reflections on the Psalms.*" *C. S. Lewis: Life, Work and Legacy,* Vol. 3. Ed. Bruce Edwards. Westport, CT: Praeger, 2007. 237-256.

Wright, Tom. *Simply Christian.* London: SPCK, 2006.

Wilson, A.N. *C. S. Lewis: A Biography.* London: Collins, 1990.

Chapter Seven

A Kneeling and a Sceptred Love:
Lewis' Perilous Passion for Inequality

Steven D. Boyer

C. S. Lewis is a great lover of hierarchy. Many casual readers may be only faintly or tacitly aware of this love: perhaps they have noticed, for example, the consistently positive way he portrays true kings and queens in the "Chronicles of Narnia". But unquestionably the love is there. Sometimes it comes out explicitly, as when he writes, "I do not believe that God created an egalitarian world. I believe the authority of parent over child, husband over wife, learned over simple to have been as much a part of the original plan [of creation] as the authority of man over beast" ("Membership" 114). More often this love is expressed implicitly, in his common portrayal of masculinity and femininity as eternal metaphysical archetypes, or in his recurrent mockery of various egalitarian educational and familial practices, or in his regular assumption that monarchy is the default form of lawful government, or in the frequent illustrations in which human dominion over animals is presupposed. It is hardly an exaggeration to say that one can find some expression of eager embrace of hierarchy on just about every page he ever wrote.

Now in my experience, this is an element in Lewis' thought that surprises many of his fans—an element, in fact, that even many self-proclaimed "friends" of Lewis would be rather hesitant to include uncritically in the Christian legacy that he has left to the world. Of course, people continue to read his work and to find it enchanting. But when they are finally forced to think explicitly about this aspect of his outlook, many people are quite scandalized. They are often most scandalized by what he says about gender relations, but it quickly becomes apparent that Lewis advocates gender hierarchy only because he delights in all hierarchy. And so thoughtful readers want to know how on earth a wise, visionary thinker like Lewis could have been duped into defending a system of social ordering that has so obviously led to catastrophe throughout human history. We think of the horrors of slavery in America, or of Russian pogroms, or of Nazi death camps. To advocate inequality is surely to align oneself with all of the most arrogant, vain, tyrannical, destructive powers in the history of the world. What could Lewis have been thinking?

I hope to address that question in this essay. For it is clear that Lewis was thinking. This was not an accidental stumble into a world whose dangers he failed to perceive; this was a self-conscious embrace of a world whose dangers he found to be worth the candle. But why did he make such a move? We are not interested (for the moment) in Screwtape's "Historical Point of View" (*Screwtape Letters* 99) or in Ezekiel Bulver's *ad hominem* explanations ("'Bulverism'" 271-73): we do not want to know who influenced Lewis, or what psychological factors colored his viewpoint. We want to know, instead, what line of reasoning he followed. I think his line of reasoning is fairly straightforward, though he does not usually lay it out very systematically, and so I shall be trying to draw together material from many different parts of the Lewis corpus, usually without citing particular texts directly (for the sake of space). Then I shall conclude with some remarks about the place of such a comprehensive hierarchical vision in the Lewis legacy for the 21st century.

The primary reason for granting so fundamental a place to inequality is theological, and its roots lie in the Christian doctrine of Creation. In agreement with the entire Christian tradition, Lewis holds that God is the "Maker of heaven and earth and of all things visible and invisible", as the Nicene Creed says. God is Creator not just in the sense that he builds the world, but also in the deeper sense that he thinks it up in the first place, and then designs and fashions it in beauty and splendor, like a consummate artist producing a masterpiece. Lewis thinks that, like every artist, God "puts himself" into his work, so that when we see the work of art properly we are also, in a sense, seeing the artist. Of course, we must have eyes to see. We must be able to look not just "at" the creation, but also "along" it ("Meditation in a Toolshed" 212), so that it serves as a medium for what is unspeakably higher than itself. But, viewed in this light, says Lewis, all of creation is a kind of "conductor" that allows a shaft of the divine glory itself to strike our senses (*Letters to Malcolm* 80, 89). Really to see the vivid brilliance of the sunset, really to feel the refreshing coolness of the brook, is in fact to perceive God's own glory—to taste and see that the Lord is good.

Note what is going on in this account. The natural world attains this astonishingly lofty, dignified position precisely insofar as she is unequivocally secondary to or in the service of the God who shines through her (*Reflections on the Psalms* 81-82). To be a reflection of God is to be filled with and to radiate God's own glory and life, and therefore, so long as Nature is a reflection, she is more glorious than a created thing has any right to be. But as soon as Nature forsakes her appropriately subordinated place, as soon as she claims to be not a reflection of divinity, but divinity as such, then she becomes a competitor with Yahweh, an idol like Baal or Molech, and all the more dangerous and damnable an idol because of her supreme beauty. This explains, for Lewis, why Christianity's approach to the natural world is as strangely complex as it is (*Miracles* 157-159). In Christianity, we find neither simple affirmation of Nature, as in a pantheistic Nature religion, nor simple negation as in some gnostic anti-Nature religion, nor again some 50-50 combination in which Nature is a little bit affirmed and a little bit denied. Instead, Christianity posits both absolute affirmation of the strongest kind *and also* absolute negation of the strongest kind, depending upon whether the one true God is rightly perceived as the real glory that shines through the created order.

In other words (and this is the crucial principle to note), the difference between startlingly strong affirmation and dreadfully fierce negation rests in nothing other than Nature's rightful subordination to her Creator. When she is what Lewis sometimes calls a "second thing" ("First and Second Things" 278-81), then she is supremely glorious. But when she is regarded as a "first thing", her glory vanishes—or, worse yet, is horribly changed into the presumptuous vanity of a false god. Seeking to become a god, she becomes a demon (*Four Loves* 20). But by contrast, to be subordinate is to be exalted, for it is to be filled with the radiant splendor that the Creator intends for his creation. Subordination is the very pathway to exaltation.

Now, if this basic theological principle describes the God-World relation at the macro-level, so that the World gloriously shines with the very glory of its Maker so long as it is rightly subordinate to its Maker, then we are perhaps not surprised to find the same principle at work at the micro level, so that the ordered majesty of the God-World relation may be echoed "in a minor key" (*Miracles* 121, 149) in all sorts of other relations *within* the created realm. This may not be precisely required logically, but Lewis thinks it certainly is justified aesthetically. When God summons the world into existence, all things gladly begin to be, and their being itself sacramentally reflects the glory and artistry of the One who summoned them. But why should this marvelous interplay of initiative and response be displayed only in the cosmic act of creation? Why not, in an on-going fashion, in a thousand refracted relations throughout the created order, with each derivative pointing back to its archetypal original? This is exactly Lewis' idea. Just as one expects to find the central theme in a piece of music repeated over and over throughout the piece—and not just repeated, but reinvented and renewed with variations and distinctives that continually draw one back to the center—so also Lewis thinks that the ordered relations within creation reflect and magnify and lead back to the order that characterizes the God-World relation as such. All legitimate command is derived from God's "Let there be . . .", and all lawful obedience is Creation's ". . . and it was so." This "fundamental polarity" (*Perelandra* 200) of divine initiative and creaturely response is replayed in all sorts of different created relations, some of them supported by actual, permanent superiority (like the relation between a human master and a dog), some supported by a more stylized asymmetry without permanent superiority (like an elderly parent's relation to an adult child—where the child is still responsible to "honor" father or mother even when the parent's superiority is long gone), but all of them—all of these created hierarchical relations—sacramentally representing the grand polarity of creation itself. By God's intricate design, creatures of all sorts are constantly occupied in the enactment of a drama that is far larger than the creatures themselves. All that I do and am may reflect greater realities than I would ever have guessed. I am not my own. I may be, in some sense, an autonomous person, but as a creature of God, I am also what Lewis calls "a thing, a made thing, made to please Another" (*That Hideous Strength* 319). And that Other is pleased to have all of creation echo and re-echo with the life-giving joy of command humbly issued and obedience gladly delivered. God has made a hierarchical world.

So the cosmic picture one gets from Lewis is of a universe that sings with the irrepressible glory of creative initiative and creaturely response, and a universe in which creatures themselves repeat the same ecstatic theme in a myriad of smaller, joyful choruses. It is a song of unmatched life and strength and beauty—and this explains why Lewis so often speaks of equality in moderately derogatory terms. Equality, he thinks, is usually *flat* equality ("Equality" 18), the lamentable absence of all of the glorious diversity that God builds into the universe, and the refusal to enter into the echoing patterns of ordered harmony by which all things participate constantly in the everlasting joy of creation itself. Against this dreary construal of equality, the shimmering elegance of "the eternal dance" (*Problem of Pain* 137) can hardly fail to dazzle by contrast.

Well, it may be dazzling, but it commonly strikes many of us as rather far removed from the real, workaday world. We begin to think that Lewis has allowed his romantic infatuation with a hierarchical, sacramental theology to blind him to plain facts. When we open our eyes and actually look around at the contemporary scene, there is nothing more obvious than the fact that an imposed hierarchy does violence to the way things really are. In the real world, wives are every bit as competent as husbands, children may be more gifted than their parents, pupils often prove more reliable than teachers, citizens can be more noble and trustworthy than those who rule them. At every point, it is a matter of plainest common sense that equality is the reality, and hierarchy an imposed ideology. It may be a beautiful ideology (in its own way), but it certainly does not describe the real world.

Lewis responds in two ways. First, he finds it hardly surprising that the enlightened "common sense" of the modern period fails to perceive the authentic spiritual and aesthetic characteristics of created relations. The modern world has been training itself for many generations *not* to see such realities, has insisted instead that any Beauty or Truth that cannot be handled by the empirical sciences is merely a subjective expression of a particular observer's physical or emotional state (*Abolition of Man* 32). Lewis reminds us, in a vivid metaphor, that when I point across the room at something, you know to look in the direction I am pointing, but a dog is notoriously committed to staring at the finger with which I point. To a dog, a finger is just a finger. And Lewis notes how common it is in contemporary educated circles to induce in oneself this "doglike mind" ("Transposition" 71), this outlook that refuses to take seriously anything not empirically demonstrable. If something like sacramental significance were present in the created order, we should almost expect that contemporary "common sense" would be blind to it.

But second, Lewis also wants to examine with a bit more care just what "common sense" actually sees, for he thinks we will discover that the shoe is really on the other foot. In every one of the "real-world" cases we noted a moment ago, what we find, Lewis thinks, is most emphatically not equality. What we find instead is an ever-present, and often dramatic, inequality, and the closer we look at individual cases, the more obvious the inequality becomes. Set any two people beside one another, and you find that they are exactly equal in no respect whatsoever: not in size or shape, not in musical talent or artistic ability, not in abstract reasoning or concrete motor skills, not in political insight or moral wisdom. At no point do we find equality; at every point we find the concrete reality of a particular person, who is different from, hence unequal to, the person next door (*Screwtape Letters* 125).

"Of course," we might want to point out, "every person is equally *human*. Each possesses a common human dignity." Yes, Lewis would reply, if you want to move away from the real, concrete person and talk about an abstract quality like "humanness", then you certainly can find equality. But notice that, in order to find it, you have had to leave concrete individuals behind. You have had to stop thinking about Dwight or Margaret or Julie or Carl as particular persons; you have begun to consider them instead as mere instances of humanity, recognizable by the DNA sequence they have in common. The more precisely and concretely we look at actual persons, the more particular, and therefore the more unequal, they turn out to be. It begins to look as if inequality is the concrete reality, whereas equality is the abstract dogma, the "legal fiction" ("Membership" 114), imposed upon that reality.

Now, this sort of observation is likely to raise our American, democratic hackles, and so I need quickly to add that Lewis very explicitly insists that this "legal fiction" of equality is an absolutely legitimate, even vital, thing in our world. He repeatedly and resolutely maintains that he is *not* opposed to equality, that he does *not* want to reinstate what he sometimes calls "the old authorities" in the contemporary world. "I should view with the strongest disapproval," he says ("Membership" 115), "any proposal to abolish manhood suffrage, or the Married Women's Property Act," or other expressions of legal equality between persons. But why? Because in a fallen world, men and women tend to take every inequality, every difference, and use it as a weapon. The legal fiction of equality is our only safeguard against the violence that fallen people inevitably work against one another. In other words, equality is primarily defensive or protective in character. Lewis says (in another memorable image), "Equality is for me in the same position as clothes. It is a result of the Fall and the remedy for it. Any attempt to retrace the steps by which we have arrived at egalitarianism and to reintroduce the old authorities on the political level is for me as foolish as it would be to take off our clothes. The Nazi and the nudist make the same mistake" ("Membership" 114).

So Lewis is all in favor of a political and social outlook that strongly insists on equality. But he is also concerned lest we unwittingly be fooled by our own rhetoric into thinking that equality is the way things really are. He emphasizes the fictional nature of equality not for the sake of any political or social agenda, but as a kind of "truth in advertising" disclaimer. If we misunderstand the nature of equality, we may unwittingly ignore the ways in which equality itself can become a destructive weapon (*Screwtape Letters* 124-26). Ask any bright junior high student whether being one of the "smart kids" has been a good or bad experience for her among her peers; ask any morally pure teenager whether his friends are aiding or undermining his purity when they advocate equality by saying, "Come on, everybody is doing it." In these and many other cases, we find an obscuring or even a hatred of real excellence, and it is grounded in a misguided insistence on equality.

Yet the real trouble with equality lies even deeper. In a quite stunning line in his address "Membership", Lewis makes the following provocative claim: "Equality is a quantitative term and therefore love often knows nothing of it" (115). Love knows nothing of equality? What can this mean? Imagine a young man and a young woman, madly in love, sitting off in a corner of the local coffee shop, gazing into one another's eyes in the way that only lovers do. How often does one expect to hear the young man romantically declare, "Oh, my Beloved, you are so . . . *equal* to other girls I know"? On the contrary, we expect him to say, "You are so . . . beautiful" or "creative" or "talented" or "elegant" or whatever her particular excellence is. To focus upon equality is to push love outside the picture altogether. The one thing that a person in love never does is to make comparisons that result in any kind of parity. It is precisely the matchless uniqueness of the object of love that makes us fall in love in the first place.

Now, with this critique of flat equality in place, we are finally in a position to sum up Lewis' rationale for a comprehensively hierarchical picture of the cosmos. Lewis holds that ordered differentiation is absolutely everywhere; and according to traditional Christianity, various ordained social hierarchies appropriately embody and stylize this differentiation. The result is that hierarchical ordering throughout creation is something to be concretely celebrated and delighted in, not abhorred, and this for at least four different reasons. It should be delighted in for *theological* reasons, because every instance of rightful subordination is a picture in miniature of the grand polarity of initiative and response that is built into the very act of creation; it should be delighted in for *aesthetic* reasons, because a dance is more beautiful than a march ("Membership" 116), and an arch is more beautiful than pebbles lying in a row ("Equality" 20); it should be delighted in for *practical* reasons, because inequalities characterize the way the world really is, and the world as it really is is good; and it should be delighted in for *moral* reasons, because "the greatest of these is love", and love resists equality at every turn. This is Lewis' argument for hierarchy, his reason for celebrating at every joyous level "the unions of a kneeling with a sceptred love" (*Perelandra* 217). And I must add that, in my estimation, this is a deeply compelling argument and an intensely moving portrait of a world more delicately nuanced and more elegantly crafted than we normally imagine.

Yet I think there is more to say as we turn to evaluate the hierarchical vision. It is compelling, yes. Moving, yes. But it is not, I think, particularly safe—and this is an important point to raise, especially among those who would count themselves as fans or "friends" of Lewis. Some of us have seen Lewis' vision and been captured by it. We have found the ordered glories of hierarchical interplay to be a spectacle of almost overpowering magnificence. Indeed, I challenge anyone with an ounce of aesthetic sensibility to read the ecstatic passage about the "Great Dance" from the end of *Perelandra* (pp. 214-19) without being moved. It cannot be done. I read, and I am swept away with the splendor of this vision. But of course, it is just here that we had better be careful. When I am swept away, my guard goes down, and my tongue wags, and I end up saying and perhaps doing things that mislead or hurt. The young man hopelessly in love tends easily to overlook flaws in his beloved that may be very serious indeed. In our world, we cannot afford to be so charitable. Hierarchy is a "beloved" who has shown that she can work catastrophe if her fallen inclinations are left unchallenged.

For this reason, I submit that Lewis' passion for inequality is a very perilous thing indeed. I for one am deeply concerned when I hear that in conservative Christian homes, where men are regarded as the Christ-like "head" of their families, the statistics for spousal abuse are often indistinguishable from those in the public at large (Tracy 590-93; Van Leeuwen 193-96). Again, I find myself very suspicious of churches that lay out, from the pulpit or in print, all of the arguments for an all-male priesthood or elder council or whatever, but that seem to have very little place in their midst for a modern-day Priscilla or Deborah to arise. Yet again, I grow rather tired of hearing from Christians about the great "dominion" mandate in Genesis 1 when I am not also hearing about the scandalous use and abuse of animals in the American meat industry or in experimental research. It will be recalled that Lewis, the great advocate of hierarchy, wrote a short pamphlet for the New England Anti-Vivisection Society in which he argued *against* animal experimentation, on the ground that, even if Christian principle permitted it, the actual practice in the real, not-very-principled world was inevitably destructive ("Vivisection" 226-27).

The point here is a simple one: in a fallen world, the love of hierarchy is death-dealing if it is not held sharply and vigilantly in check. This is a point that we fans and "friends" of Lewis need to take with utmost seriousness.

But of course, the opposite point needs also to be made—and it is the one that Lewis himself most often makes. There may still be plenty of authoritarians out there, but the public intellectual currents of our day are overwhelmingly moving in an egalitarian direction, and most of us are in one way or another carried along with them, whether we realize it or not. Somewhere along the line, our culture is in desperate need of a loud, clear summons that can awaken again that love of hierarchy that its abuse throughout history so constantly threatens to deaden. And I think we rightly demand from critics of hierarchy some indication that their criticism does not spring from this sort of deadness. I have in mind especially the multitude of Christian discussions of gender, where I want to insist, in Lewis' own words, that we should "watch the faces, mark well the accents, of the debunkers" of hierarchy, for some of these may easily be men and women of enlightened "common sense", "whose tap-root in Eden has been cut" ("Equality" 20). I want the critics to show first that they understand *hierarchy* well enough to love it; then and only then can they try to show that they understand *gender hierarchy* well enough to debunk it.

Of course, making both of these points side by side may well suggest that I am on something of a fool's errand. I want those who are suspicious of hierarchy to fall in love with it; and I want those who are in love to be a bit more suspicious (at least practically). I am not particularly optimistic about my success. Inevitably, the domineering authoritarian who needs to hear the message of equality tends to hear only that equality is not the deepest reality, whereas the militant egalitarian who needs to learn to love hierarchy tends to hear only of its abuses. Part of our fallen condition is the quickness with which we find ways of using absolutely *every* good thing to our own destruction. There simply is no safe path to walk.

Nevertheless, if there is no safe path, then it is absolutely crucial that we make as clear as we can the particular dangers that attend each path—and especially the dangers that attend the path most often presumed to be safe. Here, I think, is where Lewis' approach proves to be invaluable. Ours is an egalitarian age, in which the virtues of equality and the vices of hierarchy are hammered into our heads from earliest days. We may thank God for the blessings of such an age. Yet in this context a voice like Lewis' may provide just the right reminder of the importance of our egalitarian rhetoric, while also pointing to the glorious reality that is deeper than that rhetoric. It may serve to level the playing field so that the host of issues associated with hierarchy in our day (and they are Legion) may be given something like a fair hearing despite their stormy and polarized context. By taking this part of the Lewis legacy seriously we may learn really to rejoice in hierarchy, while at the very same time we zealously resist every fallen abuse of hierarchy. For abuse will come, as surely as the cold of winter; and we must guard against it by wearing the warm clothing of legal equality. But, as Lewis says ("Equality" 20), let us be sure to *wear* equality, and let us undress every night.

WORKS CITED

Lewis, C. S. *The Abolition of Man, or, Reflections on education with special reference to the teaching of English in the upper forms of schools.* 1947. New York: HarperCollins, 2001.

—. "'Bulverism', or, The Foundation of 20th Century Thought." *God in the Dock: Essays on Theology and Ethics.* Ed. Walter Hooper. Grand Rapids: Eerdmans, 1970. 271-77.

—. "Equality." *Present Concerns.* Ed. Walter Hooper. New York: Harcourt Brace Jovanovich, 1986. 17-20.

—. "First and Second Things." *God in the Dock: Essays on Theology and Ethics.* Ed. Walter Hooper. Grand Rapids: Eerdmans, 1970. 278-81.

—. *The Four Loves.* New York: Harcourt Brace Jovanovich, 1960.

—. *Letters to Malcolm: Chiefly on Prayer.* New York: Harcourt Brace Jovanovich, 1964.

—. "Meditation in a Toolshed." *God in the Dock: Essays on Theology and Ethics.* Ed. Walter Hooper. Grand Rapids: Eerdmans, 1970. 212-15.

—. "Membership." *The Weight of Glory and Other Addresses.* Rev. Ed. Ed. Walter Hooper. New York: Macmillan, 1980. 106-20.

—. *Miracles: A Preliminary Study.* Rev. Ed. 1960. New York: Touchstone, 1996.

—. *Perelandra: A Novel.* New York: Scribner, 1996.

—. *The Problem of Pain.* 1943. New York: Touchstone, 1996.

—. *Reflections on the Psalms.* New York: Harcourt Brace Jovanovich, 1958.

—. *The Screwtape Letters* (with "Screwtape Proposes a Toast"). 1943, 1959. New York: Touchstone, 1996.

—. *That Hideous Strength: A Modern Fairy-Tale for Grown-Ups.* New York: Collier, 1946.

—. "Transposition." *The Weight of Glory and Other Addresses.* Rev. Ed. Ed. Walter Hooper. New York: Macmillan, 1980. 54-73.

—. "Vivisection." *God in the Dock: Essays on Theology and Ethics.* Ed. Walter Hooper. Grand Rapids: Eerdmans, 1970. 224-28.

Tracy, Steven R. "Patriarchy and Domestic Violence: Challenging Common Misconceptions." *Journal of the Evangelical Theological Society* 50 (2007): 573-94.

Van Leeuwen, Mary Stewart. "Opposite Sexes or Neighboring Sexes?:

What Do the Social Sciences Really Tell Us?" *Women, Ministry and the Gospel.* Ed. Mark Husbands and Timothy Larsen. Downers Grove, IL: InterVarsity Press, 2007. 171-99.

Chapter Eight

Wilderness, Arcadia and Longing:
Mythic Landscapes and the Experience of Reality

Kip Redick

Journey narratives rooted in significant landscapes are pervasive in the stories of Narnia, Malacandra, Perelandra, and Orual's Glome and its Grey Mountain. The opening of C. S. Lewis' culminating work, *Till We Have Faces*, integrates landscape and divinity. Orual begins writing her book by telling the reader of its purpose: "I will accuse the gods, especially the god who lives on the Grey Mountain" (3). Orual's self-introduction cannot be separated from her description of Glome's landscape and its numinous aspect. She, the sacred, and the landscape unfold intersubjectively as her complaint spills forth. She writes that the city of Glome is located on the river Shennit and near the foothills of the Grey Mountain, where "the god of the Grey Mountain, who hates me, is the son of Ungit" (4). Ungit, the local fertility goddess, is comparable to the Greek Aphrodite. The Grey Mountain and its mysterious hidden valley are as integral to the retelling of the myth as are Psyche and the god of the mountain themselves.

Lewis' mythopoeic construction of vivid landscapes associated with spiritual journeys enlivens the reader's interaction with characters and places, and intensifies a desire for transcendent experience. Lewis writes, "Nature has that in her which compels us to invent giants: and only giants will do" (Hooper 8). He goes on to note that "Gawain was in the northwest corner of England" where "giants came *blowing* after him on the high fells" (8). One complaint made against *The Three Musketeers* is that "there is no country in the book . . . there is no feeling that London differs from Paris" (7). Lewis' mythic landscapes introduce a milieu that is more than location, a *topos* or mere geographical description. Place in Lewis' landscapes becomes *chora*, a living presence, a participant in the action.

Lewis notes that what flows into us from myth *is* reality; in experiencing a myth we come close to understanding reality in the concrete, not through abstract theorizing but through vicarious participation ("Myth Became Fact"). The concrete experience of reality that flows into us is rooted in vivid descriptions of landscape. Longing, that experience Lewis called *Sehnsucht*, is mediated through participation, whether vicarious or directly, in particular kinds of landscape. Longing is a response to this participation in anticipation of communication that transcends mythopoeia. The distinction between understanding place as *topos* versus *chora*, between mere location and living presence, will be used to examine Lewis' landscapes. Wilderness and Arcadian landscapes will be shown to mediate longing as the approach to a transcendent experience of the real.

Lewis' own foundational experience of longing is clearly associated with and mediated by encounters with landscape. There are two different instances of the awakening of longing recalled in his autobiography *Surprised by Joy*. Of the first account Lewis writes:

> Once in those very early days my brother brought into the nursery the lid of a biscuit tin which he had covered with moss and garnished with twigs and flowers so as to make it a toy garden or a toy forest. That was the first beauty I ever knew. What the real garden had failed to do, the toy garden did. It made me aware of nature-not, indeed, as a storehouse of forms and colors but as something cool, dewy, fresh, exuberant. . . . As long as I live my imagination of Paradise will retain something of my brother's toy garden. (7)

In this case the art form introduced an appreciation for the beauty of nature, not in an abstract reckoning, but as something concrete. The second instance involves a direct, rather than vicarious, experience of the landscape. Lewis writes:

> And every day there were what we called "the Green Hills"; that is, the low line of the Castlereagh Hills which we saw from the nursery windows. They were not very far off but they were, to children, quite unattainable. They taught me longing–*Sehnsucht*; made me for good or ill, and before I was six years old, a votary of the Blue Flower. (7)

Longing Defined

In *Bright Shadow of Reality: Spiritual Longing in C. S. Lewis,* Corbin Scott Carnell defines Lewis' special use of *sehnsucht* as more than nostalgia or yearning. In Lewis' writings it is "A sense of separation from what is desired, a ceaseless longing which always points beyond" (23). Here the transcendent aspect of longing is clearly evident. Carnell goes on to show that though Lewis' sense of longing was awakened as a six-year old looking at the Castlereagh Hills, the feeling associated with those unattainable hills evolved and was informed through literature and scholarship.

Key to the understanding of transcendence was the idea of the numinous that Lewis found in Rudolph Otto's *Idea of the Holy* (Carnell 96). In his interpretation of sacred experience Otto proposes to call the human response to the Holy, this "feeling of dependence," "'creature-consciousness' or creature-feeling. It is the emotion of a creature, submerged and overwhelmed by its own nothingness in contrast to that which is supreme above all creatures" (Otto 10). A further elaboration of this feeling results in Otto's articulation of the human experience of the Holy as that of *mysterium, tremendum,* and fascination.

The Holy as wholly other "is quite beyond the sphere of the usual, the intelligible, and the familiar . . . filling the mind with blank wonder and astonishment" (26). The feeling associated with the Holy transcends human capabilities of rationalizing and so must be approached through symbolic language, as in myth, or through the symbolic action of our imaginations in experiencing particular places as mythic landscape. Any attempt to rationalize this symbolism falls flat. Otto writes, "Both imaginative 'myth', when developed into a system, and intellectualist Scholasticism, when worked out to its completion, are methods by which the fundamental fact of religious experience is, as it were, simply rolled out so thin and flat to be finally eliminated altogether" (26).

Lewis' Narnia books illustrate Otto's articulation, especially in the interrelationship between the creatures of Narnia and Aslan. In *The Lion, the Witch, and the Wardrobe*, on finding out Aslan is a lion Susan asks, "Is he—quite safe? I shall feel rather nervous about meeting a lion." Mrs. Beaver responds, "That you will, dearie, and no mistake, if there's anyone who can appear before Aslan without their knees knocking, they're either braver than most or else just silly." Lucy then joins the conversation, "Then he isn't safe?" And Mr. Beaver answers, "Course he isn't safe. But he's good" (86). Communication of the numinous requires mythopoeia, which produces a vicarious experience of transcendence, and in Lewis' writings the focus is on a separation from the desired thing that produces a "ceaseless longing which always points beyond" (Carnell 23).

Sehnsucht, referred to by Carnell as the dialectic of desire, leads the participant to an experience of yearning, a longing to live in the world disclosed by the myth and imbued by the numinous. Symbolism is needed because direct communication of this world is inadequate. As mystics have continually noted, the numinous cannot be evoked dialectically, but myth, a kind of extended metaphor, opens us to a vicarious experience of the numinous. *Sehnsucht* is never quenched by the mediate objects of longing but only by the actual focus of longing. Lewis writes in *The Weight of Glory*, "if we are made for heaven, the desire for our proper place will be already in us, but not yet attached to the true object, and will even appear as the rival of that object" (29). In speaking of the human attempt to console longing, Lewis writes that we take "revenge on it by calling it names like Nostalgia and Romanticism and Adolescence" (30). He goes on, "Our commonest expedient is to call it beauty and behave as if that had settled the matter" (30). We look to books, music, or other media of beauty, but there is a danger here, for these, he writes, "will betray us if we trust to them; it was not in them, it only came through them, and what came through them was longing" (30). Sacred books themselves are in the same category, for they use the same symbolic action, pointing to that which transcends experience: Lewis writes, "Heaven is, by definition, outside our experience, but all intelligible descriptions must be of things within our experience. The scriptural picture of heaven is therefore just as symbolical as the picture which our desire, unaided, invents for itself; heaven is not really full of jewellery any more than it is really the beauty of Nature, or a fine piece of music" (33).

This desire for transcendence is focused on something other than an abstract intellectual reckoning, which turns toward a system of human production and thereby excludes the numinous. Otto notes, as previously indicated, that this systemic intellectualist Scholasticism eliminates the experience of the Holy (27). Desire is rooted in a need to encounter and commune. In "Myth Became Fact" Lewis writes, "This is our dilemma–either to taste and not to know or know and not to taste–or, more strictly, to lack one kind of knowledge because we are in an experience or to lack another kind because we are outside it" (65). In *The Weight of Glory* Lewis writes:

> We do not want merely to see beauty, though, God knows, even that is bounty enough. We want something else which can hardly be put into words–to be united with the beauty we see, to pass into it, to receive it into ourselves, to bathe in it, to become part of it. That is why we have peopled air and earth and water with gods and goddesses and nymphs and elves–that, though we cannot, yet these projections can enjoy in

themselves that beauty, grace, and power of which Nature is the image. (42-43)

Although we seek communion with God through the medium of nature, Lewis cautions that nature is not the focus of that communion. As embodied beings we are creatures integrated into nature and thereby communicate via the symbols of nature. We relate to God through our embodiment as indicated in scripture: "Nature is only the image, the symbol; but it is the symbol Scripture invites me to use. We are summoned to pass in through Nature, beyond her, into that splendour which she fitfully reflects" (44).

The search for relationship, a communion wherein we pass "into that splendour," is mediated by these various objects, mythic landscape being an important element. Mythic landscape provides a place through which pilgrims pass, or from which they derive their yearning. Making these mediate objects the focus of the pilgrimage leaves the longing unfulfilled and moves the quest to the objects instead of the real focus of *sehnsucht*. The mediate objects are themselves a creation of human beings; they are partly art. They are imaginative associations of *sehnsucht*. Owen Barfield describes this idea in Lewis:

> The longing for a "paradisal" reunion with the Absolute, or with the spirit informing the life of both man and nature, is, he contends, native to the human spirit and is one that embodies itself in symbols at all levels (including of course the sexual one). It is a crucial element in man's faculty of imagination . . . Symbols are symbols of each other, as well as of that which both symbols embody; and the longing for reunion with nature, though it is archetypal to most other longings, is itself only a kind of symbol for the ultimate archetype, which is precisely that quality. It is only when we experience that indefinable quality, as and for itself, that we experience what Lewis called "joy." (56)

The object of *sehnsucht* is beyond the intellectual and emotional reach of each and every human being. Barfield calls it "unattainable" (56). Stephen Thorson says that "Joy, or Desire, had kept Lewis searching for the Object of that Desire. Eventually he came to realize that what he desired with all his heart could not be fulfilled in this world at all" (5).

But Lewis is no Gnostic and does not reject this world in attempting to fulfill the longing. He sees nature as the created world that reflects the numinous and is therefore filled with symbolic potential. Nature's inherent power points to the ultimate power. Nature is capable of producing the feeling that cannot be quenched therein. Rudolph Otto's discussion of the numinous involves an analogous feeling, the sublime, resulting from the difficulty of describing the numinous (41). The sublime is more than some great "force or magnitude in spatial extent," it is also "at once daunting, and yet again singularly attracting, in its impress upon the mind" (41-42). The sublime is also a category used by landscape aestheticians to describe effects produced by wild places.

Greek and Roman Landscape Rhetoric

Lewis as medieval scholar would be familiar with landscape as a commonplace in Latin literature. Pastoral rhetoric of medieval Europe, according to Ernst Robert Curtius, reflects a view of landscape rooted in Greek and Roman literature (184). An ideal landscape was experienced through the filter of this rhetorical idea stretching from the Homeric hymns to the paintings of the sixteenth century. The mythic world depicted by Homer integrated nature and divinity. Each aspect of the natural world was embodied by Nymphs or other personalities. Some personalities associated with the wild forests caused dread to enter the hearts of people who traveled therein. But more domesticated places offered peace. Curtius writes,

> from Homer's landscapes later generations took certain motifs which became permanent elements in a long chain of tradition: the place of heart's desire, beautiful with perpetual spring, as the scene of a blessed life after death; the lovely miniature landscape which combines tree, spring, and grass; the wood with various species of trees; the carpet of flowers. (186)

Shepherds populate pastoral Arcadia in the landscapes of classical poetry giving rise to more and more pleasing imagery (195). Curtius writes that the *locus amoenus*, or pleasance, a commonplace found in Roman poetry,

> forms the principal motif of all nature description. It is . . . a beautiful, shaded natural site. . . . In Theocritus and Virgil such scenes are merely backgrounds for the ensuing pastoral poetry. But they were soon detached from any larger context and became subjects of bravura rhetorical description. (195)

The *locus amoenus* is a buffer between the wild forest and the urban centers. Pastoral poetry's deep influence had established the beauty of Arcadia:

> Of all the antique poetical genres, it [pastoral poetry] had, after the epic, the greatest influence. . . . The shepherd's life is found everywhere and at all periods. It is a basic form of human existence; and through the story of the Nativity in Luke's gospel it made its way into the

Christian tradition too. It has—and this is very important—a correlative scenery: pastoral Sicily, later Arcadia. (187)

Lewis' view of landscape would have been influenced by medieval scholarship, but also by being English and experiencing the countryside in walks. English landscape aestheticians provided a rich repository of critique that influenced experiences of those who regularly walked through the countryside. Aesthetic dialogue became a filter by which poets and other writers experienced their landscape.

English Landscape Tradition

English aesthetic rhetoric explored landscapes through an innovative, critical vocabulary. Ideas associated with the "picturesque," "beautiful," and "sublime" came to the forefront as an attempt to articulate the aesthetic value of landscape art, both painting and gardening. Claude Lorrain's (1600-1682) paintings became associated with the beautiful and Salvator Rosa's (1615-1673) with the sublime (Manwaring 54). E. H. Gombrich points to Paolo Pino, who writing in 1548 gave us "the first formulation of the idea of the 'picturesque'" (*Norm and Form* 116), but the English refined the terminology.

A search for a new criterion whereby beauty could be understood to reside in nature ensued amongst English aestheticians. Joseph Addison (1672-1719) looked to the classics. He writes that Homer "strikes the imagination wonderfully with what is Great," Virgil "with what is Beautiful," and Ovid "with what is Strange" (Hunt and Willis 144), three different ways of distinguishing those places which affect the imagination.

Addison, picking up the theme of the sublime developed by Longinus, began to use the sublime to describe landscape, but it was Edmund Burke (1729-1797) who further articulated the idea of the sublime in relation to landscapes that cause strong emotion. Burke's comprehensive attempt to distinguish between the aesthetic categories of the sublime and the beautiful were articulated in *A Philosophical Inquiry into the Origin of Our Ideas of the Sublime and Beautiful*, published in 1756. Burke's inquiry rests at least in part on the work of Longinus, whose influence had long been established in England: Marjorie Hope Nicolson notes that though Longinus was first available in England after 1554, there was little interest before 1674 (30).

Burke characterizes the sublime as the strongest emotion that can be produced, caused by something that we would call awesome:

whatever is fitted in any sort to excite the ideas of pain and danger, that is to say, whatever is in any sort terrible, or is conversant about terrible objects, or operates in a manner analogous to terror, is a source of the *sublime*; that is, it is productive of the strongest emotion which the mind is capable of feeling. (39)

The resulting passion is astonishment, which is said to be "that state of the soul, in which all its motions are suspended, with some degree of horror. . . . the mind is so entirely filled with its object, that it cannot entertain any other, nor by consequence reason on that object which employs it" (57).

Causes of astonishment in nature result from dark, confused, and uncertain images that have a greater power over the imagination than those things in nature that are clear (62). The sublime is said to come "upon us in the gloomy forest, and in the howling wilderness . . ." (66). Consistent with this view is Burke's assessment of color as productive of the sublime. Here he says, "an immense mountain covered with a shining green turf, is nothing, in this respect, to one dark and gloomy; the cloudy sky is more grand than the blue; and the night more sublime and solemn than day" (81-82).

The category of the beautiful is said to be the cause of love. Examples of the beautiful producing love are small, delicate, smooth, or polished objects. Comparing the beautiful and the sublime Burke writes:

> the sublime, which is the cause of the former, always dwells on great objects, and terrible; the latter on small ones, and pleasing; we submit to what we admire, but we love what submits to us; in one case we are forced, in the other we are flattered, into compliance. In short, the ideas of the sublime and the beautiful stand on foundations so different, that it is hard, I had almost said impossible, to think of reconciling them in the same subject, without considerably lessening the effect of the one or the other upon the passions. So that, attending to their quantity, beautiful objects are comparatively small. (113-114)

The beautiful and the sublime are neither categories of reason nor do objects that appeal to the reason produce them. Objects of nature producing an experience of the beautiful and the sublime appeal to the senses and excite emotion.

Capability Brown (1716-1783), whose name was derived from references to the "capabilities" he saw inherent in particular landscapes, dominated English gardening between 1750 and 1783. Brown's vision for the potentiality of a landscape was filtered by paintings such as those by Claude, but he did not attempt to construct a painted scene where the existing landscape did not cooperate. Brown moved away from absolute sculpting, as in Versailles where the original scene was obliterated, and toward harmonizing the conceptual with the actual. The tension between altering a landscape so that the conceptual harmonizes with rather than dominates the indigenous aspect of the place characterized the aesthetic debate in landscape art. Brown reshaped the English countryside, creating such a vast change that his landscapes influenced aesthetic criticism. Along with Addison and Burke, Brown helped to set the stage for characterizing and distinguishing between the categories of the beautiful, the picturesque, and the sublime.

Elizabeth Manwaring's study of the influence of Italian landscape painting on English aesthetic taste makes clear that the letters and literature concerning landscape scenery of the mid to late eighteenth century were filled with allusions to the paintings of Claude, Rosa, and Poussin, and these allusions, often in reference to the picturesque, point to the similitude between English landscapes and the compositions of Italian landscape paintings. Manwaring notes that the writings of the "cult of the picturesque" show how far visual rhetoric went in influencing perceptions of nature.

Gombrich, referencing Paolo Pino, notes that Italian landscapes were less valued for pictures than "the wild tracts of land" of the north. Pino's mediated experience of "wild tracts of land" came from the paintings of Northern Europeans. Gombrich writes, "sixteenth century landscapes, after all, are not 'views' but largely accumulations of individual features; they are conceptual rather than visual" (*Norm and Form* 116). Paintings train the eye to appreciate the picturesque. Late eighteenth century criticism established paintings by Claude, Rosa, and Poussin as ideal in their depiction and characterization of landscapes. The "Claude-glass," a small device used to frame landscapes by those engaged in countryside walks, rendered an actual scene into something like one of the paintings of the masters.

William Gilpin's (1724-1804) tour of the Wye became well known in publications starting in the 1780s. He described landscapes as picturesque, by which he meant "that kind of beauty which *would look well in a picture*" (Manwaring 185). The theme of the picturesque chained out into the public and by 1800 Gilpin's book was in its fifth edition (185). Manwaring quotes Gilpin as describing nature saying, "her general colouring, and her local hues, are exquisite. In composition only she fails" (187).

Richard Payne Knight (1750-1824), and Uvedale Price (1747-1829) elaborated on the picturesque and clearly distinguished between the picturesque, the beautiful, and the sublime. Price followed Burke in attributing smoothness and diminution to the beautiful, while darkness and limitlessness were associated with the sublime. The picturesque was said to be somewhere in between the two, associated with "roughness and sudden variation" (198). Refining these aesthetic categories opened human understanding to a new way of perceiving nature in relation to scenic beauty. The aesthetic categories of landscape art helped to identify and produce a new understanding of natural places, extending the classical *locus amoenus*, satyr and nymphs attending, with places that were either beautiful, picturesque, or sublime.

Lewis, as scholar and poet, follows in this tradition and his stories are filled with mythic landscapes that are informed by a refined understanding of the aesthetic categories of those landscapes. In *The Four Loves* he writes that nature lovers receive from her "an iconography, a language of images. I do not mean simply visual images; it is the 'moods' or 'spirits' themselves—the powerful expositions of terror, gloom, jocundity, cruelty, lust, innocence, purity—that are the images" (19). His landscapes are *chora* rather than *topos*, places that are imbued with a living presence rather than merely a geographical surface. Belden C. Lane, in writing about the experience of place as ordinary versus extraordinary, calls attention to two Greek words for place, *topos* and *chora*. *Topos* refers to "a mere location, a measurable, quantifiable point, neutral and indifferent," whereas *chora* meant "an energizing force, suggestive to the imagination, drawing intimate connections to everything else in our lives." Lane notes that the difference between the two result from "participation in deliberate ritual activity" that "invariably occasions the transition from experiencing a place as *topos* to encountering that same place as *chora*" (39). The reader of Lewis' fiction participates through the deliberate action of engaging the text, where landscapes become more than mere locations. Lewis' description of place as *chora* transforms geography into mythic landscape.

Narnia

Narnia is both a place and a world, a landscape of forests, moors, mountains, deserts, oceans, and islands. The reader is introduced to the creation of this world in *The Magician's Nephew*, wherein Aslan sings Narnia into existence. Soon thereafter Digory and Polly, riding the flying horse Fledge, soar above the landscape on their quest to retrieve an apple from a sacred garden. Looking down they see lawns, rocks, heather, trees, rivers, hills, and "beyond those hills a great moorland sloped gently up and up to the horizon. On their left the mountains were much higher, but every now and then there was a gap when you could see, between steep pine woods, a glimpse of the southern lands that lay beyond them, looking blue and far away" (174). Polly notes that the name of the mountain region is Archenland, a place name that has meaning for readers who have already completed *The Horse and His Boy*.

Each of the books involves a quest, a journey through some part of the vast landscape. In *The Lion, the Witch and the Wardrobe* the children must journey to the Stone Table, atop a tall hill "where only tall trees grew, very wide apart," and from its "green open space" the children could see in every direction, including far to the East a vast sea (136-137). It is here at the sacred site of the Stone Table that the children first glimpse Aslan, described as being both good and terrible at the same time (140). *The Horse and His Boy* has two talking horses and two humans journeying across the vast desert of Calormen toward the horses' homeland of Narnia and the boy, Shasta's homeland of Archenland. In *Prince Caspian* the original children from *The Lion, the Witch, and the Wardrobe*, Peter, Susan, Edmund, and Lucy, rally the old Narnians to fight the Telmarine usurpers in the clearing at the old Ford of Beruna. *The Voyage of the Dawn Treader* involves a journey at sea, exploring various islands, and finally coming to the end of the world where Reepicheep, a Narnian mouse, "quivering with happiness" (266), paddles his coracle into the beyond. The journey in *The Silver Chair* requires the children, Eustace and Jill, along with a Marsh-wiggle named Puddleglum, to cross a great moor and navigate vast underground caverns.

After traveling across Ettinsmoor for ten days the children and Puddleglum come to a place on the northern edge of the moor where the country changes. Looking down there is "a long, steep slope into a different, and grimmer, land. At the bottom of the slope were cliffs: beyond these, a country of high mountains, dark precipices, stony valleys, ravines so deep and narrow that one could not see far into them, and rivers that poured out of echoing gorges to plunge sullenly into black depths" (85). In each case the landscape is integral to the narrative action and in some cases induces a numinous aspect.

Of the walled garden at the top of a high hill in *The Magician's Nephew* Lewis writes, "you never saw a place which was so obviously private" (187). The garden is described in such a way as to emphasize the numinous rather than a *locus amoenus*. At the end of *The Last Battle*, after moving further in and further up, the characters converge on the top of a high mountain from which all of Narnia is visible. From this vantage those gathered discover they have arrived at the place where their life long yearning had been focused. Below are the shadowlands, here at the top they are in the true Archenland.

Space Stories

Lewis' Space Trilogy is also filled with mythic landscapes. In the first story, Ransom, the protagonist of the series, is shanghaied to Mars by a power-hungry scientist named Weston and a greedy businessman named Devine. Mars is inhabited by three intelligent species who refer to their planet as Malacandra. Weston and Devine, in an attempt to gain favor with one of the species inhabitants of Malacandra, intend to offer Ransom as a human sacrifice. Ransom's escape provides the story with a journey theme. In the second story, Ransom is shuttled to Venus, called Perelandra, by spirit beings known as *eldila*. Ransom meets a woman who is the Eve character of Perelandra. Eventually the antagonist, Weston, arrives and the two engage in a kind of spiritual battle over the future of Perelandra's inhabitants. Both the journey on Malacandra and the cosmic struggle on Perelandra involve an interrelation between the persons and the landscape, in each case the mythic aspect integrates people and place. I will not explore the third book of the series here.

A. Out of the Silent Planet

One of Ransom's first reactions to Malacandra relates to the landscape: "Before anything else he learned that Malacandra was beautiful" (42). Ransom describes the mountains as improbably shaped and that the "mere oddity of the prospect was swallowed up in the fantastic sublime" (53). His discovery of the gorge, called a *handramit*, is described in vivid language: "Like a rope of jewels the gorge spread beneath him, purple, sapphire blue, yellow and pinkish white, a rich and variegated inlay of wooded land and disappearing, reappearing, ubiquitous water" (63). Looking up into the high country, Ransom notes that the shining "place rose, remote and smooth and tranquil, like another and more spiritual world" (64).

As in Narnia, the Malacandrian story involves a mythic quest. Hyoi, the *hrossa* acquaintance of Ransom, describes a spiritual journey in the Malacandrian landscape:

> I do not think the forest would be so bright, nor the water so warm, nor love so sweet, if there were no danger in the lakes. I will tell you a day in my life that has shaped me, such a day as comes only once, like love . . . I went far, far up the *handramit* to the land where stars shine at midday and even water is cold. A great waterfall I climbed. I stood on the shore of Balki the pool, which is the place of most awe in all worlds. The walls of it go up for ever and ever and huge and holy images are cut in them, the work of old times. There is the fall called the Mountain of Water. Because I have stood there alone, Maleldil and I, for even Oyarsa sent me no word, my heart has been higher, my song deeper, all

my days. . . . There I drank life because death was in the pool. (75)

Ransom himself journeys up and out of the *hadramit* and across the vast highlands. The description of climbing up the mountains to the tower of Augray gives a similar prospect to the Greek holy place Delphi:

> He was only twenty yards from the almost perpendicular bases of the mountain spires, too close to them to see their tops. A sort of valley ran up in the re-entrant between two of them at the place where he had emerged: an unclimbable valley consisting of a single concave sweep of stone, which in its lower parts ascended steeply as the roof of a house and farther up seemed almost vertical. At the top it even looked as if it hung over a bit, like a tidal wave of stone at the very moment of breaking; but this, he thought, might be an illusion. He wondered what the *hrossa's* idea of a road might be. (87)

Both of these places allow the reader to vicariously experience that creature-feeling described by Otto. We identify with Hyoi, knowing that our most intense living experiences have often been associated with the *tremendum*. We walk with Ransom and imagine a sublime landscape that terrifies and invites. Higher up the mountain Lewis describes Ransom as "cutting his way up into a silent arctic world, and had already passed from an English to a Lapland winter" (88). Here "the landscape was terrifying." Lewis goes on, "Among the *hrossa* he had almost lost the feeling of being on a strange planet; here it returned upon him desolating force. It was no longer 'the world,' scarcely even 'a world': it was a planet, a star, a waste place in the universe, millions of miles from the world of men" (88).

After crossing the desolate landscape in the higher elevations of Malacandra Ransom sees a new *handramit* and its description is of a more hospitable place:

> The beauty of this new *handramit* as it opened before him took his breath away. It was wider than that in which he had hitherto lived and right below him lay an almost circular lake–a sapphire twelve miles in diameter set in the border of purple forest. Amidst the lake there rose like a low and gently sloping pyramid, or like a woman's breast, an island of pale red, smooth to the summit, and on the summit a grove of such trees as man had never seen. (105)

The island itself is described as being warm, sweet smelling and reminded Ransom of Earth "and gardens in summer" (109). Having passed through the fierce landscapes of the highlands, Ransom arrived at the paradisiacal island garden. It is a place set apart, the place where direct communication with the arch spirit of Malacandra happens.

B. Perelandra

Perelandra is a different world. Rather than an old world, its mythology is in its genesis. The ocean is the first place Ransom experiences, the womb of the new world. Ransom describes the ocean scene:

> The sky was pure, flat gold like the background of a medieval picture. It looked very distant–as far off as a cirrhus cloud looks from earth. The ocean was gold too, in the offing, flecked with innumerable shadows. The nearer waves, though golden where their summits caught the light, were green on their slopes: first emerald, and lower down a lustrous bottle green, deepening to blue where they passed beneath the shadow of other waves. (35)

Just as in *The Voyage of the Dawn Treader*, Lewis returns to the ocean as mythic landscape. The sea has always been a chora of numinosity.

After floating for some time, Ransom discovers floating islands. The island that Ransom lands upon is described as a dry surface, consisting of "something very like heather, except for the colour which was copper" (40). Being alone on the island he writes, "The sense of his solitude became intense without becoming at all painful–only adding, as it were, a last touch of wildness to the unearthly pleasures that surrounded him" (42). The last phrase distinguishes this paradise from the myth of Eden. These islands, though fruitful and attractive, are not landscapes where persons find themselves a home; they are not a *locus amoenus*.

There is an apophatic description of eating the fruit of the place. The taste was a "new *genus* of pleasures, something unheard of among men, out of all reckoning, beyond all covenant. For one draught of this on earth wars would be fought and nations betrayed. It could not be classified. . . . 'Not like that' was all he could ever say to such inquiries. . . . to repeat a pleasure so intense and almost so spiritual seemed an obvious thing to do" (42). But Ransom decides it would be a kind of perversion to continue eating.

In addition to these floating islands, Perelandra is described as having a fixed land. A large portion of the narrative involves a kind of cosmic battle between Ransom and Weston, who has become the Unman, wherein they struggle over the mythic future of the new world. The Unman attempts to cause Perelandra's first woman to fall into the same trap that befell Eve by convincing her to spend the night on the fixed land, which is forbidden. Ransom describes the fixed land as having

> a steep narrow valley with low cliffs and outcroppings of reddish rock and, lower down, banks of some kind of moss and a few trees. The trees might almost have been terrestrial: planted in any southern country of our own world they would not have seemed remarkable to anyone except a trained botanist. Best of all, down the middle of the valley–and welcome to Ransom's eyes and ears as a glimpse of home or of heaven–ran a little stream, a dark translucent stream where a man might hope for trout. (78)

The further elaborated descriptions of fixed land, an island, reveal Perelandra as a young planet (186). Toward the end of the story, after the triumph of good over evil, Ransom climbs the mountains of the fixed island (191-192). The reader is given a picture of a landscape that might have been here on earth had the first mythic couple obeyed the command not to eat of the forbidden fruit.

Till We Have Faces

I think that Lewis' *Till We Have Faces* best exemplifies longing and mythic landscape. As indicated in the introduction to this paper, in the opening of the book the landscape becomes an integral part of the story where divinity and mountain coalesce. Orual makes her case writing, "I will accuse the gods, especially the god who lives on the Grey Mountain" (3). She then describes the city of Glome as being on the river Shennit and near the foothills of the Grey Mountain, where "the god of the Grey Mountain, who hates me, is the son of Ungit" (4).

As Lewis was introduced to longing by the Castlereagh Hills, Orual and Psyche are introduced to just such an experience by their Greek teacher, the Fox. He takes the girls into the hills whereof Orual writes:

> We were often out all day in summer on the hill-top to the south-west, looking down on all Glome and across to the Grey Mountain. We stared our eyes out on that jagged ridge till we knew every tooth and notch of it, for none of us had ever gone there or seen what was on the other side. Psyche, almost from the beginning (for she was a very quick, thinking child), was half in love with the Mountain. (23)

Psyche indicates that she will marry a king who will build her a castle of "gold and amber up there on the very top" (23). It is Psyche then who awakens to the longing, and Orual struggles throughout the book to understand the experience of the numinous.

The Fox trains Orual to use rationality to quench the fire of longing. Psyche's longing is not rational, and we find her in a kind of hallucination looking to the mountain for solace. While under the influence of a fever she talks of "her gold and amber castle on the ridge of the Grey Mountain" (33). However, the Fox does not always have the whole truth: "He calls the whole world a city. But what's a city built on? There's earth beneath. And outside the walls? Doesn't all food come from there as well as all the dangers? . . . things growing and rotting, strengthening and poisoning, things shining wet . . ." (70). The Fox's rationality does not disclose the truth that is the object of longing. He even plays a part in convincing Orual to distrust her own brief encounter with the numinous, a moment in which she glimpsed the gold and amber castle. Instead, it is reason that tells Orual that some ranger has abducted her sister.

The god of the Grey Mountain, the son of Ungit, is also known as the Brute, or Shadow-Brute. He is more than a personification of the terrible place, the place and the god become interchangeable. The Brute is first introduced and is associated with the Grey Mountain when the chief shepherd's story is recounted: "'Your own chief shepherd on the Grey Mountain saw it the night the lion came. He fell upon the lion with a burning torch. And in the light of the torch he saw the Brute–behind the lion–very black and big, a terrible shape'" (47).

Psyche offends Ungit and a sacrifice is required for appeasement. In describing the "Great Offering" needed to appease the jealous goddess the priest says, "'The victim must be given to the Brute. For the Brute is, in a mystery, Ungit herself or Ungit's son, the god of the mountain; or both'" (48). Psyche must be sacrificed to the Brute. She articulates a feeling of longing for death, and Orual asks her about the implied lack of happiness. Psyche responds, "Not that kind of longing. It was when I was happiest that I longed most" (74). Her longing is associated with the hills overlooking Glome. She remembers the "colour and the smell, and looking across at the Grey Mountain in the distance? And because it was so beautiful, it set me longing, always longing. Somewhere else there must be more of it" (74). Thus the Grey Mountain is but a symbol of something beyond, something more real.

In talking about the ritual that would take Psyche to the Grey Mountain she exclaims, "I am going, you see, to the Mountain. You remember how we used to look and long?" (75). She goes on, "The sweetest thing in all my life has been the longing to reach the Mountain, to find the place where all the beauty came from" (75). Psyche then refers to this desire as a "longing for home" (76).

During the ritual of sacrifice Orual becomes sick and is not able to attend. Weeks later she and the soldier Bardia climb the Grey Mountain in an attempt to retrieve the body of Psyche. She describes the wilderness landscape that she and Bardia pass through while climbing the mountain (95). From the barren top she looks down at Glome and all else viewed from the prospect of the Grey Mountain and describes her feeling: "The sight of the huge world put mad ideas into me, as if I could wander away, wander forever, see strange and beautiful things, one after the other to the world's end" (96). Orual's longing manifests itself in a desire to journey.

The wilderness landscape at the top stands in stark contrast to the lower elevations that had affected Psyche's longing. Orual describes a desolate landscape at the top of the Grey Mountain, sublime in its aspect:

> We were so high now that, though the sun was very strong, the wind blew bitterly cold. At our feet, between us and the Mountain, lay a cursed black valley: dark moss, dark peat-bogs, shingle, great boulders, and screes of stone sprawling down into it from the Mountain—as if the Mountain had sores and these were the stony issue from them. The great mass of it rose up (we tilted our heads back to look at it) into the huge knobbles of stone against the sky, like an old giant's black teeth. The face it showed us was really no steeper than a roof, except for certain frightful cliffs on our left, but it looked as if it went up like a wall. It, too, was now black. Here the gods ceased trying to make me glad. There was nothing here that even the merriest heart could dance for. (97-98)

An evocation of Otto's *tremendum* and Burke's sublime continues once they reach the place of the ritual sacrifice where Bardia says, "We are very near the bad part of the Mountain—I mean the holy part. Beyond the tree, it's all god's country, they say" (100). Bardia's experience of the place stands in contrast to Orual's. Lane notes that persons may tred on sacred places without entering them, "recognition is existentially, not ontologically discerned. The identification of sacred place is thus intimately related to states of consciousness" (19). The participation of place may range from mere topography void of living presence, through its evocation of emotions such as astonishment as articulated by aestheticians, and to its association with the numinous. Orual's more aesthetic versus Bardia's clear religious experience of the Grey Mountain ushers the reader toward an ambiguous interpretation of the place. The reader begins to question whether the power of the place is the result of the human mind projecting emotional experience onto it, or the place itself is associated with power. This questioning thrusts the reader into a vicarious participation with the place. The reader must choose how to relate to, how to experience the Grey Mountain.

The tree that held Psyche for the Brute stands vacant, no human body is there, nor is there evidence of the leavings of wild animals. Lewis' description of the mountain landscape is of *chora*, an energizing force, filling the reader's imagination with the intense experience of the sublime. Orual and Bardia search the area and discover a new prospect, a valley on the far side of the peak. Looking down into this valley is described as "looking down into a new world" (100). The valley and landscape beyond are further described as being "warm, blue lands, hills and forests, far below us. The valley itself was like a cleft in the Mountain's southern chin . . . There was gorse in bloom, and wild vines, and many groves of flourishing trees, and great plenty of bright water-pools, streams, and little cataracts" (101). Bardia then says that "this may well be the secret valley of the gods" (101). The sublime mountaintop gives way to a paradisiacal valley, a *locus amoenus*. The juxtaposition of wild, windswept mountain versus lush, green river valley accentuates Bardia's sacred experience. The Grey Mountain is the boundary between profane Glome and the wholly other realm of the secret valley.

After making their way down into the valley, Orual discovers her sister living beside a stream. Psyche's experience of the place includes her gold and amber castle while Orual sees it as a wild landscape. Again, the idea of *chora* shows that each of the two sisters experiences the same place uniquely. For Orual its wild aspect is unpleasant, threatening the order of her world. For Psyche it is the place where her longing has been quenched. The myth continues to unfold and Psyche is convinced to look directly at the body of the god, an act that symbolically aims to tame the wild, to know the sacred with a human understanding. The result is banishment from the valley, exile from the *chora* that reveals sacred reality. Psyche and Orual spend their lives journeying. They have tasted of the real but did not recognize it and so must approach understanding in the context of a search. The sacred journey will cultivate their longing for the unattainable.

Conclusion

In each of the stories recounted here the landscape has been shown to be integral to communicating the special idea of longing that Lewis identified as *sehnsucht*. The most clear case is Lewis' final work, *Till We Have Faces*, where the Grey Mountain awakens longing in both Psyche and Orual, but its manifestation takes on divergent characterizations. For Psyche it is the unattainable distant mountain that produced a longing for that "somewhere else where there must be more of it" (74). That somewhere else turned out to be the mysterious valley beyond the mountain. For Orual the wild, barren top provoked in her a desire to "wander away, wander forever, see strange and beautiful things, one after the other to the world's end" (96). These mythic images and their moving the human heart toward a transcendent longing are described by Lewis in *The Weight of Glory*, "We do not want merely to see beauty, though, God knows, even that is bounty enough. We want something else which can hardly be put into words–to be united with the beauty we see, to pass into it, to receive it into ourselves, to bathe in it, to become part of it" (42-43). *Sehnsucht*, the dialectic of desire, is a rhetoric which leads the pilgrim step-by-step toward the ultimately real. Plato writes in the *Phaedrus*: "For the colorless, formless, and intangible truly existing essence, with which all true knowledge is concerned, holds this region and is visible only to the mind" (124). For Lewis the region is manifest through symbols that also engage our passion. Humans seem to perceive themselves trapped in a world where that which appears hides that which must really be there. St. Paul writes that there will be a time when we do see "face-to-face" (I Cor. 13:12). This implies that we do not see yet. But everywhere the search continues, and we journey through mythic landscapes in our quest to see.

WORKS CITED

Barfield, Owen. *Owen Barfield on C. S. Lewis*. Middletown: Wesleyan Univ. Press, 1989.

Burke, Edmund. *A Philosophical Enquiry into the Origin of Our Ideas of the Sublime and Beautiful*. Ed. James T. Boulton. Notre Dame: Univ. of Notre Dame Press, 1968.

Carnell, Corbin Scott. *Bright Shadow of Reality: C. S. Lewis and the Feeling Intellect*. Grand Rapids: Eerdmans, 1974.

Curtius, Ernst Robert. *European Literature and the Latin Middle Ages*. Trans. Willard R. Trask. Princeton: Princeton University Press, 1953.

Gombrich, E. H. *Art and Illusion: A Study in the Psychology of Pictorial Representation*. Bollingen Series XXXV:5. New York: Princeton Univ. Press, 1961.

—. *Norm and Form: Studies in the Art of the Renaissance*. 2nd ed. London: Phaidon Press, 1971.

—. *The Story of Art*. 12th Rev. ed. London: Phaidon Press, 1972.

Hooper, Walter. *On Stories and Other Essays on Literature*. San Diego: Harcourt Brace & Co., 1982.

Hunt, John Dixon and Peter Willis, eds. *The Genius of the Place: the English Landscape Garden 1620-1820*. New York: Harper and Row, Publishers, 1975.

Lane, Belden C. *Landscapes of the Sacred: Geography and Narrative in American Spirituality*. Baltimore: Johns Hopkins Univ. Press, 2001.

Lewis, C. S. *The Four Loves*. San Diego: Harcourt Brace & Co., 1988.

—. *The Horse and His Boy*. New York: HarperTrophy, 1954.

—. *The Last Battle*. New York: HarperTrophy, 1956.

—. *The Lion, the Witch, and the Wardrobe*. New York: HarperTrophy, 1950.

—. *The Magician's Nephew*. New York: HarperTrophy, 1955.

—. "Myth Became Fact." *God in the Dock*. Ed. Walter Hooper. Grand Rapids: Eerdmans, 1970. 63-67.

—. *Out of the Silent Planet*. New York: Scribner Paperback Fiction, 1996.

—. *Perelandra*. New York: Scribner Paperback Fiction, 1996.

—. *Prince Caspian*. New York: HarperTrophy, 1951.

—. *The Silver Chair*. New York: HarperTrophy, 1953.

—. *Surprised by Joy: The Shape of My Early Life*. San Diego: Harcourt Brace & Co., 1984.

—. *Till We Have Faces: A Myth Retold*. New York: Harcourt Brace Jovanovich, 1956.

—. *The Voyage of the Dawn Treader*. New York: HarperTrophy, 1952.

—. *The Weight of Glory*. New York: HarperOne, 1980.

Manwaring, Elizabeth W. *Italian Landscape in Eighteenth Century England*. New York: Oxford Univ. Press, 1925.

Nicolson, Marjorie Hope. *Mountain Gloom and Mountain Glory: The Development of the Aesthetics of the Infinite*. New York: W. W. Norton and Co. Inc., 1959.

Otto, Rudolph. *The Idea of the Holy: An Inquiry into the Non-Rational Factor in the Idea of the Divine and it Relation to the Rational*. 2nd Ed. London: Oxford Univ. Press, 1952.

Plato. "*Phaedrus*." *The Rhetorical Tradition: Readings from Classical Times to the Present*. Eds. Patricia Bizzell and Bruce Herzberg. Boston: Bedford Books, 1990. 113-143.

Thorson, Stephen. "Truth, Myth, and Revelation in Lewis." *The Bulletin of the New York C. S. Lewis Society*. 21:6 (April 1990): 1-6.

Part III

THE BAPTISED COSMOS: NARNIA & THE RANSOM TRILOGY

Apparently, then, our lifelong nostalgia, our longing to be reunited with something in the universe from which we now feel cut off, to be on the inside of a door which we have always seen from the outside, is no mere neurotic fancy, but the truest index of our real situation. And to be at last summoned inside would be both glory and honour beyond all our merits and also the healing of that old ache.

The Weight of Glory

Chapter Nine

The Spirit of Comedy in *The Chronicles of Narnia*

Samuel Joeckel

On the last day of a C.S. Lewis course I teach at my university, I routinely ask my students, "What were you most surprised to learn about Lewis during the course of this semester?" Many student responses are predictable, touching upon some of the more controversial aspects of the Lewis corpus: for example, Lewis's views on Scripture (too low for some of my more theologically conservative students); Lewis's attitude toward women (sexist according to some of my students of a feminist bent); Lewis's contested position on salvation (a position that too closely resembles universalism for students who wonder how a guy like Emeth can get into the Real Narnia); or Lewis's love of pubs and pints (scandalous for the teetotalers in the classroom). Last May, one student caught me off-guard, however, when she proclaimed that she did not realize Lewis was so funny. Indeed, we often forget that Lewis loved to laugh. Though, historically, Christianity and humor have not exactly strolled arm in arm down the primrose path together, Lewis was a man with a sense of humor, a man who said that his favorite sound was that of male laughter. Though this humor is evident in nearly all of Lewis's works, this paper will explore the spirit of comedy in *The Chronicles of Narnia*. The paper will; specifically the connection the narrative structure of the Narnia stories towith ancient Greek fertility rituals from which, according to one popular thesis, Greek dramatic comedy descends. The paper will also also attempt to describe moments of comedy in the more popular sense of the term—that is, comedy not only as a literary form but strictly as an affective response, one that manifests itself in the form of laughter, which, as this paper intends to remind us, was indeed, one of Lewis's favorite sounds.

The precise origins of dramatic comedy are not certain, but one prominent theory holds that comedy originated from Dionysian rituals. Before examining how these rituals—and thus moments of comedy—manifest themselves in the Narnia stories, we would do well to consider the troublemaking god after whom the rituals are named. Dionysus/Bacchus makes a few cameos in the *Chronicles*. In *The Lion, the Witch and the Wardrobe*, Mr. Tumnus the faun tells Lucy that, during summer in Narnia before the White Witch cast a spell causing a never-ending winter, revelries took place in the woods; "and sometimes," says Tumnus, "Bacchus himself …would come to visit them …and then the streams would run with wine instead of water and the whole forest would give itself to jollification for weeks on end" (17). In *Prince Caspian*, in an epiphanic moment during which Aslan reveals himself to the Pevensie children, Bacchus and a riotous train of revelers dance across Aslan's How. The narrator gives us this description of Bacchus: "One [of the revelers] was a youth, dressed only in a fawn-skin, with vine-leaves wreathed in his curly hair. His face would have been almost too pretty for a boy's, if it had not looked so extremely wild. You felt, as Edmund said when he saw him a few days later, 'There's a chap who might do anything—absolutely anything.'" (167). Attending Bacchus is a group of girls, "as wild as he" (167); these girls are undoubtedly the Maenads, Bacchus's female devotees. It is not until Bacchus's raucous procession is out of sight that the children realize who the vine-wearing, wine-drinking god is; the following conversation between Susan and Lucy ensues:

> 'I say, Su, I know who they are.'
> 'Who?'
> 'The boy with the wild face is Bacchus… Don't you remember Mr. Tumnus telling us about them long ago?
> 'Yes, course. But I say, Lu—"
> 'What?'
> 'I wouldn't have felt safe with Bacchus and all his wild girls if we'd met them without Aslan.'
> 'I should think not,' said Lucy. (169)

Susan and Lucy have reason not to feel safe. A brief overview of the figure of Dionysus might reveal how Aslan's shoulder-rubbing with Dionysus might give one pause. Walter Otto writes, "All of antiquity extolled Dionysus as the god who gave men wine. However, he was known also as the raving god whose presence makes man mad and incites him to savagery and even to lust for blood" (49). Marcel Detienne describes Dionysus as the god who "snatches his victim by surprise, who trips his prey and drags it down into madness, murder, and defilement…" (2). To begin at the beginning, Dionysus was the offspring of Zeus and the mortal Semele. When Dionysus was in utero, Semele died when Zeus appeared to her in a theophany. However, Hermes saved Dionysus by sewing him up in Zeus's thigh, where he underwent gestation for another three months and then was successfully delivered. When she Zeus' wife, Hera, heard of Dionysus' existence, a jealous Hera she commanded the titans to tear Dionysus into pieces, boiling his body parts in a cauldron. However, Dionysus' grandmother Rhea resurrected the boy, who was raised by nymphs on Mount Nysa, thus accounting for his effeminacy. From this time on, much of Dionysus' existence was spent overseeing orgiastic rituals and waging war on those who deny his godhood. In Euripedes's *The Bacchae*, women start rumors that Dionysus was not the son of Zeus. "Therefore," proclaims Dionysus,

> ...I've stung them
> with madness, and goaded them raving from their houses.
> They're living on the mountain now, delirious,
> dressed, as I've compelled them to be dressed,
> in the garments of my rituals. (4)

The Women Thus Become Maenads.

Dionysus then directs his wrath toward Pentheus, King of Thebes, who, as Dionysus rages, "is warring with divinity / by excluding me from rituals / and not invoking my name in prayers" (4). Dionysus brings madness upon not only Pentheus, who subsequently dons women's clothing, but the entire city of Thebes, eventuating in Pentheus's brutal death: he is torn to pieces—at the hands of his own mother as well as the Maenads. On another occasion, Dionysus' vindictiveness is directed toward Athens. Because the Athenians would not recognize his statue, he afflicted the entire male population with a "painful state of erection that nothing seemed to alleviate" (Detienne 32).

My thesis holds that Dionysus' role in Narnian history might have a specific purpose, a role that becomes apparent when we investigate the connection between Dionysus and the development of Greek comedy. As stated previously, the precise origins of dramatic comedy are not certain, but one prominent theory holds that comedy originated from Dionysian rituals. These were fertility rituals that involved various activities to promote healthy crops and an abundant harvest: activities that included sexual unions (to tell the land symbolically to be fertile), human sacrifice (of those who represent sterility), and phallic processions (which may help us understand why Dionysos meted out such a stiff punishment for the Athenians). (See, for example, F. M. Cornford's *The Origins of Attic Comedy*.) Most of the elements of these Dionysian rituals thus find their way into dramatic comedy, from

Aristophanes to Shakespeare. The human to be sacrificed as representative of sterility and thus hostile to fertility is depicted in dramatic comedy as the figure of the killjoy, who is often a repressed, dour-faced, prudish villain who blocks young lovers from marriage. In addition, dramatic comedy often concludes with a feast, a wedding, and the promise of children, all of which are symbolic of the triumph of fertility.

Turning now to the *Chronicles*, we can see how this historical evolution—from Dionysian fertility rituals to dramatic comedy—constitutes the subtext to Bacchus's appearances as well as the wine-drinking celebrations in the Narnia stories. For example, in *The Horse and His Boy*, the villainous king of Calormen, King Rabadash, receives his comeuppance when Aslan changes him into a donkey. Then, consistent with the conventions of comedy, once the killjoy figure is muted, weddings are announced and a great celebratory feast ensues: "Meanwhile...everyone was very glad that [Rabadash] had been disposed of before the real fun began, which was a grand feast held that evening on the lawn before the castle, with dozens of lanterns to help the moonlight. And the wine flowed and tales were told and jokes were cracked..." (238). The removal of Rabadash represents the restoration of society, during which celebrations and wine-induced merriment establish a spirit of comedy (in the generic sense of the term) wherein marriages are announced that bring the promise of children and the victory of fertility over sterility.

The patterns of comedy are also seen in *Prince Caspian*. As the Narnian forces defeat the evil King Miraz and his army, Bacchus is summoned to free a river god from the Fords of Beruna, a god that had been enchained by a river bridge. Bacchus and his Maenads splash into the water and wreak havoc on the bridge: "Great, strong trunks of ivy came curling up all the piers of the bridge, growing as quickly as a fire grows, wrapping the stones round, splitting, breaking, separating them" (221). As in Greek myth, Bacchus here is capable of great destruction; his vines operate like tentacles, ripping the bridge from its foundations. In addition, Bacchus is also figured in this passage as a liberator. In dramatic comedy, Bacchus-as-liberator translates into a liberation from repressive social conventions, resulting in the creation of a topsy-turvy world that often defies reason, order, propriety, common sense, and predictability. (One thinks, for example, of Aristophanes's *Lysistrata* or Shakespeare's *A Midsummer Night's Dream*.) By destroying the bridge, Lewis's Bacchus operates more at the service of the plot; after all, Aslan needs a force powerful enough to take down the bridge. In addition, Bacchus lacks the moral ambiguity he possesses in Greek myth: Bacchus destroys the bridge so that good can triumph over evil.

However, as Bacchus proceeds through Narnia, his wild disregard for constraint and order become more apparent, suggestive of his originally dubious moral character (at least as suggestive as one can expect in a book for children). As Bacchus and his train dance in celebration of Narnia's victory over King Miraz, they come across a school instituted under Miraz's rule: a school, explains the narrator, "where a lot of Narnian girls, with their hair done very tight and ugly tight collars round their necks and thick tickly stocking on their legs, were having a history lesson" (213). Lewis's language here evokes the repressive morality and confining social milieu against which the spirit of comedy militates: "hair done very tight," "tight collars round their necks," and "thick tickly stockings" constitute constrictions upon the body that are prohibitive to fertility. With the help of Aslan's roar, Bacchus once again employs his ivy, this time to take down the school. Once it is destroyed, most of the students ("prim little girls") flee in terror—an effect that Bacchus's presence has on many in the original myths. However, one student asks to join the procession: "Instantly [the girl] joined hands with two of the Maenads, who whirled her round in a merry dance and helped her take off some of the unnecessary and uncomfortable clothes that she was wearing" (214). One hears in the echoes of this narration the original phallic processions, orgiastic celebrations, and wine- and lust-induced insanity that were hallmarks of the rites of Dionysus.

Among those who flee in terror at the sight of Bacchus is Miss Prizzle, who, as the strict, sour-faced, joyless teacher of the school, resembles the killjoy figure of dramatic comedy. Her name itself, Prizzle, sounds like 'prissy.' Also, when one of the students exclaims that there is a lion outside the school, Miss Prizzle chastises the student for "talking nonsense" (213). Resistant to nonsense, Miss Prizzle is also inimical to the spirit of comedy.

The Telmarine soldiers—who opposed the Narnian forces—also possess attributes of the killjoy. Like Miss Prizzle, the Telmarines are humorless and morose. They are described as "sulky" (229) and "hat[ing] and fear[ing] people, who "hate and fear running water just as much as they hated and feared woods and animals" (224). Their disposition is at odds with the feast and celebration with which the narrative concludes; thus, consistent with killjoy figures in dramatic comedy, the Telmarines are expelled from the metaphorical stage. Aslan creates a magic door which leads them to the world from where they came.

The feast and celebration from which the Telmarines are expelled are, of course, the exclusion of the Telemarines from the feast and celebration is a key structural elements to any dramatic comedyelement.

Lewis goes into great detail in describing the food and drink that Bacchus and the Maenads create through a "magic dance of plenty": "sides of roasted meat that filled the grove with delicious smell, and wheaten and oaken cakes, honey and many-colored sugars and cream as think as porridge and as smooth as still water.... Then, in great wooden cups and bowls and mazers, wreathed with ivy, came the wines; dark, thick ones like syrups of mulberry juice, and clear red ones like red jellies liquefied, and yellow wines and green wines and yellow-green and greenish-yellow" (225-226). How can such a bacchanalia not lead to intoxication? And though *Prince Caspian* does not conclude with a wedding and the consequent promise of children, the *denouement* does include the sustaining and prolonging of life. During the procession, Bacchus encounters a dying woman. Dipping a pitcher into the cottage well, the vessel emerges filled not with water but the "richest wine, red as re-currant jelly, smooth as oil, strong as beef, warming as tea, cool as dew" (217). Quaffing Bacchus's wine, the woman is healed.

As noted earlier, Susan makes it clear that she would not feel comfortable with Bacchus and the Maenads if Aslan were not present. I wish to read this comment as I consider this discomfort to be a fictional emblem. The presence of Aslan sanctifies Bacchus's transgressive tendencies, sublimating the behavior that would be clearly antithetical to Lewis's orthodoxy. Aslan's close proximity to Bacchus is thus necessary. In *Surprised by Joy* Lewis claims that George MacDonald baptized his imagination (181). I want to suggest that in the *Narnia* stories it is Aslan who baptizes Bacchus's rituals, cleansing them of murder, mutilation, and licentiousness. Once purged of these elements, what still remains is significant: not only wildness but the spirit of comedy, which serves to de-stabilize and disrupt. In fact, enough of this wildness and potential for de-stabilization and disruption exists to keep characters from feeling too safe, for as Edmund says of Bacchus, "'There's a chap who might do anything—absolutely anything'" (167).

I maintain, then, that the spirit of comedy in the Narnia stories often serves to de-stabilize and disrupt. Briefly consider one of the most famous comic moments in the stories. After Aslan rises from the dead in *The Lion, the Witch and the Wardrobe*, he enjoys a romp with Susan and Lucy. The lion and the children run, scramble, and wrestle, laughing all the while. The obvious interpretation here is of course that the laughter in this scene proceeds from a sense of joy knowing that Aslan is alive and not dead. However, humor theory might shed some original light on this scene. In 1819, Arthur Schopenhauer (of all people) provided an early definition of the Incongruity Theory of humor: "The cause of laughter in every case is simply the sudden perception of the incongruity between a concept and the real objects which have been thought through in some relation, and laughter itself is just the expression of this incongruity" (77). We see how this theory applies toIn Aslan's romp scene. Aslan as , the all-powerful creator and providential sustainer of Narnia seems incongruous to the Aslan playing tag with two kids in an outdoor romper room. Lucy could not make up her mind whether, as Lewis writes, "it was more like playing with a thunderstorm or playing with a kitten…" (179). The parallel structure of this sentence sets up the seeming incongruities.

On a profound level, iIncongruity has a conceptual kinship to Christianity. While the Incongruity Theory makes use of words like 'contradiction' and 'discrepancies,' Christianity appeals to paradox. Consider some of the central paradoxes of Jesus' teachings: the first shall be last (Matthew 20:16), those who serve will be the greatest (Luke 20:16), life comes through death (John 12:25), etc. Peter Berger identifies these sorts of paradoxes as "holy folly" (190). For my purposes, incongruities and paradoxes, as important concepts in the spirit of comedy, destabilize facile understandings of transcendence. Simply put, Aslan (or God) cannot be put into a box.

In *The Lion, the Witch and the Wardrobe*, Susan asks Mr. and Mrs. Beaver if Aslan is safe. "'Course he isn't safe," replies Mr. Beaver, "But he's good" (86). One finds this same sort of quality in Lewis's Bacchus: unsafe, not tame. My sense is that Lewis has not only a mythopoeic but a theological attraction to this sort of wildness, which frustrates expectations, defies common conceptions, and makes room for mystery, paradox, and comedy. This wildness is a quality that marks the Holy Other, which itself cannot be tamed, controlled, compressed into a theological box, or reduced, in one way or another, by human reason. Jane Harrison writes that with Dionysus "came a 'return to nature,' a breaking of bonds and limitations and crystallizations, a desire for the life rather of the emotions than of the reason, a recrudescence if maybe of animal passions" (444). The imagination of Lewis the romantic, the myth-maker, the "votary of the Blue Flower," as he describes himself in *Surprised by Joy* (7), resonates with such a life of the emotions and the breaking of limitations and crystallizations. Bacchus, like Aslan, is not tame, and that means the imagination can run wild, eventuating in theological insight as well as rich moments of comedy.

WORKS CITED

Berger, Peter. *Redeeming Laughter: The Comic Dimension of Human Experience*. New York: Walter de Gruyter, 1997.

Detienne, Marcel. *Dionysos at Large*. Trans. Arthur Goldhammer. Cambridge: Harvard University Press, 1989.

Euripedes, *The Bacchae*. Trans. C. K. Williams. New York: Farrar Straus Giroux, 1990.

Harrison, Jane. *Prolegomena to the Study of Greek Religion*. New York: Meridian Books, 1957.

Lewis, C.S. *The Chronicles of Narnia*. 7 vols. New York: HarperTrophy, 1994.

—. *Surprised by Joy*. San Diego: Harcourt Brace, 1984.

Otto, Walter F. *Dionysus: Myth and Cult*. Trans. Robert B. Palmer. Bloomington: Indiana University Press, 1965.

Schopenhauer, Arthur. *The World as Will and Idea*. Trans. R. B. Haldane and J. Kemp. London: Routledge & Kegan Paul, 1957.

Chapter Ten

A High and Lonely Destiny:
Sources for Jadis, the White Witch,
in *Milton's Paradise Lost* and Spenser's *The Faerie Queene*

Elizabeth Baird Hardey

In the *Chronicles of Narnia*, C.S. Lewis teaches his readers both about Aslan and his "other name," and about much else that was important to him spiritually, personally, and professionally, including the literature that he respected and enjoyed. Everything Lewis read and loved, no matter its literary weight, was likely to be woven into his fiction. It is unlikely that anyone, even Lewis himself, could readily identify every text that finds its way into the *Chronicles of Narnia*, but two of the most influential sources for the series are clearly Edmund Spenser's *The Faerie Queene* and John Milton's *Paradise Lost*. Lewis did not include material from these classic works of Western literature merely in order to indoctrinate young readers with blatant literary criticism nor even to ensure that these crucial works of Western literature and thought received adequate attention. Just as his books are Christian in nature because Lewis was himself a Christian, and because his books feature British protagonists because Lewis was himself British, the *Chronicles* echo Milton and Spenser naturally as a result of Lewis's lifelong affection for and appreciation of their work.

Evil in the Chronicles is given a thorough and well-developed treatment that echoes *The Faerie Queene* and *Paradise Lost*. The most successful of Lewis's villains, and the only one to appear in more than one installment of the series, is Jadis, the White Witch. Jadis is most certainly another incarnation of the same bad mother archetype who rears her sometimes ugly head in fairy and folk tales as wicked stepmother and sorceress. Jadis is a powerful archetypal figure: beautiful, vain, cruel, and powerful. Spenser and Milton, certainly also drawing upon archetypal sources, created villains who lend a number of characteristics to Jadis.

The Faerie Queene's Duessa, one of Spenser's masterpieces, is clearly an influence in the creation of Jadis. Like Duessa, the White Witch appears with all the trappings of royalty and an usurped name. As Lucy reports, "She calls herself the Queen of Narnia though she has no right to be queen at all" (*The Lion, the Witch, and the Wardrobe* 37-38). Duessa, too, wears a stolen name, Fidessa, "Borne the sole daughter of an Emperour" (I.ii.22.7) until she is tried and convicted in Book V. Her crown and richly caparisoned steed are props of royalty as deceptive as the Witch's: "Like a Persian mitre on her hed/ She wore, with crownes and ouches garnished,...Her wanton palfrey all was overspread/ With tinsel trappings, woven like a wave,/ Whose bridle rung with golden bels and bosses brave" (I.ii.13.4-5, 7-9). Interestingly, both villainesses have bells on the harnesses of their animals, reflecting the brashness of their assumed identities, and their deceptively cheerful appearances. The Witch, when she sets about the serious business of pursuing Peter, Susan, Lucy, and the Beavers, orders her dwarf slave to prepare her sledge using the harness without the bells (*The Lion, the Witch, and the Wardrobe* 94). Her true nature has been exposed, and the pretext of a pleasant sleigh ride is discarded in favor of deadly silence and stealth. Once her hand has been revealed, she is no longer concerned about making herself appear royal and harmless. Like Duessa, who makes her "speedy way" (I.v.19.9) to get aid from Night, Jadis is a "terribly practical" (*The Magician's Nephew* 72) person who uses disguise when she must, but who essentially uses whatever means she has at her disposal in order to achieve her aims of power and destruction.

Although Jadis is certainly physically attractive, she is not painted as quite the sexual creature that Duessa is. The fact that Jadis is not as alluring as Duessa is clear from the color schemes attached to each character. While the White Witch's reindeer have golden horns and scarlet harness, she is almost completely without color, especially the sensual reds and purples that dominate the descriptions of Duessa and her garb. Only the Witch's mouth is red, perhaps a reference to her consumption of the "forbidden" fruit from Aslan's Garden, or to her use of enchanted food. In addition, her red mouth marks one of her most powerful weapons: words which often twist and distort the truth in order to influence others. Though her physical strength is astonishing, she only resorts to flinging people across rooms, tearing crosspieces off lamp-posts, and knocking policemen in the head with clubs when she discovers that her ability to turn people to dust with "horrible words.... was not going to work" (*The Magician's Nephew* 80). Indeed, the doomsday weapon with which she wiped out her entire native world of Charn was the Deplorable Word. Her mouth, then, is clearly a powerful weapon, and appropriately an alarming color, for red is the color of danger. In her very first appearance in *The Lion the Witch, and the Wardrobe*, she represents both sensual desire, in the form of addictive sweets and a warm seat on a cold day, as well as a very real threat that Edmund only stops perceiving when his desire overcomes his good sense. Other than the one spot of shocking red, Jadis is completely devoid of color.

Duessa is distinguished by red, but in much larger quantities: "A goodly Lady clad in scarlot red, Purfled with gold and pearl of rich assay" (I.ii.13.12-3). The dissimilar color patterns in the two antagonists emphasize the natures of their seductive powers. While Jadis lures mainly with words, Duessa uses her whole deceptive person. Yet, they are both seducers who utilize magic to achieve their goals. Both tempt protagonists by offering them something physically desirable and sensually fulfilling. In Duessa's case, she offers "the shield, and I, and all"(I.v.11.10) to the Redcrosse knight. Edmund, as a child, is lured by the Turkish Delight and by the power the Witch promises to give him over the siblings he resents for what he perceives as their mistreatment of him. In *The Magician's Nephew*, Digory, struggling with the reality of his mother's terminal illness, has been sent on a mission to retrieve an apple that, once planted, will produce a tree to protect Narnia from the evil Jadis represents. He is tempted by the healing and normalcy offered by Jadis if he keeps the Apple of Protection rather than returning it to Aslan as ordered. His longing is not, in and of itself, wrong, but, when manipulated by those whose motivations are power and pride, even the most innocuous human tendencies can turn dangerous. Jadis and Duessa promise the protagonists what they think most desirable and attempt to convince them that they want it more than anything else. Although these promises are exactly what Redcrosse, Edmund, and Digory most want, they are as false as Duessa and Jadis themselves. Duessa's cry of encouragement is apparently a general one since she has made overtures to both Redcrosse and his opponent, the pagan knight Sans joy, evidently to ensure that whichever knight wins will take her. In addition, as her later defeat reveals, Duessa's beauty and physical charms are illusions covering her hideous true form. Edmund's Turkish Delight is merely bait to bring him and his siblings under the Witch's power. It is also candy without any nutritional value whatsoever. Even Digory's mother would not experience a true healing from Jadis's proffered apple. These villainesses' temptations are no more valid than their identities and titles.

Both Jadis and Duessa also possess a brand of magic that opposes and perverts nature, reflecting the sterility of their characters. Duessa, for all her sexual imagery and appearance as a lusty young woman, is not a fertile being.

Under her beautiful disguise, she is old, misformed, and not even human. Mr. Beaver emphasizes the fact that the Witch is "no Daughter of Eve" (*The Lion, the Witch, and the Wardrobe* 77) but descended from giants and the Jinn, though she pretends to be human. In Mr. Beaver's opinion, her heritage is further evidence of how dangerous she is. She herself tells Edmund that she has no children of her own, and thus no heir (*The Lion, the Witch, and the Wardrobe* 34). Of course, since she has no intentions of dying, she does not require an heir. She prefers the false immortality given by the forbidden apple she has consumed, rather than the natural immortality achieved by reproduction. To Lewis, sterility, particularly within sexuality, is the antithesis of all that is good or genuine. One of his most insightful analyses of sterile and therefore joyless sex lies in his examination of the artifice within the Bower of Bliss in the second book of *The Faerie Queene*: "There is not a kiss or an embrace in the whole island: only male prurience and female provocation" (*The Allegory of Love: A Study in Medieval Tradition* 332). He incorporates this sterile corruption of nature, or cold artifice, into Jadis. Her magic in *The Lion, the Witch and the Wardrobe* is most clearly manifested in her snow spell and her magic wand. The spell, like Duessa's transformation of Fraudubio and Fraelissa into trees, is a perversion of nature. Jadis creates a hundred-year winter without a Christmas, thus extending a small portion of the calendar and suppressing the other three seasons. She favors only the non-productive winter, removing the festal holiday of Christmas with its vibrant reds and greens of blood and growth and its celebration of holy birth, as well as its astrological importance as the winter solstice. Jadis despises change, so Christmas and its emphasis on transformation is most unwelcome She is terrified of any celebrations or expressions of life. In fact, her fury with the Christmas party is the essential moment when Edmund realizes what a bad bargain he has made in joining her, for she resents even the possibility of Father Christmas's arrival, as well as the lively rejoicing that she calls "gluttony... waste...self-indulgence" (*The Lion, the Witch, and the Wardrobe* 112). It is, importantly, the baby squirrel's refusal to deny that Father Christmas has arrived that drives the Witch over the edge so that she draws blood biting her own lip before unleashing the fury of her wand upon the festive group. For the sterile and cold Jadis, reminders of life, particularly from children, must be silenced. So too, Duessa contorts nature by her tree enchantment and her manipulation of life and death for the mortally stricken Sans joy. Certainly, counteracting the forces of mortality and turning people into other things is a perversion and corruption of nature. However, by transforming Fraudubio and Fraelissa specifically into trees, rather than into birds or animals, Duessa also makes them unable to marry and mate. Duessa's victims are reduced to a virtually unmoving state in which gender, and therefore mating, is irrelevant. Closely resembling this transformation is the power contained in Jadis's wand, the power to turn living beings into stone. By transforming people into stone, Jadis nullifies their lives, their very identities, and freezes them just as she has the landscape with her snow spell. Jadis's castle courtyard resembles a cemetery more than a yard. Both women use different techniques to achieve their ends, but they share the impetus to sterilize and freeze, to contort nature and defy the progress of time.

The heritage of the two characters is also similar. Duessa is "the daughter of Deceit and Shame" (I.v.26.10). Jadis's descent from Lilith is a connection to the Hebraic and Babylonian archetype of Adam's first wife "cast out of Eden for insubordination and doomed to roam the world [as] a malevolent spirit" (Price 3) The Lilith demon is also credited with murdering infants, pregnant women, and lost children. Both Duessa and Jadis, then, are descended from the embodiments of evil traits. These are traits that they themselves possess. Duessa is both deceitful and shameful, tricking everyone she meets and concealing her true, hideous form, while the White Witch overturns the true hierarchy of Narnia and attempts to kill children who are lost in the forest. Duessa claims to be the daughter of an Emperor, yet her true parents are both negative and powerful, placing her in Night's esteem. When Digory views the rulers of Charn in the Hall of Images, it is clear that Jadis is descended from a long line of rulers whose faces progress from good and happy to wicked and happy, and at last to wicked and unhappy. Like Jadis herself, they have remained proud and strong, but at the cost of their happiness and emotional well-being. Both Jadis and Duessa are members of distinguished but tainted royal families.

Their true names ring with this negative, lofty heritage as well: "Duessa" accurately echoes her dual nature, her literal two-faced aspect, and has a distinct hissing sound from the doubled "s," calling to mind a serpent; "Jadis," like many names of Lewis's creation, also has an important sound to it, reminding the reader of jade, with its connotations of being jaded, or cynical, and perhaps of the "false jade," or duplicitous woman, as the thwarted Prince Rabadash calls Susan in *The Horse and his Boy*. This connection is even clearer when the books are read in their original publication order since Jadis's name is only revealed in *The Magician's Nephew*. In addition, the French word "jadis" is usually translated "formerly," or even "once upon a time." This association echoes her aloneness, her chosen "high and lonely destiny" (*The Magician's Nephew* 62) as the last queen of her once-mighty world. By her own selfish and cruel choices, she is the last surviving inhabitant of Charn and of her ruling family. Their names remind the reader that these villainesses are tricksters, and that their heritage, while noble, is also shameful, sub-human, and completely ingrained within their characters. Mr. Beaver's strong opinions about beings that are not quite human would apply both to the supernaturally birthed Duessa and to her disguise, which masks her hideousness and her "foxes taile, with dung all fowly dight;/ and her feet most monstrous/ for one of them was like an Eagles claw/...The other like a Beares uneven paw" (I.viii.48.4-6,8). The inhuman nature of both villainesses makes them appropriate antagonists for Lewis's Sons and Daughters of Adam and Eve, and for Spenser's Una, whose royal parents are typified Adam and Eve figures, the queen and "mighty king of Eden" (I.xii.26.2). Inhuman witches, both descended from corrupt if notable families, contrast completely with fully human protagonists descended from "The Lord Adam and the Lady Eve" (*Prince Caspian* 212). Unlike the witches, the human protagonists understand and accept their heritage, both noble and tainted, rather than concealing it.

The false queen of Narnia is also powerfully reminiscent of Duessa's queen, Lucifera, and her House of Pride. To Edmund, Jadis describes her house as a boy's paradise with "whole rooms of Turkish Delight" (*The Lion, the Witch, and the Wardrobe* 34). The reality, however, is a cold, dimly lit castle with only the sinister wolf, Fenris Ulf (or Maugrim), and a pair of subservient dwarfs as courtiers. Edmund's promised feast is actually a condemned prisoner's portion--bread and water--foreshadowing his planned execution by Jadis. For both the White Witch and Lucifera, the castle or house is a place of deception:

> It was a goodly heape for to behould,
> And spake the praises of the workmans wit;
> But full great pity; that so faire a mould
> Did on so weak foundation ever sit. (I.iv.5.1-4)

The fact that the towers of Jadis's castle look like sorcerer's caps (88) is a clear indication that it is not to be trusted. Both palaces are beautiful on the surface, yet both offer only death, literally destroying victims and displaying their bodies as clutter. Lucifera's house "digests" the victims of pride, leaving them to languish in its dungeon as "wretched thralles" (I.v.51.1) or tossed on the "Donghill of dead carcases" (I.v.53.8), in such numbers that "Scarse could he[the Redcrosse knight] footing find in that fowle way (I. V. 53.1-2); Jadis's castle is full of statues, her previous victims, who serve as trophies and as warnings. The statues are eventually restored, but until the return of

Aslan, they are as cold and lifeless as corpses. Edmund even mistakes Fenris Ulf, one of the only living creatures in the castle, for a stone wolf. Despite his fears, Edmund, like Redcrosse, enters where he really does not belong. Neither character heeds the evidence that chances of escaping the castles are not good. The broad entrance to House of Pride is deceptive, since few who enter ever escape: "Great troupes of people traveiled thitherward/ Both day and night, of each degree and place,/ But few returned" (I. Iv.3.1-3). Mr. Beaver's description of the fate of the White Witch's guests is similar: "There's not many taken in there that ever comes out again" (73). Like the entrance to Lucifera's palace, the "great iron gates" of Jadis's castle stand "wide open" (*The Lion, the Witch, and the Wardrobe* 89) since neither woman wants to keep anyone out: it is escaping, not entering, these castles that presents problems. Like any clever predator, both Jadis and Lucifera know that a good trap starts with an open door. The allure of both Jadis and Lucifera masks their true natures and the very real threats they pose, but it is also indicative of their exceptional confidence and deadly pride. Neither sorceress feels that she can be defeated.

Pride is clearly one of the strongest of Jadis's characteristics. While she is already a well-rounded character in her first appearance in *The Lion the Witch and the Wardrobe*, in *The Magician's Nephew* her coming to Narnia is detailed, and her pride is even more apparent. When Digory and Polly awaken the Witch from suspended animation among her ancestors, she assumes that she has been sent for by some powerful magician. The reality, that she has been stumbled upon by two lost children who have been the guinea pigs in the careless experiment of a dabbling magical bungler, is so intolerable to her that she cannot fathom its possibly being true. Her pride creates an interpretation of events that is completely wrong, but more flattering than the truth. The destroyed condition of Charn is a result of Jadis's pride during her sister's attempt to gain the throne: "At any moment I was ready to make peace--yes, and to spare her life too, if only she would yield me the throne. But she would not. Her pride has destroyed the whole world"(*The Magician's Nephew* 60). Ironically, it is actually Jadis, and her pride, rather than her sister's, that wipe out every trace of life in Charn. Rather than surrendering to her sister, who technically won the last war, she uses the power of the "Deplorable Word," connecting her to the most sinister antagonist available from either *The Faerie Queene* or *Paradise Lost*.

Jadis, so unable to accept defeat that she chooses destruction for her whole world, is reminiscent of Milton's Satan. She certainly prefers reigning in hell to serving in heaven. Her throne, in a dead castle in a dead city of a dead world, is a meaningless one, but it is a throne. The notion of servitude is clearly as foreign to Jadis as it is to Satan, who declares, "To bow and sue for grace/ with suppliant knee, and deify his power who from the terror of this arm so late/ Doubted his empire/ that were low indeed" (I.111-14). When Polly, shocked at Jadis's use of the Deplorable Word, asks about the common people of her world who died, she replies, "I was the Queen. They were all *my* people. What else were they there for except to do my will" (61). Her pride is more than vanity, for, as Lewis attests in *Mere Christianty*, vanity is not nearly so dangerous as Pride: "As long as you are proud you cannot know God. A proud man is always looking down on things and people; and, of course, as long as you are looking down, you cannot see something that is above you" (24). Jadis looks down on everyone and everything. She, like Satan, refuses to acknowledge any power or authority other than herself, but also refuses to accept full responsibility for the events she sets in motion. Though she wants all the power, she wants none of the blame, and she consistently blames others for her own actions. Satan also does not acknowledge that it is his pride that has led to the downfall of his followers; instead he blames God. Even when he encourages the fallen angels to "Awake, arise, or be for ever fall'n" (I. 330), Satan is not concerned about their well-being; he is trying to keep his army intact for a possible future attack. Pride, more than any other sin, is responsible for the downfall of Satan and for the fall of humanity. Both characters, exhibiting diabolical pride, want to be served rather than to serve anyone, and they are not at all concerned with anyone else's suffering in their ascents to power. Jadis further resembles Satan in her perception of herself as a tragic figure with "a high and lonely destiny" (*The Magician's Nephew* 62). This clearly mirrors Satan's first appearance in the first book of *Paradise Lost*, which emphasizes his "mighty stature" (I.221) and his form of an "Archangel ruined" (I.592). Lewis's concern over the heroic interpretation of Satan is one of the primary tenets of *A Preface to Paradise Lost*. It is not surprising that Satan has a role in the creation of Lewis's most fully realized and intriguing villain, as he always contended that Satan was both villainous and unheroic.

Lewis also indicated that Satan cannot be truly heroic because he makes such a fool of himself, much in the same way a spoiled child is foolish in its tantrums. Both Jadis and Satan, although they may be read in some contexts as admirable, become unheroic. Jadis, particularly in *The Magician's Nephew*, is clearly a majestic and impressive creature, a "dem fine woman" (186) as Uncle Andrew calls her, whose beauty and power take one's breath away; but when she slays Aslan–her moment of triumph–she exhibits no heroism or even superior strength. Her adversary is a willing sacrifice whom she has shaved, muzzled, and tied down. She is not a hero, or even an antihero; she is a bully and a coward. Despite heroic interpretations by Romantic Era authors, Satan also picks on the helpless. He does not confront Adam and Eve together, nor does he approach Adam first. He does not use weapons to kill the first humans or force them to do his will. Instead, he sets out to divide and conquer, starting with Eve, whom he perceives as less able to resist him: "behold alone/ The Woman, opportune to all attempts,/ Her husband, for I view far round, not nigh,/ Whose higher intellectual more I shun,/ And strength" (IX. 480-3). Satan's comments not only indicate that he has a low opinion of Eve and thinks she is less intelligent than her husband, but also reveal that he is a coward, afraid to face Adam whom he perceives as the more critically perceptive and physically powerful of the two. Clearly Satan does not appear to be the same brilliant general who made war in heaven; rather, he is afraid of confronting anyone whom he believes may be a match for him, even a newly made human who lacks experience with his kind. Lewis's deep concern with the reading of Satan as a hero is exhibited in his points about the unheroic descent Satan voluntarily undertakes "from hero to general, from general to politician, from politician to secret service agent, and thence to a thing that peers in at bedroom or bathroom windows, and thence to a toad, and finally to a snake--such is the progress of Satan" (*A Preface to Paradise Lost* 95). Jadis goes through a similar descent. When the books are read in chronological order, rather than publication order, Jadis goes from queen to mass murderess, to criminal in London, to lurking evil in Narnia, to witch, and finally to a tormentor of animals, little children, and helpless enemies, no more noble or heroic than Hansel and Gretel's witch with her candy house and oven.

One of Jadis's most obviously Satanic moments is in *The Magician's Nephew* when Digory encounters her in the mountaintop garden he has entered to fetch the Apple of Protection. The garden is walled, and its only gates bear the inscription: "Come in by the gold gates or not at all,/ Take of my fruit for others or forbear./ For those who steal or those who climb my wall/ Shall find their heart's desire and find despair" (157). After Digory enters properly, he finds Jadis, who has apparently come over the wall and is just finishing an apple that makes "a horrid stain" on her mouth (159). Jadis's implied vaulting of the wall is almost identical to Satan's entry to Eden in Book IV of *Paradise Lost*: "Due entrance he disdained, and in contempt,/ At one slight bound high overleaped all bound/ Of hill or highest wall, and sheer within/ Lights on his feet" (ll 180-183). This method of entry also marks both of them as criminals, for, as Jesus indicates in John 10:1, one who eschews the gate and "climbs in by some other way is a thief" (NIV). Both characters move from the violation of a sacred garden to the temptation of a protagonist who belongs there. While Lewis's feminizing of the tempter role can be seen as a blending of Eve's sin and the serpent's guile, it is intriguing that Jadis, a woman, is so clearly Satanic. Such a role, while equating a female villain with the ultimate personification of evil, also casts her in a role of power.

The Biblical temptation scene is, of course, the basis for both Milton's and Lewis's temptation tableaus. However, it is Milton's garden and tree and Satan's temptation that appear in *The Magician's Nephew*. Even the logical fallicies employed by Satan are mirrored by Jadis. Satan flatters Eve as "Goddess humane" (IX.732) and tries to twist the purpose of the heavenly injunction against eating from the tree to a rule against eating from any tree. One of his most persuasive tropes is that of testimony, claiming to have eaten the fruit himself and experienced intelligent thought and speech as a result. Though it is easy to condemn Eve for falling for the serpent's wiles, his testimony is impressive, since he really is speaking to her. In addition, Eve has never experienced dishonesty and thus has no reason to think the serpent a liar. Jadis appeals to Digory's love for his mother, making the implication that not taking the apple to his mother will make Digory a bad son. She also uses her own experience with the apple to tell Digory of its value: "I have tasted it; and I feel such changes in myself that I know I shall never grow old or die" (161). Unlike Eve, Digory is a child of a fallen world who has experience with lying and does not merely take the Witch's word for truth. He must see Jadis actually eating the apple. While Satan lies about having eaten the fruit, Jadis lies about its results. Although the fruit makes her strong and virtually immortal, it also brings her despair. The apple has such a negative effect on her that the Tree of Protection Digory plants from one of these apples creates in her a horror so great that she cannot enter Narnia for generations. Aslan also confirms that the Witch's claims of the apple's effects are erroneous for one who stole the fruit, telling Digory that had he stolen an apple for his mother "it would have healed her; but not to your joy or hers. The day would have come when both you and she would have looked back and said it would have been better to die in that illness" (*The Magician's Nephew* 175). Since the apples, as Aslan says, always work according to their nature, the Witch's lie is partially mixed with truth, making it, like Satan's deception and the twisting of God's word, all the more insidious. The most significant difference in the two episodes is the result. Digory, unlike Eve, is already a fallen human being, a "son of Adam," and by resisting temptation simply resists one sin, while Eve's failure brings about the fall of herself and her descendants.

Though the intended victims respond differently, and thus experience different fates, the two temptation sequences both set in motion drastic changes for individuals and entire worlds. Satan's successful seduction of Eve transforms the newly created Earth from a reflection of Heaven into a flawed, mortal planet. Jadis, while unable to convince Digory to eat an apple, profoundly affects Narnia by her own consumption of the forbidden fruit since the long but miserable life it gives her enables her to outlive the Tree of Protection and to eventually cast her powerful winter spell, marking Narnia forever with her theft of the throne and hundred-year rule of cruelty and cold.

In addition to the role of tempter, Jadis, like Satan, is also an usurper. Lewis valued hierarchy, particularly as expressed in Milton's epic, and usurping is a disturbance of a moral hierarchy as well as an act of pride and aggression. Like Jadis, Satan also wants to have power over his peers, but he refuses subordination to one who is his natural superior: As Lewis observes in *A Preface to Paradise Lost*, "He wants hierarchy and does not want hierarchy"(96) Satan's fallen state is exposed in his assertion that he is not a created being, and therefore not under God's command to worship the Son. Jadis, too, pursues the ultimate goal of pride by usurping power. She refuses to acknowledge Aslan as king, though all true kings of Narnia recognize that the Lion is the High King. In *The Lion, the Witch, and the Wardrobe*, she is clearly not the rightful ruler because she cannot inhabit the true capital of Cair Paravel. Her fortress, which she calls a house, rather than a castle, is clearly inferior to the splendor and beauty of Cair Paravel, but since she is not at all human, and therefore not the rightful Queen, she must rule from a secondary castle. Like Satan, who has lost the glories of heaven and must create an inferior kingdom, but one all his own, Jadis lives in a castle that is a strong fortress, but lacks warmth, comfort, or any amenities one would expect to be accorded a queen. Usurpers, such as Jadis and Satan, inevitably convince themselves that their seats of power, though inferior to the true capitals of rightful monarchs, are somehow superior, just as they are convinced of their own right to power that is not truly theirs.

Like all usurpers, Jadis is also a bully. Once she realizes that Digory's Uncle Andrew is not an all-powerful magician, she makes him her tool and looks for a way to conquer London, both verbally and physically assaulting anyone who gets in her way. As usurpers, both Jadis and Satan hate humanity, which is favored over each of them. Satan views God's newly created beings as replacements for himself and his fallen angel colleagues, and Jadis can never be a true queen of Narnia because "there isn't a real drop of human blood" in her body (*The Lion, the Witch, and the Wardrobe* 77). Because of this, she cannot fulfill the order set in place at the creation of Narnia: the rule of a human being. She also knows that her life and her reign will end with rightful human rulers on the four thrones at Cair Paravel, and she seeks to destroy all "Sons and Daughters of Adam and Eve" who enter Narnia in order to ensure a continuation of her already unnaturally long life. Satan feels that humanity has been created to take over his position and that humans are both dear to God and vulnerable to corruption. Satan does not merely seek to destroy humans but to pervert them into objects of grief for God rather than blessings: "on him who next/ provokes my envy, this new favorite/ Of Heav'n, this man of clay, son of despite,/ Whom us the more to spite his Maker raised/ from dust: spite then with spite is best repaid"(IX.174-8). Jadis also attempts this ploy with Edmund, using him as a pawn to bring her his brother and sisters. Edmund, despite being warned by Lucy that Jadis is not the true queen, is fooled by her trappings and her food, lured to treason by her promises to make him first a prince, and then a king under her; however, his true destiny actually is to become king, but a king under Aslan, the true High King over all High Kings, not under an usurper. Jadis's methods are not dissimilar from Satan's temptation of Eve as a design to corrupt Adam and thus all of humanity. Instead of immediately killing humans, the rightful heirs of both Eden and Narnia, both Satan and Jadis prefer to corrupt and contaminate the people they envy and the kingdoms they covet.

Despite their attempts to corrupt or destroy the forces of good, Jadis and Satan are both thwarted and even, against their intended plans, bring about good. The White Witch, having killed Aslan, believes that she is victorious. As she strikes the fatal blow, she sneers, "Understand that you have given me Narnia forever…In that knowledge, despair and die"(*The Lion, the Witch, and the Wardrobe* 152). However, by killing Aslan, she has invoked the "Deeper Magic from Before Time," an injunction dictating that a willing victim, giving himself up for another's fault, will be resurrected. While this echoes Christ's sacrifice, and thus *Paradise Regained* rather than *Paradise Lost*, the Witch's apparent triumph resembles Satan's determination to be busy about doing evil and his assumption that he can actually destroy God's plan. Both antagonists, however, underestimate the power of divine good to produce positive results from the most malicious of schemes. Like Satan's thwarted plans that bring about the greater good of Christ's incarnation, sacrifice, and resurrection, Jadis's evil intentions actually bring about the good she fears. Edmund, whom she assumes will be killed without Aslan's protection, actually destroys her magic wand in combat after being reunited with his siblings. The resurrected Aslan, whom Jadis believes to be dead and no threat, releases her statue prisoners and becomes the instrument of her destruction. As Lewis wrote in one of his many letters to Catholic priest Don Giovanni Calabria, "all, either willingly or unwillingly, do the will of God: Judas and Satan as tools, or instruments, John and Peter as sons" (Lewis and Calabria 32).

Jadis, one of the most subtle and most carefully drawn villainesses in all literature, echoes Spenser's and Milton's villains, both male and female. While Lewis, Milton, and Spenser all incorporate antagonists throughout their texts, the villains who appear first remain the most impressive and the most challenging. Milton's Satan, though accompanied by demons and accomplices, remains from his first appearance as a fallen, embittered ex-angel, the dominant force of evil–and of energy–throughout the poem. Although all of Spenser's knights face particular foes, Redcrosse's antagonists, particularly Duessa, seem far more complex than some of the later creations. Likewise, Lewis's recurring Jadis is more sophisticated and well-rounded than characters like Shift the Ape and Rishdah Tarkaan. This falling off of adversarial power does not negate the very real and threatening presence of the antagonists. Rather, it serves as a reminder that evil can lurk in flashy and complex figures like Satan, Duessa, and Jadis, or in the brute force of a Blatant Beast, or the tricks of an Ape. All are equally likely to bring good to its knees; the Christian, the knight, and the child must be wary.

WORKS CITED

Christopher, Joe. *C. S. Lewis*. Boston: Twayne Publishers, 1987.

Ford, Paul F. *Companion to Narnia*. New York: MacMillian Publishing Company, 1986

Kort, Wesley A. *C.S. Lewis Then and Now*. Oxford: Oxford UP, 2001.

Lewis, C.S. *The Allegory of Love: A Study in Medieval Tradition*. Oxford: Oxford University Press, 1958.

—. "Edmund Spenser." *Fifteen Poets*. London: Oxford University Press, 1951.

—. *An Experiment in Criticism*. Cambridge: Cambridge University Press, 1965.

—. *English Literature in the Sixteenth Century Excluding Drama*. New York: Oxford University Press, 1954.

—. *The Horse and His Boy*. New York: Scholastic Inc., 1988.

—. *The Last Battle*. New York: Scholastic Inc., 1988.

—. *The Lion, the Witch and the Wardrobe*. New York: Scholastic Inc., 1988.

—. *The Magician's Nephew*. New York: Scholastic Inc., 1988.

—. *Mere Christianity*. New York, HarperSanFrancisco, 1952, 2001.

—. *A Preface to Paradise Lost*. London: Oxford University Press, 1979.

—. *Prince Caspian*. New York: Scholastic, Inc., 1988.

—. *The Silver Chair*. New York: Scholastic, Inc., 1988.

—. *Spenser's Images of Life*. Ed. Alastair Fowler. Cambridge: Cambridge University Press, 1967.

—. *Studies in Medieval and Renaissance Literature*. Collected by Walter Hooper. Cambridge: Cambridge University Press, 1966.

—. *Surprised By Joy*. New York: Harcourt, Brace, and Company, 1955.

—. *The Voyage of the 'Dawn Treader'*. New York: Scholastic Inc., 1988.

— and Don Giovanni Calabria. *The Latin Letters of C.S. Lewis*. Trans., ed. Martin Moynihan. South Bend, Indiana: St. Augustine Press, 1998.

Manlove, Colin. *Christian Fantasy: From 1200 to the Present*. Notre Dame: University of Notre Dame Press, 992.

Milton, John. *Paradise Lost.* Ed. Scott Elledge. New York: W.W. Norton and Company, 1993.

Price, Merdith. "'All Shall Love Me and Despair.' The Figure of Lilith in Tolkien, Lewis, Williams, and Sayers." *Mythlore: A Journal of J.R.R. Tolkien, C.S. Lewis, Charles Williams and the Genres of Myth and Fantasy.* 31 (Spring 1982): 3-7

Spenser, Edmund. *Edmund Spenser's Poetry.* Ed Hugh Maclean. New York: W.W. Norton and Company, 1982.

—*The Faerie Qveene.* Ed. A. C. Hamilton. Text ed. Hiroshi Yamashita and Toshiyuki Suzuki .London: Pearson Education, 2001.

Chapter Eleven

From Vampire to Venus:
C.S. Lewis' Christian Affirmation of the Body

David Rosenberg

A month before the centenary of C.S. Lewis' birth on November 29, 1998, a scathing article on the writer appeared in the British newspaper *The Guardian*. The article, entitled "The Dark Side of Narnia," was penned by children's writer and author of the *His Dark Materials* trilogy Philip Pullman, who claimed that the Narnia cycle "is one of the most ugly and poisonous things I've ever read." In particular, Pullman's allegations centered on what he calls "one of the most vile moments in the whole of children's literature," the conclusion of the final book in the cycle, *The Last Battle*. Within this scene, the Christ-surrogate Aslan the Lion announces to the child protagonists in Narnia that within the "Shadowlands" (our Earth), they have died in a railway accident:

> Lucy said, "We're so afraid of being sent away, Aslan. And you have sent us back into our own world so often."
>
> "No fear of that," said Aslan. "Have you not guessed?"
>
> Their hearts leaped and a wild hope rose within them.
>
> "There *was* a real railway accident," said Aslan softly. "Your father and mother and all of you are – as you used to call it in the Shadowlands – dead. The term is over: the holidays have begun. The dream is ended: this is the morning. (228)

Following the apocalyptic battle with the Calormenes and their god Tash, the children have joined Aslan/Christ in an afterlife imagined as a restored Narnia. Pullman claims that this "slaughter of characters" equates to "propaganda in the service of a *life-hating* ideology" (my emphasis), and that, within the Narnia Chronicles in general, the main lesson learned by the reader is that "death is better than life" ("The Dark Side of Narnia"). In his essay "The Kingdom of Heaven," also delivered as a speech in early 2000,

Pullman further explains that the notion of the Shadowland Earth as a dim copy of Aslan's Narnia is a "state of mind which, unless we're careful, can lead to a thoroughgoing hatred of the physical world." The fact that Lewis, through the mouth of his character "the wise old professor," ascribes a more tangible reality to the world of the afterlife leads, in Pullman's view, directly to a depreciation of the concrete world around us.

Such a denigration of the physical world implicates first and foremost the body and sexuality. Pullman also protests Lewis' portrayal of Susan Pevensie in the pages of *The Last Battle*. Within the narrative, Susan's brother Peter asserts that "'my sister Susan is no longer a friend of Narnia'" and when asked why, her sister Jill states, "'She's interested in nothing nowadays except nylons and lipstick and invitations. She was always a jolly sight too keen on being grown-up.'" (169). Pullman concludes from this passage that Lewis "didn't like women in general, or sexuality at all, at least at the stage in his life when he wrote the Narnia books" ("The Dark Side of Narnia"). The world of sensuality and the body, particularly the female body, seems for Pullman to be excluded from the "Kingdom of Heaven" as it is portrayed in the Narnia books. By way of contrast with this "Kingdom," Pullman's "Republic of Heaven," a term adopted from *His Dark Materials*, disposes of the idea of a divine monarch, leonine or otherwise: "...(The republic of Heaven) enables us to see this real world, *our* world, as a place of infinite delight, so intensely beautiful and intoxicating that if we saw it clearly then we would want nothing more, ever. We would know that this earth is our true home, and nowhere else is" ("The Republic of Heaven").

In the final book of the *His Dark Materials* trilogy, *The Amber Spyglass*, Pullman writes what could be described as a (pre-) teenage sex scene within a "Botanical Garden" reminiscent of the pre-lapsarian Eden:

> And she lifted the fruit gently to his mouth. She could see from his eyes that he knew at once what she meant, and that he was too joyful to speak. Her fingers were still at his lips, and he felt them tremble, and he put his own hand up to hold hers there, and then neither of them could look; they were confused; they were brimming with happiness.
>
> Like two moths clumsily bumping together, with no more weight than that, their lips touched. Then before they knew how it happened, they were clinging together, blindly pressing their faces toward each other...
>
> The word *love* set his nerves ablaze. All his body thrilled with it, and he answered her in the same words, kissing her hot face over and

over again, drinking in with adoration the scent of her body and her warm, honey-fragrant hair and her sweet, moist mouth that tasted of the little red fruit. Around them there was nothing but silence, as if all the world were holding its Breath. (416-17)

The physical union between the protagonists Lyra and Will, which Pullman has claimed amounts to nothing more than the kiss described in the above lines (Meacham, "The Shed Where God Died"), provides a kind of alternate myth of the Fall, in which the union of the two teenagers signifies salvation for a world afflicted by the depletion of cosmic life-forming "Dust." The consummation of the love Lyra and Will feel for one another ushers in a "Republic of Heaven" no longer located in Lord Asriel's parallel world above the earth; instead, this future society is a direct transfiguration of the world of Lyra and Will's birth.

Pullman's final claim in "The Dark Side of Narnia" charges Lewis with the "colossal impertinence, to put it mildly, of hijacking the emotions that are evoked by the story of the Crucifixion and Resurrection in order to boost the reader's concern about Aslan in *The Lion, the Witch, and the Wardrobe*." Pullman objects to the parallel Lewis draws between Aslan's death at the hands of the White Witch and Christ's crucifixion, and sees this as a kind of plagiarism of the Biblical narrative.

This last allegation reveals the agenda behind Pullman's polemic against Lewis. The "life-hating ideology" Pullman describes is nothing more nor less than Lewis' Christian faith. The problem he has with Lewis' (admittedly heavy-handed) Christian allegory reveals Pullman's problem with the Christian faith itself. In a 2001 interview with Alona Wartofsky of *The Washington Post*, Pullman reportedly states, "I'm trying to undermine the basis of Christian belief itself...Mr. Lewis would think I was doing the Devil's work." To Helena de Bertodano of the British newspaper *The Daily Telegraph* he states, "...if there is a God and he is as the Christians describe him, then he deserves to be put down and rebelled against."

Pullman's *His Dark Materials* trilogy has been described by Washington Post staff critic Michael Dirda as an "anti-Narnia" (see Grenier, "Philip Pullman's Dark Materials"). Pullman clearly models his primary antagonists, the Magisterium, after the Catholic Church and has the witch Ruta Skadi proclaim "for all of the Church's history...it's tried to suppress and control every natural impulse, And when it can't control them, it cuts them out... every church is the same: control, destroy, obliterate every good feeling" (*The Subtle Knife*, 50).

In an interview with Archbishop of Canterbury Rowan Williams, Pullman has announced that *His Dark Materials* attempts to get away from "the notions of sin that are bound up with our physicality supposedly," and goes on to say that "the Fall is something that happens to all of us when we move from childhood through adolescence to adulthood...I wanted to find a way of presenting it as something natural and good, and to be welcomed, and, you know – celebrated, rather than deplored." In Pullman's view, the denigration of sexual maturity and the "real world" go hand-in-hand as part of an insidious mechanism of religious institutions, which he describes elsewhere as "a kind of subset of the totalitarian mind against which the thrust of (*His Dark Materials*) is moving" (Bertodano, "Faith and Fantasy").

Pullman's contention that religion, specifically Christianity, condemns human sexuality and "natural impulse" so as to promote a worldview in which death is privileged over life, is certainly not new. In German letters, such a critique stretches at least as far back as the eighteenth century and the so-called "Classical" period of German literature, in particular with the writings of those famous partners in aesthetics Friedrich Schiller and Johann Wolfgang von Goethe. Representative poems from these authors register an aversion to Christianity and a turn back to Classical Greece as the model for an aesthetics of life-affirming beauty, inspired in large part by the writings of Johann Joachim Winckelmann in his 1755 *Thoughts on the Imitation of Greek Artwork in Painting and Sculpture*. Both Goethe and Schiller claim in these poems a clear preference for the pre-Christian Classical aesthetic and argued for a revival of this aesthetic in their era as a possible palliative for a society fully indoctrinated in what they saw as the Christian negation of life.

In Schiller's "Die Götter Griechenlands" ("The Gods of Greece"), the narrator mourns the loss of the Classical aesthetic in the modern and announces that Christianity has "removed divinity from nature," leaving behind only a "shadow"; European culture is now transformed from a society practicing the "fullness of life" to one governed by the "soulless word" (*Sämtliche Werke* 1, 56). In Schiller's poem, the primacy of the spirit and the Christian belief in a world beyond has drained the sensual world of life and subjected it to the coldness of reason (*logos*).

Goethe's "Die Braut von Korinth" ("The Bride of Corinth") recounts in ballad form the tragic consequences of the transition from paganism to Christianity on the love affair between two childhood friends in ancient Corinth. The "bride," who is sent to a convent by her newly-converted mother, dies and returns as a blood-drinking vampire. Goethe insinuates that the new religion has a poisonous effect on her youthful sexuality that condemns her to an existence of living death; the narrator describes the mother's dedication of her daughter to the new faith as a sacrifice of "youth and nature" to "heaven" (*Werke: Auswahl in zehn Teilen* 1, 111). At the conclusion of the poem, the bride drains the blood of her lover and both are cremated at the altar of the pagan gods.

German-Jewish writer Heinrich Heine, responding in large part to the anti-Semitism of German Christians around him, inherited the preference for Classical paganism over Christianity exhibited by his literary predecessors Goethe and Schiller. With Heine one can first see evidence of a psychological interpretation of the history of religion: what he calls the "Christian idea" first instigates a split in man's self-perception. To Heine, pagans experienced a harmony of mind and body unknown to what he calls "us moderns," who "still feel cramps and weaknesses in our members" (*Historisch-kritische Gesamtausgabe der Werke* 8, 16-17) from the illness that divided body from spirit/mind (the German word *Geist* means both "mind" and "spirit"). Heine thus views the world following the advent of Christianity as sick, cut off from its body and subject to the demands of an immaterial spirit that viewed that body as the representative of death. He terms the fascination with the Christian Middle Ages in the works of his immediate forerunners the German Romantics as an an "evil specter, which steps into our midst in the full light of day to suck the red life from our breast" (240); the poem resonates with Goethe's vampire maiden in "The Bride of Corinth."

The line of continuity in the German critique of Christianity's relationship to life and the body stretches from the writings of Schiller and Goethe through Heine to the philosophy of Friedrich Nietzsche, who has offered the most comprehensive and influential critique of Christianity to date. Nietzsche's writings discuss the "revaluation" that occurs with the triumph of Christianity in history, in which "feeling good because one is strong" no longer is an end in itself as in the pagan world, but instead links up with a self-destructive guilt that causes the pre-Christian masters of society to give their power to the weak and feeble. In "The Antichrist," Nietzsche writes:

> Christianity was the *vampire* [italics mine] of the *imperium Romanum:* overnight it undid the tremendous deed of the Romans – who had won the ground for a great culture *that would have time...* This was [Paul's] moment at Damascus: he comprehended that he *needed* the belief in immortality to deprive 'the world' of value, that the concept of 'hell' would become master even over Rome – that with the 'beyond' one *kills life.* (*The Portable Nietzsche* 648-50)

In Nietzsche's thought, Christianity fully transforms into the societal vampire of world history, joining up with Pullman's more contemporary remarks concerning the "life-hating ideology" promoted by the Christian Church.

The discerning reader will by now have perhaps faulted me for moving a discussion of Pullman into a specifically German context; after all, Pullman comes out of a specifically British tradition, and even cites Milton and Blake as the formative influences on his worldview. However, it is my contention that Nietzsche, as the most incisive modern critic of the Christian religion, serves as the immediate context for Pullman's polemic against Lewis and Christianity. Pullman's remarks concerning the "life-hating ideology" of the Narnia cycle, and the words that he puts in the mouth of witch Ruta Skadi, should even be read as contemporary re-statements of Nietzsche's thought.

To further support this view, in *The Amber Compass* protagonists Will and Lyra kill the God-figure called "the Authority," an act that helps to bring about the realization of the "Republic of Heaven." The scene evokes Nietzsche's most famous formulation, "Whither is God?...I shall tell you. *We have killed him*---you and I...God is dead" (95). Pullman opens his "Republic of Heaven," by stating, "...the children's books I love are saying something important about the most important subject I know, which is the death of God and its consequences...the old assumptions have all withered away... the idea of God with which I was brought up is now perfectly incredible." Pullman's *His Dark Materials* could thus be considered a kind of Nietzschean children's series that actively attempts to spread the conviction (for Pullman, the enlightened realization) in the minds of its readers that the Christian god is no longer valid for our day and age.

To recap, the central claim of Pullman's Nietzschean critique states that the Christian belief in the afterlife gives preference to a world of the "beyond" over the world in which we are embodied here and now. This "vampiric" world drains life and vitality from the world of embodiment and orients the Christian believer to a life lived only in anticipation of death. The critiques of Pullman and Nietzsche specifically target the Pauline division between "flesh and spirit" as found in Romans 8: 5-6 and 12-13, constituting a critical reading of the Biblical text that I here include in full:

> For those who live according to the flesh set their minds on the things of the flesh, but those who live according to the Spirit set their minds on the things of the Spirit. To set the mind on the flesh is death, but to set the mind on the Spirit is life and peace...So then, brothers, we are debtors, not to the flesh, to live according to the

flesh. For if you live according to the flesh you will die, but if by the Spirit you put to death the deeds of the body, you will live.

To Pullman and Nietzsche, the world of the "flesh," or the world of embodiment, is to them the only verifiable reality. Thus, the world of the "Spirit" is mere illusion, either instilled by psychology, culture, or a combination of the two. With these assumptions firmly in place, Pullman and Nietzsche read Paul literally: since they do not accept the possibility of a life of the "Spirit" beyond death, Paul's preference for the Spirit seems to them simply a preference for, and orientation towards, death.

In what follows, I examine Lewis' specifically Christian understanding of the relationship between the worlds of "flesh and Spirit" as a possible rebuttal to Pullman's renewal of the Nietzschean critique of Christianity within the controversial arena of contemporary children's literature. As might be already apparent, there is no arguing with the viewpoint espoused by Pullman and the thinkers that precede and shadow his critique; no academic means of neatly proving their criticisms unfounded or wrong. As Lewis states at the conclusion of *The Problem of Pain*, "We are very shy nowadays of even mentioning heaven. We are afraid of the jeer about 'pie in the sky,' and of being told that we are trying to escape from the duty of making a happy world here and now into dreams of a happy world elsewhere. But either there is 'pie in the sky' or there is not. If there is not, then Christianity is false, for this doctrine is woven into its whole fabric" (*The Complete C.S. Lewis Signature Classics*, 638-9).

In the end, what a reading of Lewis' views on sexuality accomplish is a witness to a truth that must be taken on faith, as the "assurance of things hoped for, the conviction of things not seen" (Hebrews 11:1). Christian scholarship must first and foremost acknowledge the central role of a faith in its epistemology opposed to an order of knowledge that "proves" things empirically. On the other hand, the thought that "God is dead" also involves a certain kind of faith, this time in the infallibility of the order of human knowledge and empirical certainty. When the assertion is made that what we can perceive and touch is more true or real than that which we can only intuit, the assertion itself claims an immunity from the kinds of "first assumptions" it claims faith alone must make.

What if one starts, however, with the "first assumption" that the world of the Spirit is more tangible than that of the flesh, and that the body without this Spirit can indeed be only understood as a kind of vampire or existence of living death? To mention an event that Pullman accords near-mythic status, Lewis' conversion starts from such an assumption, that "one famous night after a long conversation with his friends Hugo Dyson and J.R.R. Tolkien, (Lewis came) to the conclusion that the story of the Gospels was a myth like those he already cherished, 'but one with this tremendous difference: that it really happened'" ("The Dark Side of Narnia").

We can find the complete account of Lewis' conversion in his autobiography *Surprised by Joy*. He was once a man who, having been brought up as a nominal Christian, ceased to believe, even hated, the notion of a divine "Interferer" (172). However, an emotion he calls "Joy" remained to continually provoke an indefinable longing within him for something beyond what could be concretely experienced. Lewis initially christens this longing by the German name *Sehnsucht*, a favored trope of the German Romantics.

In *Surprised by Joy*, it is through writing (the children's book *Squirrel Nutkin* and the poetry of Longfellow), and myth (Norse/Germanic myth, also the pantheon of the Greeks), but also through contemplation of nature and music (Wagner) that the feeling of Joy first comes to Lewis. Lewis describes Joy as a desire that nevertheless "is the fullest possession we can know on earth...the very nature of Joy makes nonsense of our common distinction between having and wanting. There, to have is to want and to want is to have" (166). Paired with the longing that always points to something that cannot be fully attained on earth, is a sense that the longing itself is our only true and permanent possession. Unlike the understanding of that line of German criticism I have just sketched out, the longing for and glimpse of Heaven afforded by Joy does not depreciate the material world, but instead becomes the defining quality of materiality. For Goethe and Schiller, Freud and Nietzsche, the history of man has been the history of a movement from harmony to disharmony for which Christianity has been largely to blame. Man has thereby moved from a habitation within embodied existence to a life lived mostly within the mind, a move that accomplishes a dissociation of man from his body. For these thinkers, it is a desire to get back to the origin, to inhabit once again the body from which we have been separated, that causes the specific anguish of human existence.

For Lewis, the separation between body and mind is only possible from a viewpoint that attempts to salvage an idea of the body devoid of the Spirit that gives it life. As he puts it in *The Four Loves*, man is halfway between "angel and tomcat," and the longing that is Joy or *Sehnsucht* expresses this truth. The body's awareness that it contains that aspect of the Spirit known as Joy becomes not a source of unending anguish, but rather the sole means by which one can envision and even experience in the "here and now" the premonition of the future redemption of the embodied world.

The move from paganism to Christianity is therefore for Lewis not a "regression." To Lewis, a supposed harmony between body and spirit would have always been illusory, the interpenetration of matter and spirit best expressed not in some fantasy of a prior harmony, but rather in the paradoxical want and possession of Joy. The proper object of Joy is not the "celebration or affirmation" of the body or material world that Pullman desires; it is that figure, to borrow the language of Karl Barth, that is wholly Other and can never be fully comprehended by the order of human knowledge and experience.

How does sexuality fit into this discussion of Joy as a manifestation of the divided nature of man between flesh and spirit? Does Christianity, and in particular, Lewis' understanding of Christianity, denigrate, even proclaim a hatred for every "natural impulse" or "good feeling," as Pullman asserts?

Lewis makes what might seem a surprising confession to some at this point – that he "came to know by experience" that the longing he describes as Joy is "not a disguise for sexual desire" (169). Those who might imagine a prudish Lewis or a Lewis that did not like "sexuality at all" must stop short at the proclamation that "I learned this mistake to be a mistake by the simple, if discreditable, process of repeatedly making it" (Ibid). Sexual desire and its satisfaction result in a physical pleasure that does not at all serve to quell the longing evoked by what Lewis calls Joy: "You might as well offer a mutton chop to a man who is dying of thirst as offer sexual pleasure to the desire I am speaking of...Joy is not a substitute for sex; sex is very often a substitute for Joy" (170).

For Lewis, the sensual and the erotic are re-defined as subordinate to the lover's attachment to the beloved. In his *The Four Loves*, sexual appetite and its satisfaction, the "animal act" of sexuality, is differentiated from "Eros" and named "Venus":

> To the evolutionist Eros (the human variation) will be something that grows out of Venus, a late complication and development of the immemorial biological impulse. We must not assume, however, that this is necessarily what happens within the consciousness of the individual. There may be those who have first felt mere sexual appetite for a woman and then gone on at a later stage to "fall in love with her." But I doubt if this is at all common. Very often what comes first is simply a delighted pre-occupation with the Beloved... Sexual desire, without Eros, wants it, the thing in itself;
>
> Eros wants the Beloved.

> The *thing* is a sensory pleasure; that is, an event occurring within one's own body.
>
> We use a most unfortunate idiom when we say, of a lustful man prowling the streets, that he "wants a woman." Strictly speaking, a woman is just what he does not want. He wants a pleasure for which a woman happens to be the necessary piece of apparatus. How much he cares about the woman as such may be gauged by his attitude to her five minutes after fruition (one does not keep the carton after one has smoked the cigarettes). Now Eros makes a man really want, not a woman, but one particular woman. In some mysterious but quite indisputable fashion the lover desires the Beloved herself, not the pleasure she can give. No lover in the world ever sought the embraces of the woman he loved as the result of a calculation, however unconscious, that they would be more pleasurable than those of any other woman. (93-4)

In Lewis' thought, Venus and Eros are to be kept separate, not because they are opposed, but because Eros desires a person rather than a body; it sees a human being as an organic whole greater than the sum of its body parts, so to speak. The desire for personhood precedes the instinctual desire to use another's body to satisfy pleasure. Lewis does not denigrate sex, but accords it a role as one aspect of the total person. Mankind is not guided by a biological impulse to seek out and enjoy the body of the sexual partner as a thing in itself; rather, the biological instinct of sexual desire is conditioned by the yearning for personhood that expresses God's relationship with humanity.

Eros, in its preoccupation with person rather than body, thus offers up a foretaste and reflection of the fourth and final Love, Charity, the love of God for man. Ultimately, God gifts us with all love; it flows from Him as from the source of love itself. Without the mediating influence of Charity, Eros turns into a poisonous affair of "devouring," an insatiable instinct to possess completely the other person and to lose oneself within them. Charity helps to preserve individuality and to preserve a life-long marriage relationship patterned after Christ and the Church. (This last aspect of Eros would, of course, not enter into Pullman's calculations, as it would represent a sexual ethics centered on a dead God).

I conclude my brief discussion, however, not with Lewis the writer of non-fictive expository works, but with Lewis the writer of fiction— it is here that Pullman's accusations begin and end. To obtain a complete picture of his literary treatment of sexuality, one would have to take into account Lewis' Space Trilogy, a series that the author dubbed a "fairy-tale for adults." The trilogy is an earlier work than *The Four Loves*, but provides an important supplement to it. Lewis' reading of sexuality in *That Hideous Strength*, the final book of the trilogy, ties together those strands of Pullman's critique of Lewis we have been considering. The German tradition of exalted paganism, the criticism of the world of the "beyond," the alleged denigration of sexuality, is dealt with in one and the same stroke.

In the novel, protagonist Jane is transformed from a non-Christian to a Christian wife.

The catalyst for this transformation appears as the vision of a "red-cheeked, wet-lipped" woman, giant-sized and surrounded by cavorting dwarves (301-2). In her discussion with Ransom, the hero of the Space Trilogy, Jane discovers that the woman is an image of what her sexuality will become – indeed, already has become – if she does not become a Christian wife; in other words, if she does not acknowledge the guiding influence of a loving God as the source of her desire. The world of the earthly Venus – blooming nature as well as sexual pleasure – must become, if it remains solely pagan, "untransformed, demoniac" (311); in the language of *The Four Loves*, Venus, and the Eros that flows from it, when devoid of Charity join in a "love" that devours the parties involved, reminiscent of the fates of the vampire bride and her lover in Goethe's poem "The Bride of Corinth."

Now that Maleldil (the Christ of the Space Trilogy) has come, the world of sexuality in *That Hideous Strength* has been transformed by the infusion of Charity or God-love. Interestingly, Maleldil is portrayed, as Aslan with his fauns and centaurs, as having sealed a pact of friendship with the pagan world. Unlike the works of the Germans from Goethe to Nietzsche, the pagan world and the Christian world are not hostile antagonists. The gods of pagan myth do not represent, as in Milton's *Paradise Lost* and in the convictions of certain fundamentalists, minions of Satan lording it over an unsuspecting humanity. Rather, "It was these earthly wraiths of the high intelligences that men met in old times when they reported that they had seen the gods" (313). The pagan gods are seen as emissaries – earthly copies – of Heaven.

Following the conversation between Jane and Ransom, we see the archon of planet Perelandra, or Venus (who was the subject of the second book in the series) descend on St. Anne's under the lordship of Maleldil/Christ. It is in this scene that Lewis explores the mystery of marriage as a reflection of God (Ephesians 5:32), and it is here that the valuable supplement to his treatment of the four loves can be found:

> And now it came. It was fiery, sharp, bright and ruthless, ready to kill, ready to die, outspeeding light: it was Charity, not as mortals imagine it, not even as it has been humanised for them since the Incarnation of the Word, but the translunary virtue, fallen upon them direct from the Third Heaven, unmitigated. They were blinded, scorched, deafened. They thought it would burn their bones. They could not bear that it should continue. They could not bear that it should cease. So Perelandra, triumphant among planets, whom men call Venus, came and was with them. (320-1)

The description here is of the unmitigated love of God the Father, the source from which Lewis' four loves spring. In the Space Trilogy Venus, or the raw power of human sexuality, is transformed by Charity into an expression of divine love. It is really in this love that not only body and spirit, but also the principles of masculine and feminine, still sharply differentiated, are reconciled to form full complements of one another.

One could easily compare these reflections with the conclusion of *The Four Loves*:

> We were made for God. Only by being in some respect like Him, only by being a manifestation of His beauty, loving-kindness, wisdom, or goodness, has any earthly Beloved excited our love...In Heaven there will be no anguish and no duty of turning from our earthly Beloveds. First, because we shall have turned already; from the portraits to the Original, from the rivulets to the Fountain, from the creatures He made lovable to Love Himself. (139)

Lewis repeats at the conclusion of *The Four Loves* what he had said earlier in *The Problem of Pain*: that "the dream of finding our end, the thing we were made for, in a Heaven of purely human love could not be true unless our whole Faith were wrong" (ibid). In Lewis' Christian vision of life and love, hopes placed in this world, the world of exile and of renunciation, the "valley" in Lewis' phrase, ultimately result in an inversion that Jane experiences and which is the central theme of *That Hideous Strength*.

At the same time, an inversion of the German critique from Goethe to Nietzsche takes place. The "grey formalized world" really belongs not amongst those "joy-killing Christians," but instead among the skeptics and rational academics that would view the body as an end in itself devoid of the spirit in which it lives, moves, and has its being. The "vivid perilous world" is experienced only by those whom those same skeptics accuse of embracing death. The world of vitality is the world of stained glass, the world of the Church, as Jane discovers. Certainly not a Church in the religious sense (something Pullman may appreciate) – Jane notes that Ransom and his court "never talked about Religion," rather, "they talked about God" (315). In this world that is the inverse of Pullman's view of Christianity as "life-hating ideology," Goethe's vampire bride of death is transformed into the promise of a "splendor of virility and richness of womanhood unknown on earth" (Lewis, *Perelandra*, 179), made possible only through the transfiguring love of a God that contains, inhabits, and overshadows the sensual world.

WORKS CITED

Bertodano, Helena de. "I Am Of The Devil's Party." *Telegraph* 29 Jan. 2002 <www.telegraph.co.uk/arts/main/jhtml?xml=/arts/2002/01/29/bopull27.xml:2>.

"Faith and Fantasy." *Encounter* 24 Mar. 2000 <www.abc.net.au/rn/relig/enc/stories/s510312.htm>.

"The Dark Materials Debate: Life, God, the Universe" *Telegraph* 17 Mar. 2004 <www.telegraph.co.uk/arts/main.jhtml?xml=/arts/2004/03/17/bodark17.xml>.

Goethe, Johann Wolfgang von. *Werke: Auswahl in zehn Teilen,* ed. Eduard Scheidemantel, vol. 1. Berlin : Deutsches Verlagshaus Bong & Co., 1909.

Grenier, Cynthia. "Phillip Pullman's Dark Materials." *Crisis: Politics, Culture, and the Church* Oct. 2001 <http://www.crisismagazine.com/October2001/feature4.htm>.

Heine, Heinrich. *Historisch-kritische Gesamtausgabe der Werke* (DHA) ed. Manfred Windfuhr, vol. 8. Hamburg: Hoffmann und Campe, 1973.

The Holy Bible, English Standard Version.

Lewis, C.S. *Perelandra.* New York: Scribner, 2003.

—. *Surprised by Joy.* New York: Harcourt Brace, 1955.

—. *That Hideous Strength.* New York: Scribner, 2003.

—. *The Four Loves.* New York: Harcourt Brace, 1960.

—. *The Last Battle.* New York: HarperCollins, 1994.

—. *The Problem of Pain. The Complete C.S. Lewis Signature Classics.* San Francisco: HarperCollins, 2007.

Meacham, Steve. "The Shed Where God Died." *Sydney Morning Herald* 13 Dec. 2003. <http://www.smh.com.au/articles/2003/12/12/1071125644900.html>.

Nietzsche, Friedrich. *The Portable Nietzsche,* ed. and trans. Walter Kaufmann. New York: The Viking Press, 1954.

Pullman, Philip. *The Amber Spyglass.* New York: Random House, 2000. "The Dark Side of Narnia." *The Guardian* 1 Oct. 1998 <http://www.crlamppost.org/darkside.html>.

"The Republic of Heaven." *The Horn Book Magazine*, Nov./Dec. 2001 <www.hbook.com/magazine/articles/nov01_pullman.asp>. *The Subtle Knife*. New York: Random House, 1997.

Schiller, Friedrich. *Sämtliche Werke in 14 Bänden*, ed. Gotthilf Lachenmaier, vol. 1. Berlin und Leipzig: Th. Knaur, 1892.

Wartofsky, Alona. "The Last Word. Philip Pullman's Trilogy for Young Adults Ends With God's Death, and Remarkably Few Critics." *The Washington Post* 19 Feb. 2001: C01.

Chapter Twelve

Why Wells is from Mars, Bergson from Venus: Mapping Evolution in the Space Trilogy

Stephen Schwartz

In his popular series of "interstellar romances," C.S. Lewis presents his readers with a clear line of continuity and development as they proceed from one volume to the next. The continuity rests primarily on the conflict between the Christian protagonist, Elwin Ransom, and his two ruthless foes—the physicist Weston and the venture capitalist Devine—who are first introduced in *Out of the Silent Planet* (1938) and then resurface in the two sequels, Weston in *Perelandra* (1943) and Devine (as Lord Feverstone) in *That Hideous Strength* (1945). The sense of development is most apparent in the gradual transformation of the hero, who progresses from a perplexed captive to an anointed agent of divine redemption, confronting the demonic powers that threaten the beneficent order of the created universe. Equally important, however, are the largely neglected changes that occur in Ransom's enemies and in the modern "evolutionary" or "developmental" model they explicitly represent. In *Out of the Silent Planet,* Ransom's antagonists are associated with the popular "materialist" view of the evolutionary process—the infamous "struggle for existence"—especially as it appears in H.G. Wells's portrayal of interplanetary invasion in *The War of the Worlds* and elsewhere. The two villains use the presumption of their own evolutionary superiority to justify the conquest, displacement, or even the extermination of other rational beings, whether they are members of other species, as they are on Mars (Malacandra), or "inferior" members of our own species here on earth.[1] In *Perelandra* Ransom once again encounters Weston, who has been converted to "biological philosophy" and now espouses the vision of perpetual cosmic progress as it appears in Henri Bergson's "creative evolution" and the British "emergent evolution" that followed in its wake. At first glance, the physicist's conversion may seem a distinction without a difference, since the encounter between Ransom and Weston (or rather the Satanic Unman who gradually takes possession of Weston's mind) rapidly descends, as it does in the first book, into a mortal conflict between Christian tradition and modern apostasy. Nevertheless, as readers of Lewis' "interstellar romances" we should not be too quick to shrug off the evil professor's newfound faith. In his other writings, Lewis discriminates carefully between the "materialist" (or "mechanistic") view of "orthodox Darwinism" ("Is Theology Poetry?" *The Weight of Glory* 136) and the "organic" (or "vitalist") view of creative/emergent evolution, and though he is critical of each of these stances, he refuses to equate the one with the other. Moreover, the distinction between "Wellsianity" (his term) and "Bergsianity" (my term) plays a constitutive role in the Space Trilogy. As we shall see, certain features of Lewis' Malacandra suggest that this spiritually uncorrupted planet should be regarded as the "sublimation" or "taking up" (*Reflections on the Psalms* 112; 117) of the Wellsian war between the species, while the distinctive temporal dynamism of Perelandra may be considered a sanctified version of "creative evolution" itself. In line with his Augustinian view that "bad things are good things perverted" (*Preface to* Paradise Lost 66), Lewis transforms first the "mechanistic" and then the "vitalist" views of evolution into pristine worlds that make their terrestrial counterparts appear as parodic distortions of unspoiled and divinely created originals. In this respect the distinction between Wellsianity and Bergsianity illuminates not only the changing character of the evil powers in the two "interstellar romances" but also some of the most salient differences between the "unfallen" worlds which Lewis envisions on Mars and Venus before returning to earth in the final volume of the series.

I

To appreciate the difference between "materialist" and "vitalist" views of the evolutionary process, we must take a closer look at "creative evolution" and the function it served in early twentieth-century culture. The term itself is associated specifically with the philosopher Henri Bergson, whose *Creative Evolution* (1907) became one of the most influential books of the period.[2] Bergson's theory of evolution developed out his pioneering reformulation of the concept of time, which upset the traditional priority of Being over Becoming and paved the way for the British movement of "emergent evolution"—most notably Samuel Alexander's *Space, Time and Deity* (1920) and C. Lloyd Morgan's *Emergent Evolution* (1923)—who modified the

Darwinian paradigm to allow more room for novelty, discontinuity, and creative development in the evolutionary process. Bergson also laid the foundation for the subsequent explorations of temporal process that appear in the later works of Alfred North Whitehead—*Science and the Modern World* (1925) and *Process and Reality* (1929)—and (though unacknowledged at the time) in the French "existentialists" of the thirties and forties. Moreover, as the ostensible "middle way" between "materialist" and "religious" points of view, Bergson's "vitalist" or "Life-Force philosophy" (*Mere Christianity* 34-35) played a significant if controversial role in early twentieth-century religious thought. As we shall see, in his early years Lewis read Bergson with much enthusiasm, and his often favorable remarks even after his midlife conversion to Christianity indicate some of the ways that *Perelandra* takes up the philosopher's vision of creation as a process of continuous and innovative development.[3]

On the basis of his first two books, *Time and Free Will* (1889) and *Matter and Memory* (1896), Bergson established a significant reputation as a critic of "positivism," demonstrating that the "mechanistic" procedures designed to explore the physical world are insufficient for the study of mental life. In contrast to association psychologists, whose picture of the mind as a collection of discrete impersonal "atoms" is modeled on the laws of physics, Bergson shows that consciousness in "real duration" (*durée réelle*) is not a sequence of isolatable moments but rather a seamless continuity in a "constant state of becoming," and is therefore irreducible to the forms of explanation employed in the physical sciences. In an intellectual milieu still dominated by positivism, Bergson's early works appealed to many younger intellectuals who flocked to his lecture and referred to him as the "liberator"—the philosopher who redeemed Western thought from the nineteenth century's "religion of science." But soon after the turn of the century Bergson's thought began to develop along lines that would alienate many of his early admirers by extending the idea of real duration from the human mind to the natural universe itself. In *An Introduction to Metaphysics* (1903), he maintains that absolute reality does not reside in a system of unchanging forms constituted by the "intellect" but in the mobile flux given to us directly in "intuition." This "inversion of Platonism" offered a dramatic challenge to traditional ways of thought, and its implications became explicit several years later with the appearance of *Creative Evolution*.

In his wide-ranging and enormously influential magnum opus, Bergson simultaneously dismantles the Darwinian theory of evolution, which is based on the "mechanistic" explanations of the intellect, and proposes an alternative view in which real duration provides a model for the intuitive grasp of the perpetual movement of life itself. Tracing the problems of nineteenth-century positivism back to the origins of Western philosophy, Bergson claims that by its very nature the rational intellect reduces time to a function of space and that, as a consequence of this spatializing function, it treats the past and the future as calculable functions of the present. In other words, the intellect is an ingenious instrument for organizing and arranging the existing products of creation, but its inability to comprehend processes involving true novelty and unforeseeable change account not only for the problems of traditional metaphysics but also for the failure of modern scientific theories of evolution. In place of the latter, Bergson postulates the existence of creative spiritual impetus, the *élan vital,* that spontaneously produces novel forms of life. Just as the human mind develops continuously in "real duration," the natural universe is impelled by a "vital impetus" that perpetually raises creation to new and previously unpredictable levels of development.

Creative Evolution was a huge popular success, and its author soon became an international celebrity. The basis of Bergson's remarkable appeal lay in his synthesis of opposing points of view. Under his spell the presumably unbridgeable gap between religious and naturalistic viewpoints appeared to dissolve into mere illusion. Bergson achieved this feat by simultaneously spiritualizing the biological and naturalizing the spiritual realms. After reading his book one could believe that the Darwinian model is essentially a consequence of the mechanistic nature of the intellect, and that the *élan vital* makes more sense of the entire evolutionary process. One could also discard the traditional metaphysical conception of God as a product of the intellect, which leads us to identify reality with stasis rather than dynamic process, and proceed to reenvision the Divine as a creative spirit that realizes itself progressively in the natural order. As it turned out, this middle way between the "spiritual" and the "material" achieved a considerable if momentary following, but as a means of reconciling opposing points of view it was often treated as a suspicious compromise on both sides of the ideological spectrum. Bergson's Catholic followers, such as Jacques Maritain and Charles Péguy, continued to applaud his distinction between the "mechanistic" realm of matter and the "vital" realm of human existence, but at the same time they condemned him for collapsing the essential distinction between the "vital" and the "religious" realms by reducing the divine to an immanent life-force.[4] Hence the Bergsonian synthesis proved to be an unstable compound, and with the outbreak of World War I, the cultural climate began to change dramatically, and by the time the war was over the ethos that could support the notion of an immanent spiritual impetus had seriously eroded. While the distinction between "mechanistic" and "vital" processes continued to play a significant role in postwar thought, the extraordinary vogue of Bergsonism began its steady descent.

Ironically, C.S. Lewis' interest in Bergson began while he was recovering from battlefront wounds in 1918, and the young scholar continued reading Bergson intermittently in the years that followed.[5] As might be expected, after his conversion in the early thirties Lewis assumed the more critical stance of Maritain and Péguy, affirming Bergson's separation of the mechanistic and vital realms but rejecting the virtual equation between the vital and the spiritual. According to the Christian Lewis, creative evolution is a "modern form of nature religion" ("The Grand Miracle" *God in the Dock* 86). Its distinctive appeal lies in its "in-between view," which promises to deliver us from the "material" while diluting the "religious" into an emotionally uplifting but undemanding sense of "striving" or "purposiveness" in the natural universe (*Mere Christianity* 34-35). Nevertheless, even as he dissects the dangers and temptations of "Life-Force philosophy," Lewis never reduces Bergsianity to mere Wellsianity. In one of his classic accounts of the latter, he maintains that "the Bergsonian critique of orthodox Darwinism is not easy to answer" ("Is Theology Poetry?" *The Weight of Glory* 136). He also treated Bergson himself with considerable if qualified respect, customarily distinguishing the philosopher's own works from its various popularizations by George Bernard Shaw and others. In his autobiography, *Surprised by Joy* (1956), Lewis is quite open in his praise as he recalls his initial response to Bergson in 1918:

> The other momentous experience was that of reading Bergson in a Convalescent Camp on Salisbury Plain. . . . [It also] had a revolutionary effect on my emotional outlook. Hitherto my whole bent had been toward things pale, remote, and evanescent; the water-color world of Morris, the leafy recesses of Malory, the twilight of Yeats. The word "life" had for me pretty much the same associations it had for Shelley in *The Triumph of Life*. I would not have understood what Goethe meant by *des Lebens goldnes Baum*. Bergson showed me. He did not abolish my old loves, but he gave me a new one. From him I first learned to relish energy, fertility, and urgency; the resource, the triumphs, and even the insolence, of things that grow. I became capable of appreciating artists who would, I believe, have meant nothing to me before; all the resonant, dogmatic, flaming, unanswerable people like Beethoven, Titian (in his mythological pictures), Goethe, Dunbar, Pindar, Christopher Wren, and the more exultant Psalms. (*Surprised by Joy* 198)

For the young agnostic caught between a dreamy late Romanticism and the horror of the trenches, Bergson's way of infusing nature with spirit appears to have worked like a charm. In his later life Lewis may have become more critical of Bergson, but he respected the difference between the mechanistic and vitalist views of the evolutionary process. In the Space Trilogy, this distinction becomes crucial as we proceed from Ransom's first adventure in *Out of the Silent Planet* to his new expedition in *Perelandra*. More importantly, this distinction is evident not just in the villain's dubious awakening to the *élan vital* but in the uncorrupted worlds that Lewis constructs on Mars and Venus. Indeed, the new Eden on Perelandra may be regarded as Lewis' own paean to "the resource, the triumphs, and even the insolence, of things that grow"—a celebration of the vital realm that reaches its highest expression in the "*animal rationale*" (*Perelandra* 178) who presides over the rest of creation. The Adversary may preach the gospel of "creative" or "emergent" evolution, but Lewis designs his own version of creative evolution by endowing his imaginary world with a principle of dynamic change in which even the evolutionary lapses, including the spiritual catastrophe that has overtaken our own fallen planet, are transfigured into something new and more marvelous by the redeeming act of God.

II

It is well known that Lewis endows his "other worlds" on Mars and Venus with attributes drawn from the "medieval model" of the cosmos—the "heavens which declared the glory" (*Out of the Silent Planet* 34)—and populates them with unfallen rational creatures free from the fears and temptations that plague our own wayward species. Therefore it may seem surprising that these imaginary planets derive some of their most salient features from the same modern "evolutionary model" espoused by the terrestrial invaders. Seen from this perspective, each of the two unspoiled worlds with which Ransom is associated appears not as the polar opposite but the "beatific" transfiguration of the specific phase of the evolutionary model to which it stands opposed. In *Out of the Silent Planet*, the solidarity of Malacandra's three rational species may be seen as the "sublimation," or "working-up" (RP 112) into a first principle, of Wells's Darwinian vision of evolution as a relentless "struggle for existence." Similarly, Maleldil's creation of Perelandra's fluid and ever-progressing paradise may be regarded as the "up-grading" (*Reflections on the Psalms* 116) of Bergson's hospitable and temporally dynamic vision of cosmic development. Furthermore, as a consequence of this artistic strategy the naturalistic theories—Wellsian and Bergsonian—are transformed into parodic distortions of the unfallen worlds for which they ironically provide the model: the interspecies amity of *Out of the Silent* appears as an archetype that turns Wells's "struggle for existence" into a perverse copy of the real thing; while the new paradise in *Perelandra* reduces Bergson's "creative evolution" to a degraded form of the authentic temporal order that Maleldil has created on Venus.[6]

In *Out of the Silent Planet*, Weston has not yet been converted to Bergson's "biological philosophy." His self-defined mission is simply to perpetuate his "race" by extending the Darwinian "struggle for existence" from our world to other sectors of the universe. Hence it is no accident that Lewis creates a Martian cosmopolis in which reason transcends biological differences, a civilization comprised of three rational species—each with its own distinctive anatomy and temperament—that live separately but peacefully in a Divinely ordered universe. Lewis' Malacandrans know nothing of the evolutionary struggle on our own planet, but once Ransom arrives on Mars his obsessive concern with the order of the "species"—their origins, development, and modes of relationship—indicates that Lewis is not only transporting us from a fallen to an uncontaminated world but also "taking up" (*Reflections on the Psalms* 116-117) the Wellsian view of Nature "red in tooth and claw" into a cosmic vision in which the various species are bound together in universal brotherhood. Significantly, the Malacandrans have not been immune to the natural perils that plague our own terrestrial existence. As a result of an ancient invasion by the fallen archangel who still reigns over the earth, they have adapted to environmental change and learned to compensate for the irreparable physical damage to the surface of their planet. In the process they have also acquired the discipline and courage to overcome the insecurity—and above all the fear of death—that impels the mistrust and violence of life on our own "silent" planet. Moreover, at least one of their rational species exercises these martial virtues in the ritual of the hunt, a form of "unfallen" violence that expresses the ancient kinship between rational and irrational creatures and enhances the joy of life through the very risk of death. In this respect the imaginary world of Malacandra is a composite entity—an uncorrupted planet akin to our own visions of the terrestrial paradise, but also an "up-grading" of the evolutionary struggle for existence into an "original," or "archetype," which simultaneously transfigures the "biocentric" view of universal strife and parodies its one-sided character.

It may seem a long way from the Darwinian survival of the fittest to the interspecies unity of Malacandra, but elsewhere in his writings Lewis shows us that it is not far fetched to consider the creation on Mars as a transfiguration of the terrestrial condition of evolutionary strife. Elsewhere in his works Lewis acknowledges the competitive brutality of the natural order, but he also maintains that in light of the Christian doctrine of creation the undeniable "cruelty and wastefulness" of Nature as we know it "may yet be derived from a principle which is good and fair, may indeed be a depraved and blurred copy of it—the pathological form which it would take in a spoiled Nature" (*Miracles* 156).[7] In the same way Lewis' Malacandra embodies the transfiguration of "spoiled Nature"—i.e. Nature as it appears in the "materialist" account of the evolutionary process—into its originary "principle." Or seen from the opposite direction, the creation on Mars may be regarded as the "archetype" of which our own "*spoiled* Nature"—the "cruelty and wastefulness" of the struggle for existence—is the "depraved and blurred copy" (*Miracles* 156). Lewis' formulation descends from the venerable tradition of Neoplatonic thought, but to conceive the interspecies unity on Mars as the archetype of our own strife-torn planet takes us closer to some of Lewis' demonstrably modern concerns. Far from simply turning back the clock to a premodern conception of the "heavens," Lewis' transfiguration of Wells's evolutionary naturalism capitalizes upon his predecessor's use of interplanetary conflict to explore the spiritual affliction at the source of our troubled relations with other members of our own species as well as the other creatures with whom we share the earth. If nothing else, Lewis is addressing the urgent issues of his own moment. The peace and equality shared by the three Martian species, who live apart but never seek to subordinate one another, underscores the opposite situation here on earth—the propensity of a single rational species to split into factions that regard each other as inherently alien, inferior, or even as creatures of a different species—an age-old affliction of our self-divided species, but raised to a boiling point by the virulent nationalism and racism of the 1930s.[8]

Perelandra offers a more readily discernable example of the "taking up" of the evolutionary model into an imagined archetype. If *Out of the Silent Planet* at once rejects and raises up Wells's "orthodox Darwinism," *Perelandra* simultaneously repudiates and "sublimates" Bergson's affirmative vision of evolutionary progress. In this second interplanetary struggle, Weston's shift from materialist "Wellsianity" to "creative evolution" is reflected in the dynamic (and remarkably Bergsonian) character of the new creation that Ransom discovers on Venus.[9] When Ransom first arrives on this newly minted world, he is as yet unaware that his role is to protect the new Eve from the demonically possessed Weston and his seductive new creed. What Ransom does discover at the outset of his adventure is that the created order on Perelandra is dramatically different from its terrestrial counterpart. In a striking departure from traditional views of the earthly paradise, Lewis presents the prelapsarian condition as a state of continuous flux, a "universe of shifting slopes" (*Perelandra* 34), and he portrays its crowning achievement— its Adam and Eve—as dynamic creatures who are fast learners and seem to develop with every passing moment. Instead of an immutable condition that precedes the fall into time and change, Lewis' new Eden is a world of perpetual movement in which the one prohibition—its Tree of the Knowledge of Good and Evil—is to avoid habitation of the "Fixed Land." This feature of the novel rarely receives the attention it deserves: when it is not simply taken for granted or chalked up as a clever conceit, it is attributed either to hints of an evolving Eden in Milton's *Paradise Lost* to the "floating islands" that appear in extant scientific accounts of Venus's atmosphere.[10] These are significant sources, but the shift from Being to Becoming on Lewis' mobile paradise is so pronounced, and the psychological, spiritual, and cosmological implications of this "inversion of Platonism" explored in such exacting detail, that a more far-reaching alternative suggests itself—that the new world on Perelandra is not merely a reconstruction of the biblical conception of paradise, nor an extrapolation from "the discarded image" of medieval cosmology, but a sublimated and Christianized form of creative evolution itself. In fact, the Bergsonian stamp appears virtually everywhere in this perpetually evolving planet. It is evident not only in the continuous development of the untarnished Green Lady—the Eve of this new Eden—but also in the ceaseless novelty and progress of Maleldil's wondrous creativity: "Never did He make two things the same; never did He utter one word twice. After earths, not better earths but beasts; after beasts, not better beasts, but spirits. After a falling, not a recovery but a new creation. Out of the new creation, not a third but the mode of change itself is changed for ever. Blessed is He!" (*Perelandra* 184). Of course this celebration of the transcendent Creator involves a significant departure from Bergson. Whereas the philosopher equates the divine with the immanent development of life itself (*élan vital*), Lewis attempts to raise Bergson's vision of perpetual development to a higher power, reversing his naturalization of the supernatural and reshaping his model of cosmic progress into a Christian vision of Becoming.

At first glance it seems strange, if not contradictory, to think of Lewis assembling his new Eden according to a blueprint provided by the enemy Himself. But such a view of *Perelandra* grows less perplexing if we consider Lewis' contemporaneous study of Milton, *A Preface to* Paradise Lost (1942). In this highly influential work Lewis overturns the Romantic reading of Milton as "of the Devil's part without knowing it" by reducing Satan from an exalted tragic hero to a parody of the God against whom he has rebelled.[11] Invoking the Augustinian notion that evil has no substantial existence and is merely a defection from the Good, Lewis shows that Milton's fallen archangel should be regarded not an authentic hero but as a warped imitation of his Creator. The same logic, which presupposes that God "has no opposite" (*Letters* II, 121; 9/12/33) may account for the otherwise baffling situation in *Perelandra*, where Lewis presents creative evolution as a dangerous distortion of the divinely ordained and beneficent temporal dynamism of his own imaginary paradise. Armed with Augustine's view that "what we call bad things are good things perverted" (*Preface to* Paradise Lost 66), Lewis took the Platonic step of conceiving an "original", or an "archetype," which "takes up" creative evolution to a higher level and simultaneously reduces it to a misshapen derivative. Put somewhat differently, just as Bergson transfigured a "mechanistic" theory of evolution still entangled in the static categories of traditional metaphysics into a new principle of Becoming, so Lewis transfigures Bergson's "vitalistic" naturalism, rejecting his reduction of the divine to an immanent creative impetus but reworking his radical reformulation of evolutionary theory into a Christian conception of continuous cosmic development.[12]

III

The first two novels of the Space Trilogy form a coherent set. In each instance the journey "into another dimension" involves the sublimation of one version of the modern evolutionary paradigm into its imagined "archetype." But does the progression from the "materialist" view of *Out of the Silent Planet* to the "organic" view of *Perelandra* tell us anything about *That Hideous Strength*, which abandons interplanetary adventure in favor of the earthbound "spiritual shockers" of Charles Williams? In the finale to the series, Ransom remains on his own planet to battle Divine and his seemingly scientific institution—the National Institute of Co-ordinated Experiments (N.I.C.E.)—whose leaders are actually conspiring with demonic powers to seize control of the evolutionary process and bring about the self-transformation of man into "God almighty . . . a being made by man—who will finally ascend to the throne of the universe. And rule forever" (*That Hideous Strength* 176). As paradoxical as it seems, the modern developmental paradigm as it appears in *That Hideous Strength* is no longer tethered to its naturalistic moorings. As the titular allusion to the Tower of Babel suggests, the N.I.C.E. transports us beyond both the "material" (Wellsian) and the "organic" (Bergsonian) realms to the "spiritual" (Babelian) plane of the supernatural "New Man, who will not die, the artificial man, free from nature" (*That Hideous Strength* 174). Strangely enough, as we progress through the Trilogy we are also progressing to seemingly higher forms of the evolutionary model itself as it aspires to ascend and in a sense return to the transcendent heights of the religious world-view it had presumably left behind.[13]

If the concluding novel of the series sustains the progression from the "material" to the "organic" conceptions of evolution in the first two novels, can we find anything in the earthbound finale corresponding to the "upgrading" of the developmental model that takes place on the unfallen planets of the first two novels? Lewis has abandoned the literary form of the previous tales, but in shifting to the "supernatural thrillers" of Charles Williams, he is turning to a fictional "formula" ("The Novels of Charles Williams" *Of This and Other Worlds* 35) in which the process of imaginary transfiguration to an original informing "principle" plays a fundamental role. Much has been made of Williams's study of magic and the occult, but the source of his fictional "formula" lies primarily in the blending of "the Probable and the Marvelous" ("The Novels of Charles Williams" *Of This and Other Worlds* 46) that began in Gothic romances of the eighteenth century. The Faustian necromancers of Williams's shockers are staples of the Gothic tradition, but at the same time Williams raises Gothic terror to a higher dimension, ingeniously using its revenants, doppelgangers, and other spectral resources to "haunt" his modern protagonists and restore the palpable presence of the divine Omnipotence—the "dreadful goodness" (*Descent into Hell* 16)—that creates and sustains the ordinary world we inhabit. Lewis follows Williams in this double use of the Gothic to portray the Faustian aspirations of the N.I.C.E. and simultaneously to reaffirm (in a peculiar mixture of Arthurian and Gothic romance) a traditional conception of the supernatural.[14] As in the "workings-up" of Wells on Mars and Bergson on Venus, the construction of a beatific "original" at the manor of St. Anne's, like the very form of the novel itself, retains many of the defining elements of the Gothic—above all, its trademark "mixture of the realistic and the supernatural" (*Letters* II, 682, 12/6/45)—that ultimately reduces the hideous techno-magical power of the

N.I.C.E. to a distorted Gothic double. In this respect, the final novel of the series employs a strategy virtually identical to that of its two predecessors.

The final volume of the Space Trilogy completes a complex but coherent pattern of confrontation and appropriation of the modern developmental paradigm. It suggests that we should conceive the three-level progression—material, organic, and spiritual—both as a "vertical" hierarchy and as a "horizontal" sequence that proceeds from one novel to the next. Along the vertical axis we encounter a set of upwards transpositions, each of which converts a distinctive version of the modern imaginary into a divinely sanctioned "original," or first "principle," which in turn reduces its modern target—ironically the very stuff out of which it has been conceived—into a parodic imitation. Along the "horizontal" axis we advance from transpositions of the "material" (Wellsian) and "organic" (Bergsonian) to "spiritual" (Babelian) forms of the developmental model as it paradoxically reascends to the transcendent heights of the religious world-view it purports to supersede.[15] Fortunately, a familiar assumption underlies the relationship between vertical and horizontal axes. Like Arthur Lovejoy (*The Great Chain of Being*, 1936) and many others, Lewis often represents the modern era in terms of a momentous historical change—the transposition of the source and center of Being from a transcendent God to the progressive development of Man. As he describes it in *The Discarded Image* (1964), it is as if the multi-tiered medieval hierarchy (of which the three-level material/organic/spiritual hierarchy is the modern counterpart) has tumbled over on its side, and as a result of this cultural transformation the traditional "vertical" relationship between lower and higher levels of Being has mutated into the "horizontal" progression from primitive to progressively more developed forms of life.[16] In the Space Trilogy, however, the modern developmental paradigm undergoes a series of self-transformations as we proceed throughout the series. As Lewis leads us from the "material" to the "spiritual" forms of this modern master myth, culminating in the techno-magical deification of man in *That Hideous Strength*, it becomes increasingly evident that he conceives evolutionary naturalism as merely a displaced and ultimately self-contradictory form of the multi-tiered cosmic hierarchy it has superseded. In the final analysis, the ostensibly "horizontal" model of perpetual progress begins to manifest (in progressively sinister fashion) the "vertical" character of its founding motivation and its ultimate aim, which lies in the ineradicable desire to transcend our finite condition and return to our spiritual homeland.

IV

If Lewis designs his imaginary worlds by "taking up" the very things he is putting down, then we must reconsider the terms of engagement that have traditionally informed the interpretation of these novels. Ever since its publication, the Space Trilogy has been read primarily in terms of a sharply defined struggle between religious and naturalistic points of view, the first associated with the "discarded image" of premodern cosmology, the second with the modern "evolutionary model" that has supplanted it. There is much to support this approach, but it also obscures the more complex process of Lewis' world-building, which would be better served by identifying the various subtypes of the evolutionary model and conceiving the conflict in each of these novels not simply as a clash between two disparate and competing principles but as a relationship between "archetype" and its misshapen "copy." In one sense, Lewis' creation of pristine "originals" out of warped reproductions is merely a skillful adaptation of an age-old polemical maneuver. As the critic Northrop Frye once described it, the Augustinian strategy of transforming the ideological enemy into a distorted derivative or demonic double reflects "the revolutionary and dialectical element in Christian belief, which is constantly polarizing its truth against the falsehoods of the heathen, but, like other revolutionary doctrines, feels most secure when the dark side takes the form of a heresy that closely resembles itself" (*The Secular Scripture,* 142). Lewis employs this conceptual maneuver to reduce the opposition to a parodic imitation, but at the same time his imagined archetypes bear witness to an irreducible element of receptivity to the very "falsehoods" he is exposing. The imaginary Malacandra is not only an unfallen planet that reflects the traditional conception of the "heavens"; it is also a transfiguration of the Darwinian "struggle for existence" into the site of a modern exploration of the means through which we establish the most basic distinctions between ourselves and other beings—and in particular, the process that makes it possible for certain human beings to relegate other members of their own kind to inferior or subhuman status. Similarly, the evolving Eden on Perelandra, which is virtually inconceivable in the absence of creative evolution, establishes the grounds of compatibility between Christian orthodoxy and a distinctively modern conception of time and temporal process. As for the conclusion of the series, scholars have long regarded *That Hideous Strength* as a "Charles Williams novel by C.S. Lewis" (Green & Hooper 205). Nevertheless, the tendency to conceive the rival powers in terms of a sheer antithesis between religious and naturalistic worldviews, medieval romance and modern realism, covers up Lewis' ambitious attempt, inspired by Williams's example, to employ the modern Gothic mix of "the Probable and the Marvellous" ("The Novels of Charles Williams" *Of This and Other Worlds* 34) in a way that does not simply revert to medieval romance but aspires to reactivate the powers of enchantment (both demonic and divine) that have been cast aside by the practitioners of modern realism. In this respect, Lewis' work should be viewed not as a casual dismissal but as a searching exploration of modern forms of thought and imaginative invention. As a result of this adjustment of our optic, we may begin to see the Space Trilogy less as the irreconcilable struggle between an old-fashioned Christian humanism and a newfangled heresy and more as the effort of a modern Christian writer to sustain and enrich the former through critical engagement with the latter.

NOTES

1. Lewis states repeatedly that his target is not the biological theory of evolution, which he regards as a "genuine scientific hypothesis" ("Funeral of a Great Myth" *Christian Reflections* 83), but the broader "developmental" paradigm which was well established by the time that *Origin of Species* appeared in 1859. In this respect he regards Darwinism as the effect rather than the cause of the evolutionary model. In general, Lewis is less concerned with the prospect of subhuman ancestry than with the ideology that consigns other human beings to subhuman status or summons up an "evolutionary imperative" to legitimate the suspension of time-honored moral law.

2. There are many expository and critical studies of Bergson, a fair portion of them from the period of his highest acclaim. Since the eclipse of his reputation in the middle third of the century, Bergson has been rehabilitated primarily through the efforts of Gilles Deleuze, and he is again receiving attention as an important and original voice in modern philosophy.

3. Lewis' much expressed fondness for Samuel Alexander is based not on the "emergent" character of his philosophy but on his largely unrelated distinction between "contemplation" and "enjoyment" in the apprehension of objects of perception. The British fascination with a dynamic conception of nature is evident not only in the "emergent" evolutionists and Whitehead (whom Lewis called "our greatest natural philosopher" [*Miracles* 139]), but also in the more philosophical writings of well-known physicists such as Arthur Eddington, who included a chapter on "Becoming" in his influential book, *The Nature of the Physical World* (1928). Peter Bowler's formidable study, *Reconciling Science and Religion: The Debate in Early-Twentieth-Century Britain* (2001), situates "emergent evolution" and related developments in the context of the broader struggle between religious and scientific viewpoints in the first few decades of the century. Until quite recently, most accounts of French "existentialism" followed the lead of Sartre and his contemporaries in excluding Bergson from the canonical list of seminal precursors, which typically includes Kierkegaard, Nietzsche, Husserl, and Heidegger among others. Contemporary scholars such as Suzanne Guerlac (*Literary Polemics: Bataille, Sartre, Valéry, Breton* [1997]) have address this problematic dismissal and confirm the formative influence of Bergson reflections on the openness of time and its relationship to human freedom upon the French philosophers of the next generation.

In this chapter Weston uses the expression "emergent evolution." Later on, Ransom refers to Weston's doctrine as "Creative Evolution" (104). Here and elsewhere, Lewis tends to use "emergent evolution," "creative evolution," and "life-force philosophy" interchangeably.

4. Bergson continued to inspire many Catholic intellectuals, particularly those who believed that the Church must eventually come to terms with modernity. But by suggesting that the *élan vital* may be equated with God, Bergson had entered into a fatal collision course with Rome, which ultimately placed his works on the Index of Prohibited Books. The hierarchical division into three planes of being—the material (or "mechanistic"), the organic (or "vital"), and the spiritual (or "theological")—which arose largely in response to Bergson, became a prominent feature of Catholic thought in early 20th-century France. Students of Anglo-American modernism may be more familiar with its exposition in T.E. Hulme's posthumous *Speculations* (1924), which influenced T.S. Eliot and other like-minded intellectuals in the twenties and thirties. See note 6 on Lewis' use of the same three-tier hierarchy.

5. The main autobiographical account appears in *Surprised by Joy* (198, 204, 211). In June 1920, Lewis mentions that he is reading Bergson in a letter to Arthur Greeves (*Letters* I, 494; 6/19/20). His diary entry for September 17, 1923 states that he is "re-reading" *Creative Evolution.* The diary also records his reading of Bergson's *Mind-Energy* (*L'Énergie spirituelle*, a collection of essays published in 1919) in January, 1924 and *Matter and Memory* in February, 1925 (*All My Road Before Me* 269, 285, 349). Other references to Bergson appear throughout his later works.

6. In his other writings, Lewis often employs the notion of "taking up" or extrapolating from a lower level to a higher one. The *locus classicus* may be found in his essay, "Transposition" (*The Weight of Glory* 25-46), which assumes a three-level hierarchical ladder and focuses on 1) the modern tendency to reduce middle-level "human" phenomena to lower-level "material" causation, and 2) the correspondences that enable us to glimpse beyond the "human" to the "divine" level. The origins of this idea lie in Plato and the longstanding neo-Platonic tradition with which Lewis was intimately acquainted. But he also drew on a fascinating modern source—the idea of the fourth dimension. In "Transposition" and elsewhere Lewis turns to Edwin Abbott's immensely influential popularization, *Flatland: A Romance of Many Dimensions* (1884), as a model for projecting beyond the (three-dimensional) world we inhabit to a higher dimension—"God's dimension" (*Mere Christianity* 143)—to which the elements on the lower plane of our own existence may provide a certain degree of comprehension. On the sometimes startling results of the movement "upwards" and "downwards" (occasionally conceived as "inwards" [Gk. "andwards"] and "outwards" [Gk. "eckwards"]), see Lewis' account of the transposition process in the passage from our time-bound experience to our comprehension of the eternal (*Mere Christianity* 149; *Miracles* 187); in the imputed "sublimation" of some of the all-too-human sentiments expressed in the Psalms (*Reflections on the Psalms* 112-116); in the transfiguration of our Old Nature into the New (*Miracles,* chapter 16); and, picking up on a cardinal point in the theological works of Charles Williams, in the Athanasian formulation of the Incarnation as proceeding "'not by the conversion of the godhead into flesh, but by taking of (the) manhood into God'" (*Reflections on the Psalms* 116).

7. It is worth quoting the entire passage: "What the Christian story does is not instate on the Divine level a cruelty and wastefulness which have already disgusted us on the Natural, but to show us in God's act, working neither cruelly nor wastefully, the same principle which is in Nature also, though down there it works sometimes in one way and sometimes in the

other. It illuminates the Natural scene by suggesting that a principle which at first looked meaningless may yet be derived from a principle which is good and fair, may indeed be a depraved and blurred copy of it—the pathological form which it would take in a *spoiled* Nature" (*Miracles* 156).

8. I consider this aspect of the novel at some length in ""Cosmic Anthropology: Race and Reason in *Out of the Silent Planet*," *Christianity and Literature* 52 (2003) 523-556.

9. The difference between the transposition of the material realm on Mars and the organic realm on Venus is evident in the physical description of the two planets as well as the celestial intelligences (Oyarsas) who preside over them. When the Oyarsas of Mars and Venus appear side by side at the end of *Perelandra,* they exhibit the traditional planetary distinction based on gender (masculine and feminine) and governing virtue (martial discipline and love), but they also bear the difference between the inorganic and the vital realms embodied by their respective planets: "The Oyarsa of Mars shone with cold and morning colours, a little metallic—pure, hard, and bracing. The Oyarsa of Venus glowed with a warm splendour, full of the suggestion of teeming vegetable life" (*Perelandra* 171).

10. According to Lewis, "the germ of *Perelandra* was simply the picture of the floating islands themselves, with no location, no story . . ." (*Letters* III, 162; 1/31/52). There is no reason to doubt that this image was the "germ" of the novel, but the picture of "floating islands" is insufficient to account for the extensive exploration of time and of the complexities of temporal experience that Lewis erected upon it. So are Milton's suggestive remarks about paradise as a progressive state in which "bodies may at last turn all to spirit, / Improved by tract of time, and winged ascend / Ethereal, as we, or may at choice / Here or in heavenly paradises dwell" (5.497-500). Lewis is heavily indebted to Milton, but it is arguable that for Lewis' readers the very focus upon his great predecessor has directed attention away from the modern elements in his invented paradise.

11. "The reason Milton wrote in fetters when he wrote of Angels & God, and at liberty when of Devils & Hell, is because he was a true Poet, and of the Devil's party without knowing it" (William Blake, *The Marriage of Heaven and Hell*). Another representative remark comes from Shelley: "Nothing can exceed the energy and magnificence of the character of Satan in "Paradise Lost." It is a mistake to suppose that he could ever have been intended for the popular personification of evil. . . . Milton's Devil as a moral being is so far superior to his God, as One who perseveres in some purposes which he

has conceived to be excellent in spite of adversity and torture, is to One who in the cold security of undoubted triumph inflicts the most horrible revenge upon his enemy, not from any mistaken notion of inducing him to repent of a perseverance in enmity, but with the alleged design of exasperating him to deserve new torments" (Percy Bysshe Shelley, *The Defence of Poetry*).

12. I develop this argument in an extended reading of *Perelandra* in . "Paradise Reframed: Lewis, Bergson, and Changing Times on Perelandra," *Christianity and Literature* 51 (2002) 569-602.

13. To attribute this sequence to the Space Trilogy does not imply that Lewis conceived it whole cloth in this manner from the outset. Based on the little evidence we have, it is more likely that the larger scheme emerged as the work progressed.

14. Lewis does not refer to the Gothic as such, but his own blend of the realistic and the supernatural is a virtual catalogue of Gothic conventions: the pervasive atmosphere of "terror," "dread," and "horror" (the terms occur frequently); nightmares that record actual events otherwise unknown to the dreamer; imprisonment and persecution in the "haunted castle," the domain of oppressive authority; the interest in the relations between love and power, and the attendant problems of marriage, family, and inheritance in a changing but intractably patriarchal society; the creation of a "monster"—"that hideous strength"—associated with lust for the kind of knowledge that confers mastery over life itself; and the ancient crypt that marks the ever present threat of a "return of the repressed"—the power of the past to haunt or invade the world of the living. The "beatific" transfiguration of the Gothic, derived from the fiction of Charles Williams, is evident in the "supernatural" shocks and surprises that constantly beset the modern sensibility of the heroine, Jane Studdock, and lead to her spiritual transformation; in the manor of St. Anne's, which is not simply an avatar of medieval romance but a carefully crafted composite of traditional and modern elements that simultaneously sublimates and satirizes the "miserific" enchantment of Belbury; and in the redemptive action of Merlin the magician, who rises from the grave to exercise divine judgment (in a characteristically excessive Gothic manner) upon the dark powers that have sought to subdue to the planet.

15. The difference between the opening and the close of the Trilogy is especially instructive in this regard. In *Out of the Silent Planet* Lewis responds to the evolutionary naturalism of H.G. Wells by constructing an imaginary world in which universal reason transcends the differences between the species and provides the basis for their mutual acknowledgement and shared

participation in a divinely ordered cosmos. By contrast, in *That Hideous Strength,* where the enemy aspires to transcend the natural order itself, the transfiguration of the myth of "development" runs in the opposite direction. The emphasis is no longer on the rational harmony that transcends our animal nature but on the affirmation of our organic, embodied, and finite condition, or rather the incarnate union of spirit and matter that constitutes our finite condition.

16. Lewis also describes this transformation as a process of "Internalisation" in which "century by century, item after item is transferred from the object's side of the account to the subject's" (*The Discarded Image* 215). Lewis' affection for "the discarded image" of premodern cosmology is apparent throughout his works, nowhere more so than in the volume of that title, where he declares "that the old Model delights me as I believe it delighted our ancestors. Few constructions of the imagination seem to me to have combined splendour, sobriety, and coherence in the same degree." It is important to remember that Lewis follows this well-known statement first with the remark that for all its appeal, this Medieval Model "had a serious defect; it was not true" (*The Discarded Image* 216); then with an examination of the interests, needs, and values behind the "new Model" (219) that replaced it; and finally with a discussion of the manner and degree to which such relatively stable but impermanent Models (roughly equivalent to the "paradigms" of Thomas Kuhn's ground-breaking study, *The Structure of Scientific Revolutions* [1963]) shape the particular forms of knowledge and the process of inquiry in each successive epoch.

WORKS CITED

WORKS BY C.S. LEWIS

All My Road Before Me: The Diary of C. S. Lewis, 1922-1927. Ed. Walter Hooper. San Diego: Harcourt, 1991.

Collected Letters. 3 vols. Ed Walter Hooper. San Francisco: Harper, 2000, 2004, 2007.

The Discarded Image: An Introduction to Medieval and Renaissance Literature. 1964. Cambridge: Cambridge University Press, 1994.

"The Funeral of a Great Myth." *Christian Reflections.* Ed. Walter Hooper. Grand Rapids: Eerdmans, 1967. pp. 82-93.

"The Grand Miracle." *God in the Dock: Essays on Theology and Ethics.* Grand Rapids: Eerdmans, 1970. pp.80-88.

"Is Theology Poetry?" 1945. *The Weight of Glory and Other Addresses.* 1949. New York: HarperCollins, 2001. pp. 116-140.

Mere Christianity. 1952. New York: Simon & Schuster, 1996.

Miracles. 1947. New York: Simon, 1996.

"The Novels of Charles Williams." 1949. *Of This and Other Worlds.* 1982. Ed. Walter Hooper. London: HarperCollins, 2000. pp.34-41.

Out of the Silent Planet. 1938. New York: Scribner, 2003.

Perelandra. 1943. New York: Scribner, 2003.

A Preface to Paradise Lost. 1942. London: Oxford, 1960.

Reflections on the Psalms. San Diego: Harcourt, 1958.

Surprised by Joy: The Shape of My Early Life. 1956. San Diego: Harcourt, 1970.

"Transposition." *The Weight of Glory and Other Addresses.* 1949 New York: HarperCollins, 2001. pp. 91-116.

OTHER WORKS

Abbott, Edwin A. *Flatland: A Romance of Many Dimensions.* 1884. New York: Penguin Books, 1998.

Alexander, Samuel. *Space, Time, and Deity.* 2 vols. London: Macmillan, 1920.

Bergson, Henri. *Creative Evolution.* 1907. Trans. Arthur Mitchell. New York: Henry Holt, 1911.

—. *The Creative Mind.* Orig. *La Pénsée et le mouvant: Essais et conferences.* 1934. Trans. Mabelle L. Andison. New York: 1946.

—. *An Introduction to Metaphysics.* 1903. Trans. T.E. Hulme. 1910. Indianapolis: Bobbs Merrill, 1955.

—. *Laughter: An Essay on the Meaning of the Comic.* 1901. Trans. Cloudesley Brereton and Fred Rothwell. New York, 1911. Rpt. *Comedy.* Ed. Wylie Sypher. Garden City, N.Y., 1956.

—. *Matter and Memory.* 1896. Trans. Nancy Margaret Paul and W. Scott Palmer, 1911. New York: Zone, 1998.

—. *Mind-Energy.* 1919. Trans. H. Wildon Carr. New York: 1920.

—. *Time and Free Will.* Orig. *Essai sur les données immédiates de la conscience.* 1889. Trans. F.L. Pogson. New York: 1910.

Blake, William. *The Complete Poetry and Prose of William Blake.* Ed. David V. Erdman. Rev. ed. Berkeley: University of California Press, 1982.

Bowler, Peter. *Reconciling Science and Religion: The Debate in Early-Twentieth Century Britain.* Chicago: University of Chicago Press, 2001.

Darwin, Charles. *On the Origin of Species.* 1859. Ed. J.W. Burrow. Harmondsworth: Penguin, 1968.

Deleuze, Gilles. *Bergsonism.* 1966. Trans. Hugh Tomlinson and Barbara Habberjam. New York: Zone, 1991.

Frye, Northrop. *The Secular Scripture: A Study of the Structure of Romance.* Cambridge, Mass.: Harvard University Press, 1976.

Guerlac, Suzanne. *Literary Polemics: Bataille, Sartre, Valéry, Breton.* Stanford: Stanford Univ. Press, 1997.

Hulme, T.E. *Speculations: Essays on Humanism and the Philosophy of Art.* 1924. London: Kegan Paul, 1936.

Lovejoy, Arthur. *The Great Chain of Being: A Study of the History of an Idea.* Cambridge, Mass.: Harvard University Press, 1936.

Milton, John. *Complete Poems and Major Prose.* Ed. Merritt Y. Hughes. Indianapolis: Bobbs-Mcrrill, 1957.

Morgan, C. Lloyd. *Emergent Evolution.* New York: Henry Holt, 1923.

Schwartz, Sanford. "Paradise Reframed: Lewis, Bergson, and Changing Times on Perelandra," *Christianity and Literature* 51 (2002) 569-602.

—. "Cosmic Anthropology: Race and Reason in *Out of the Silent Planet*," *Christianity and Literature* 52 (2003) 523-556.

Shelley, Percy Bysshe. *Shelley's Poetry and Prose.* Eds. Donald H. Reiman and Neil Fraistat. 2nd ed. New York: W.W. Norton, 2002.

Wells, H. G. *The War of the Worlds: A Critical Text of the 1898 London First Edition.* Ed. Leon Stover. Jefferson, North Carolina: McFarland, 2001.

Whitehead, Alfred North. *Science and the Modern World.* New York: Macmillan, 1925.

—. *Process and Reality.* New York: Macmillan, 1929.

Part IV

MYTHS RETOLD:
THE DISCARDED IMAGE
&
TILL WE HAVE FACES

> But in reading great literature I become a thousand men and yet remain myself. Like the night sky in the Greek poem, I see with a myriad eyes, but it is still I who see. Here, as in worship, in love, in moral action, and in knowing, I transcend myself; and am never more myself than when I do.
>
> *An Experiment in Criticism*

Chapter Thirteen

The Discarded Image:
Patterns of Truth and Fantasy

David Hogg

One of the joys of childhood is the blissful assumption that everyone must share the same view of the world. What the five-year old mind sees and the way it explains what is understood is surely standard for all. Slowly, this assumption is challenged in numerous ways, yet what is important is not *that* such presumption is challenged, but what the response is. As we mature, do we recognize that our world view is not the standard by which all others are judged, but one that is related to others by virtue of questions of universal concern, while differentiated by the answers provided? Appreciating these similarities and differences is, as C.S. Lewis was fond of pointing out, not only possible, but desirable.

To illustrate the point, Lewis draws an analogy in *The Discarded Image: An Introduction to Medieval and Renaissance Literature* with English tourists who travel to the European continent and interact only with other English tourists and delight in the "quaintness" of all that surrounds them. Such an approach to travel will surely bring its own delight, to be sure, but is something not lacking? Similarly, says Lewis, some "prefer not to go beyond the impression, however accidental, which an old work makes on a mind that brings to it a purely modern sensibility and modern conceptions" (ix-x). Drawing out the analogy a bit further, we might say that Lewis sees his work as providing something of a guide or map to the medieval landscape.

In *The Discarded Image* C. S. Lewis provides his students and future audience with a model of reality of the medieval period that emerged from his extensive knowledge of the literature and history of the period. In pursuing this end, Lewis did not disparage the craft of careful exegesis. Rather, he believed he was upholding it and bringing it into sharper relief by framing the already-existing medieval textual tradition in such a way that its details and perspectives would be highlighted for prospective readers. It was in stepping back from an examination of the particulars (the details of Medieval and Renaissance literature) that Lewis believed he could provide a map or atlas, if you like. The aim of *The Discarded Image* is not to analyze a set of specific texts, but it does draw on the particulars of the period and its literature to provide a foundation or conceptual model of the Middle Ages. In this way, Lewis' students would be aided in their comprehension and appreciation of Medieval and Renaissance literature. (It is worth nothing in passing here that Lewis did not see a great disconnect between the Medieval period and the Renaissance ["De Descriptione Temporum" 472] and that in 1954 he was appointed Professor of Medieval and Renaissance English Literature at Magdelene College, Cambridge.) In short, and to use what has for many become the common parlance, Lewis outlines the world view in which Medieval and Renaissance literature was written.

Can a Medieval World View be Identified?

Now there are some who would quibble with the whole notion of world views, raising doubts about identifying and relating context and details in any given period of history, and for such critics of Lewis' *The Discarded Image* there are basically two broad questions. First, can a medieval world view be identified? Which is to ask if a *Zeitgeist* of the period even existed. Second, if a coherent world view of the Middle Ages did exist in some form, has Lewis, in fact, identified it rightly? Taking these questions in order, let us begin by asking if a world view or *Zeitgeist* of the Middle Ages can even be identified.

Among the detractors of the notion of world views is Ian Robinson. *The Discarded Image*, Robinson contends, is problematic because any attempt to supply what he calls a "map" of medieval literary texts is fallacious. Robinson questions the very notion that a "world picture" (as he calls it) was even known, let alone shared, by any original readers. Reading, says Robinson, is an activity that takes place in the present and, as such, reading texts intelligibly is not a matter of trying to re-enter a long-lost mind set (which in his opinion is impossible), but a matter of relating texts to each other (Adey 62-63). As texts are related to one other, the reader can learn what is universal in these texts.

Before turning to consider what Lewis wrote and how it should be understood in light of this criticism offered by Robinson as well as others, it is worth lingering for just a moment to consider the irony of these arguments. It is ironic that what might be described as the "transcendency" of texts—that is, what is perceived to be universal to human knowledge and experience as understood in the present context—can only be identified and appreciated in the "immanency" of the texts. Paradoxically, the understanding of what is universal in a text requires specific expression in particular texts. If Robinson's world view informs his notions of what is universal and, presumably, important in any given text, surely that says more about a commonality between world views than about the inability of attaining to another world view. And if there is something shared between two positions, perhaps there is more opportunity for entering into others' shoes or gaining an appreciable grasp of their *Zeitgeist* than might at first be believed.

The coherence of Robinson's critiques aside, what might be said in defense of Lewis? Perhaps the first place we should go is Lewis' magisterial work, *English Literature in the Sixteenth Century, excluding Drama* (often affectionately dubbed *OHEL*). Here Lewis appears to agree with his critics. As he draws his conclusion to a close, Lewis states, "[t]he picture which I have tried to draw in this introduction is no model of neatness." Even so, Lewis complains that what he has written concerning the context and background of the literature of the sixteenth century is still "too neat, too diagrammatic, for the facts." He then proceeds to warn that we "must beware of schematizing" (*OHEL* 63). How paradoxical! On the one hand Lewis canvasses the backgrounds and contexts of the sixteenth century against which he hopes to display the variegated richness of that period's literature. On the other hand, he seems to deny the very possibility of reconstructing a coherent context in which the literature can be comfortably placed.

Here is a tension with which Lewis was willing to live. The tension lies between explaining the similarities and continuities of a body of literature while maintaining the contrasts and variations that threaten categorization. Lewis' great concern is that we not impose (in this case, on sixteenth-century literature) an external system foreign to the particulars we wish to study. As an example of such a pitfall, Lewis turns to the relationship between humanism and Protestantism. That humanism was a precursor for and integrally related to what we now call Protestantism may help our understanding, but such a view ought not to dictate our understanding. Otherwise, we should be excused if we were to read the greatest of all humanists, Erasmus, as though he were a Protestant. Humanism and its greatest proponent may help explain the rise of Protestantism or the Reformation, but that connection is neither in the order of a one-to-one correspondence, nor is it the sole and sufficient means by which religious upheaval in the sixteenth century is explained (*OHEL* 2).

Once we see that Lewis is willing not to resolve the tension between the need for organization on the one hand and the stubborn particularity of specific texts on the other, reading the rest of what he has to say in *The Discarded Image* makes more sense. Helpful here is a parallel argument in *The Oxford History of English Literature*, where Lewis states that the historian simply cannot "penetrate beyond this apparent confusion and heterogeneity, and to grasp in a single intuition the 'spirit' or 'meaning' of his period" (63). At the same time, however, he admits that "though 'periods' are a mischievous conception they are a methodological necessity" (64). Here are the two sides of the tension. If Lewis distances himself from schema and categorization, he does so without denying the utility and even necessity of such organization. This is surely an important tension to recognize in the face of charges that Lewis was either naive or dismissive.

With this point in mind, we can assert that Lewis neither changes his mind nor is he inconsistent. Instead, he evidences a consistency throughout his works. We might even say that Lewis was consistent about inconsistency. When lecturing and then writing on sixteenth English literature to an informed audience, he would downplay generalizations that might dull or dim literary senses. When lecturing to and writing for beginning undergraduates who were starting their studies with virtually no sense of the landscape, however, Lewis would emphasize the other side of the tension—namely the existence of "the spirit of the age" (*The Discarded Image* 47). The same awareness also appears in Lewis' inaugural lecture at Cambridge, *De Descriptione Temporum* (Lewis, *Essential* 473). Far from being a contradiction in his writings, we can understand this aspect of Lewis' thought as a necessary tension or paradox.

The skill required in navigating this paradox is, to a degree, summarized in the concluding paragraphs of *The Discarded Image*. In the "Epilogue" of that work Lewis states that "[n]o Model is a catalogue of ultimate realities, and none is a mere fantasy" (222). It is for this reason that Lewis can make the concomitant argument that changing models of reality is not a matter of moving from error to truth. Any given model of reality is a reflection of or development from the "spirit of the age" and the "spirit of the age" is, in turn, molded by the answers given to the questions asked. Lewis gives every indication that the relationship between each of these is dynamic and ever changing even if that change is sometimes rather slow. While Lewis does not recognize this pattern as linear, he does identify its driving force in 'the questions we ask'. (TDI, p. 223)

One helpful way to enter the zeitgeist of a work of literature is to bear Northrop Frye's comments in mind in the Massey Lectures broadcast by the

Canadian Broadcasting Company in 1962 and later published under the title, *The Educated Imagination*. Frye reminds his audience that reading literature, and especially literature that has a story or myth, requires imagination and as such is different from discursive writing (70). When we fail to see the myth that underlies a story and is intended to engage our imagination we end up asking all the wrong questions. We ask questions that center around what we are supposed to get out of it or why the author could not have written in a more straightforward and plain fashion. To ask these and other questions of myth-based literature, of which there are many examples in the literature of the Middle Ages and Renaissance, is to fail as a reader or listener of that literature. The point is not to argue with the writer as though the elements of his work are intended as pieces of "disguised information," but to accept his presuppositions so as to appreciate the whole. As Frye somewhat comically notes, even if you are told that the cow jumped over the moon, "you don't react until you've taken in all of what he has to say" (71). Readers enter a work of literature, then, in a spirit of good will, accepting the terms and conditions the text sets forth. In the big picture, Frye sees a grand myth on which all stories find their foundation, and that is the Bible—another helpful understanding for the medieval world view Lewis unpacks for his readers in *The Educated Imagination* (Frye 66).

C. S. Lewis and Northrop Frye certainly agree on the fundamental and foundational function of the Bible in producing some identifiable marks of the spirit of the Middle Ages. Lewis, however, was reticent to permit too much latitude on this point as he made clear in his essay "De Audiendis Poetis." There, Lewis reserves a paragraph to debunk what he calls a theological approach to medieval literature. He contends that some see "all medieval literature primarily, if not exclusively, as exposition of medieval Christian doctrine" (9). Accordingly, the reader is directed, for instance, to Chaucer's need to repent of *Troilus*, a none too doctrinal work! Lewis seems grateful that he does not need to pursue the matter further by concluding that "most modern readers will be in no danger of excessive leniency to it" (9).

While few would quibble with Lewis that we ought not to see all medieval literature primarily as exposition of medieval Christian doctrine, it is curious that the model of reality Lewis delineates in a number of places, but most extensively in *The Discarded Image*, is distinctly theological. The reason the medieval model of reality was so beautiful, so ordered, so sublime was surely because it was a model that resulted from theological reflection. Not always theological reflection in what we might consider the professional sense, but theological reflection in the sense of any grappling with the world and questions of truth in light of the existence and presence of the sovereign, omniscient, omnipotent God for whom order and beauty were believed to be paramount. To be sure, the gamut of medieval literature provides ample evidence of authors and works which are not centered on Christian doctrine, let alone in any way supportive of it. Moreover, it would not be overstating the case to say that many share Lewis' distaste for interpreting Medieval and Renaissance literature in terms of Christian doctrine, as though everything written were an expression of theology proper. Yet, it is highly doubtful that Lewis would deny that what we do is guided by and pervaded by what we believe.

It is for this reason that, while medieval literature is not all doctrinal or reflective of theology proper, virtually all of it is grounded in theology after all. What is more, one's being was not, in the Middle Ages, individualistically conceived, meaning that the attainment of who a person is was not a matter of personal preference with the accent falling on the personal. Rather, for the medieval man, a person was conceived within the context of divine presence. Thus I wonder if Lewis' nervousness about those who read medieval literature as doctrinal was less a concern about the pervasiveness of a fundamentally theological world view and more a concern about imposing modern constructs on ancient texts. In other words, certain works of medieval literature should not be read as illuminating, discussing or interacting with specific doctrines, but perhaps they should be read as related to, whether positively or negatively, a theological view of reality. And so we turn to the second criticism of the ideas presented in *The Discarded Image* and ask, "Has Lewis identified the medieval worldview rightly?"

Has Lewis Identified the Medieval World View Rightly?

The answer to this question has, in different ways, already been broached. The short version to this question is a qualified yes. My intention in responding in the affirmative is to highlight the enduring value of what Lewis achieved. What Lewis did most effectively in *The Discarded Image* was not provide a model of reality that was agreed on in his day nor a model that would be agreed upon in any day. Quarrels and disputes about the particulars of Lewis' model will never go away. It is not, however, the particulars of his model that deserve the most attention, even though I would argue that much of what he wrote was accurate and helpful. The enduring significance of *The Discarded Image* is, rather, that it provides a template or guide for *replicating* what Lewis had done, but not so as to *duplicate* what Lewis had done.

As intimated earlier, the "Epilogue" of *The Discarded Image* may be the most significant section of the book because it distills for the reader the methodology of what Lewis has just shown us. Over some 200 pages Lewis reveals that, even with the Greek and pagan ideas that slipped or were adopted into medieval thought, the controlling world picture out of which the literature of the time grew was theological. This is not to suggest that all those who wrote in the Middle Ages were Christians or that they all thought about the world and reality in the same way. It is to say, however, that the orientation of thought that begins with who a person is before moving to what a person does was grounded in a knowledge of God that was either admitted or lying immediately beneath the surface.

Lewis picks up on this when he describes the symmetry, balance and static beauty of the medieval cosmos. The universe is, as medieval people noted, filled with four categories of objects covering inanimate objects, plants, animals and humans. In our age, it is the description of the inanimate objects that is most puzzling. As Lewis pointed out, medieval writers had a penchant for describing all things, including rocks, as having what Chaucer called a "kindly enclyning" (*Image* 92). Does this mean that such things had some semblance of sentience? No more, replies Lewis, than we imply sentience when we speak of objects obeying the laws of physics. Indeed, it is the modern way of speaking that is more anthropomorphic than the medieval way (*Image* 94). What intrigues us here is not the manner of expression, but the reason for the expression. Why, for example, did Chaucer speak of all objects having this "kindly enclyning"? It was because even the most basic elements of the cosmos find their origin in the spiritual, and more especially in God's creative activity. Again, this does not mean that medieval people believed that inanimate objects yearned or have longings, but that they have been designed as part of the larger cosmos which is itself a reflection of a divine being. Reality is what it is because God is who he is. Granted, it was up to the theologians to explain how sin integrated into this system, but the general idea persisted.

When we turn to the medieval understanding of the planetary system we discover not only more of the same, but even further elaborations. It is sometimes assumed that the stars and planets were believed to be actual beings, possibly angels. While there were doubtless those who believed this, this interpretation of medieval astronomy is not altogether accurate. Lewis took great care to delineate how the medieval *Primum Mobile* was conceived. After discussing Aristotle, Plato and others, Lewis carries on to quote from Albertus Magnus and Thomas Aquinas in order to demonstrate that the medieval concept of intelligences or souls in planetary and stellar bodies was not confused with the intelligence or souls of humans (*Image* 115-116). The reason these bodies move as they do is because the love of God has moved them. Consequently, as medieval star gazers looked out on the night sky, they perceived these objects continually approximating "to Him in the fullest measure of which their nature is capable" (119).

Lewis aptly summarized the medieval view of the universe by contending that the "human imagination has seldom had before it an object so sublimely ordered as the medieval cosmos" (121). In all of this, Lewis was identifying that what really mattered is that what is is more important than what happens. Why something happens or how it got to where it is are significantly inferior questions than what a thing is because what is, is what it is, in relation to God. To put it another way, the ontological value of the created order was paramount. By this, we should not think that what a thing does is unimportant, for when anything does what it does rightly, it demonstrates the enervating love of God. It is the case, however, that the love of God as prime mover was subsidiary to the love of God as creator.

If I may be permitted to take a step away from Lewis and his medieval literature for just a moment, I would suggest that we see the same thing in theological works of the period. Perhaps the best example is Thomas Aquinas' five ways or so-called proofs for the existence of God. Aquinas' list of five arguments is, as he makes quite clear, not proof for the existence of God in the way that we currently think about proofs. They are, more accurately, probings. Aquinas' purpose is to offer an explanation of why things are the way they are. He believes these probings carry force because of his expectation that his readers share, at the very least, that part of his presuppositions or world view that desires to know the ontological framework that undergirds everything else we know and experience. What is significant about this expectation and its expression in the five ways is that Aquinas has never lost an audience, which may say more about commonalities between spirits of the ages then irreconcilable differences or an inability to relate to other perspectives.

When we consider *The Discarded Image* in this light, the answer to whether or not Lewis has properly identified a medieval world view takes on a new hue. Lewis not only identified the nature of the medieval spirit of the age correctly, but in doing so tried to help his contemporary and future audience see that every model of reality exists in the tension between truth and fantasy. Whereas some might like to think that their model is almost completely truth and others, by default, are all but fantasy, Lewis helps us to see that if the emphasis is on the truth even while admitting the presence of fantasy, not only is more gained, but what is gained is far richer.

The richness of medieval literature and texts in general is that they were written less to disseminate information and more to teach or guide or question. In this way, the authors of these texts are trying to prod their readers to ask questions and reflect on their place in the "spirit of the age". Indeed, historically, the greatest fallacy in reading medieval texts has been to read them as though they are solely concerned with imparting information. Thus, the commentaries of, for example, the Venerable Bede have long been considered unimaginative and largely useless because they did nothing innovative. So too with the *Catena Aurea* of Thomas Aquinas because it is little more than a collection of texts on the gospels. The list could go on with the *Glossa Ordinaria* (the standard Bible commentary from the twelfth century) or the *Sentences* of Peter Lombard (the standard systematic theology from the twelfth century). The point is that, when medieval works are read with modern eyes that do not appreciate either the "spirit of the age" or how our own spirit of the age compares with theirs, we fail as readers.

When we do not read for the questions the author is asking, we degenerate into asking what we are supposed to get out of it—as Northrop Frye suggested about myth-based literature. The genius and wonder of these texts (including both literature and theology) - their innovation - is that they are constantly begging the reader to ask questions. And not just questions in general, but questions about why the information is presented as it is and why some details are included and others are not, and so on. It is this sort of writing and reading that has as its primary priority the struggle between ultimate realities and fantasy. This struggle is lost when texts are flattened by reader-response approaches that give precedence to the readers' demands for information rather than to the questions the author is raising. The dynamic between questions and answers and world views that Lewis tried to press upon his audience is quashed and the ability to understand and interpret well is simultaneously dulled. Returning to and ending with Lewis, then, it seems to me that the fundamental difference between Lewis and critics of *The Discarded Image* is best summarized by playing on a title from one of Lewis' other works. While Lewis' critics are sitting on the bench and have put medieval texts and literature in the dock, Lewis was satisfied to place himself in the dock while his medieval predecessors, through their writing, remain on the bench.

WORKS CITED

Adey, Lionel. *C. S. Lewis: Writer, Dreamer and Mentor*. Grand Rapids: Eerdmans Publishing Company, 1998.

Frye, Northrop. *The Educated Imagination*. Toronto: House of Anansi Press, 1993.

Lewis, C. S. "The Abolition of Man." *The Essential C. S. Lewis*. Ed. Lyle W. Dorsett. New York: Macmillan Publishing Company, 1988. 429-466.

—. "De Audiendis Poetis." *Studies in Medieval and Renaissance Literature*. Comp. Walter Hooper. Cambridge: Cambridge University Press, 1998. 1-17.

—. "De Descriptione Temporum." *The Essential C. S. Lewis*. Ed. Lyle W. Dorsett. New York: Macmillan Publishing Company, 1988. 471-481.

—. *The Discarded Image: an Introduction to Medieval and Renaissance Literature*. Cambridge: Cambridge University Press, 2006.

—. *English Literature in the Sixteenth Century, excluding drama*. Oxford: Oxford University Press, 1954.

Chapter Fourteen

The Classical Sub-text to *Till We Have Faces*[1]

Ian C. Storey

C.S. Lewis received a traditional classical education. He learned Latin from his mother, was taught how to "taste" the classics as poetry from his teacher at Malvern, and studied the classical canon with Kirkpatrick at Great Bookham. At Oxford he took first "Mods" and then "Greats", the classical curriculum at that time in Oxford, receiving first-class honours on each occasion. But he did not see himself as a pure "classicist." In fact after in 1922 he was interviewed for a lectureship in Classics at University College in Reading, he wrote to his father, "pure classics is not my line" (*Letters* 1: 594-96). For Lewis classical antiquity was just one part of a larger culture, which he called "Old European, or Old Western, Culture" and which in his own words "had already begun with the *Iliad* and was still almost unimpaired when Waterloo was fought" ("*De Descriptione Temporum*" 11-12). Moreover, Lewis' first preference was for the "cold piercing appeal" of the northern myths, although he does admit the attraction of the classical myths with their "new quality ... something Mediterranean and volcanic, the orgiastic drum-beat" ("*Surprised*" 113).

Although I am concerned principally with Lewis' imaginative fiction in this paper, it would be fair to say that one cannot open any work by Lewis without finding some citation from or allusion to the classical world, one that Lewis expects to means something to the reader. In *The Space Trilogy* Lewis makes the gods of Greco-Roman myth into the governors ("Oyarsae") of the planets (Malacandra represents Mars, Perelandra Venus and so on). Part of the mythical make-up of the Narnia-stories is classical: Tumnus the Faun in *The Lion, the Witch and the Wardrobe*, the strange presence of Bacchus and Silenus in *Prince Caspian*, the Odyssey-like journey in *Voyage of the Dawn Treader*), the descent of the seekers to the world below in *The Silver Chair* with its overtones of both Orpheus and Persephone. One short-story, not sufficiently well-known or appreciated, *Forms of Things Unknown*, depends upon a knowledge of Greek myth for its shock ending to be fully effective. There exists also a fragment of his story, *After Ten Years*, which would have retold the narrative of Menelaos and Helen along the lines of the palinode of Stesichorus (see below) and of Euripides' *Helen*. But the best and fullest re-working of a classical theme is his last novel, *Till We Have Faces*.

Till We Have Faces surprises the reader who comes to it for the first time. This is not the comfortable and familiar Lewis that readers have come to know. Indeed, if one did not know that the novel was by C.S. Lewis, would his authorship be that apparent? For those used to the bright fantasies of Narnia, the dark and brooding landscape of Glome comes as an uneasy surprise; to readers of the "Ransom-trilogy" seeking a further instance of a Christian sub-text beneath a brilliant piece of imaginative fiction, the pre-Christian setting and the pagan gods present a barrier. Lewis himself was disappointed by its reception and by the lack of critical understanding of its central theme. He wrote to Anne Scott in 1960: "You gave me much pleasure by what you said about *Till We Have Faces*, for that book, which I consider far and away the best I have written, has been my one big failure with the critics and with the public" (*Letters* 3: 1160).

He gave the novel the secondary title "a Myth Retold," the myth in this case being the well-known story of Cupid and Psyche, the central panel in Apuleius' marvellous second-century AD novel, *Metamorphoses* or the *Golden Ass*.[2] The tale, told in a bandits' cave to reassure a bride who has been kidnapped on her wedding day, relates the love of the god Cupid, son of Venus, for a beautiful mortal princess, Psyche. Psyche's jealous sisters persuade her to disobey Cupid's injunction not to seek his identity nor to look upon his face. Disaster and separation inevitably take place. Psyche must undergo various trials and tribulations before the lovers are reunited at the end of the story, where Psyche becomes a god and she and Cupid produce a daughter named "Pleasure." Since *Cupido* (Cupid) in Latin means "Love" and *Psyche* in Greek means "Soul," there has always been a suspicion that this story is more than a decorative panel in a picaresque novel, that in some sense it represents in allegorical form the salvation of the Soul through Love, and that it perhaps anticipates the narrator's (Lucius) own salvation in the last book through his initiation into the cult of the goddess Isis. One problem with this interpretation is that Apuleius' deity is *Cupido*, more properly "Lust" or "Desire" rather than "Love" (*Amor*) and the daughter that they produce is "Pleasure." Another is that the humorous presentation of the Olympian gods in the Cupid and Psyche narrative is very much at variance with the earnestness of the final scenes where Lucius becomes an ascetic follower of Isis, to the exclusion of all pleasure in the world.

Lewis first mentions Apuleius' story, which he informally calls "Psyche," in a letter to his friend Arthur Greeves in January 1917 (*Letters* 1: 268-69),[3] but it was in his undergraduate days (1922-23) that he began a number of attempts to write his own version of the story, as a masque or play, or in couplet or ballad form.[4] There the project stalled until the spring of 1955, when with the inspiration and encouragement of Joy Gresham, his wife-to-be, he resumed the narrative, this time in prose. Lewis made four major changes in his account:

1. actually creating the kingdom of Glome, "a little barbarous state on the borders of the Hellenistic world of Greek culture,"[5] the River Shennit, the palace of painted brick, the house of Ungit, and brooding over all the Mountain;

2. telling the story as a first-person narrative by one of the elder sisters (Orual), the popular technique of historical fiction (the narrative told in old age);

3. making her motive not jealousy or envy, but possessive love (*storge*) gone very wrong and very bad – this is clear from his very first attempts in the 1920s;

4. having the palace of Love be visible only to Psyche, although Orual does get a brief glimpse in the moment between night and day.

Lewis did not adopt the familiar approach to myth by writers of historical fiction, that myth is misunderstood history, that behind a marvellous and amazing tale lies sober and explainable fact. This is what Plutarch does in his *Life of Theseus* when he suggests that the man-eating sow killed by Theseus on his journey to Athens was in fact a she-robber nicknamed "the sow" for her foul personal habits (9), or that the palace on Crete contained, not a mysterious labyrinth with a Minotaur at its centre, but rather the royal prison marked with double axes (*labryes*) on the wall and presided over by King Minos' lieutenant, a man named Tauros (16). Similarly Mary Renault, one of the leading writers of historical fiction in the last century, goes out of her way to give rational explanations of myth. Here is her depiction of Theseus' encounter with a centaur:

> At the next turn, I saw a sight that made me nearly jump from the saddle: a beast with four legs and two arms, with a shock-haired boy growing up from its shoulders. So it seemed, at first. Coming near, I saw how the pony grazed head down, and the child sitting up bareback had tucked his brown dirty feet into the shaggy pelt. (*The Bull from the Sea*, p. 58)

For Lewis, Apuleius' version is not misunderstood history, but misunderstood myth; Lewis was writing the myth that Apuleius got wrong.[6] He found nothing of power in Apuleius' myth, nothing (to use a word popular with the Inklings) "numinous."[7] This is not "mythologized" history, but in his own words "a real though unfocused gleam of divine truth falling on human imagination" (*Miracles* 134).

I have argued elsewhere ("Between Myth and Reality") that *Till We Have Faces* is a novel masquerading as historical fiction. Glome is set in an uncertain time and an uncertain place, and there are precious few historical allusions in the text to real persons, places, or events of the ancient world. For instance, we hear about the Trojan War (41), but nothing about the Persian Wars or the Peloponnesian War. Figures of myth are mentioned either by name (Anchises, Oedipus) or indirectly (Agamemnon [65-66]), but the historical figures of Perikles or Alexander seem to be unknown. We are introduced to the local kingdoms of Phars and Essur and Caphad, but only one Greek city, Eleusis (292), is ever named. The closest specific reference we get to the familiar classical world is an allusion to the Persian King (264-65).[8] Only two historical figures from classical antiquity are mentioned by name, Alcibiades (155 - of Bardia, who is "as amorous as Alcibiades") and Socrates (292 – "the conversation which his friends had with Socrates before he drank the hemlock"), and both seem to have become personages of legend rather than of history. What we do get are frequent allusions to Greek literature and to Greek myth rather than to Greek history, appropriate given the work's sub-title. I hope to show in this paper that these allusions are cleverly chosen by Lewis, in that they create a resonance to the larger themes of the novel.[9]

Andromeda, Helen, and Aphrodite

One brief sentence by the Fox about Psyche contains three such allusions: "Prettier than Andromeda, prettier than Helen, prettier than Aphrodite herself" (32). The influential dramatic versions of the story of Andromeda by Sophocles and Euripides have been lost, and we must rely on the account given in Apollodoros' compendium of myth dating from the second or third century AD:

> [Perseus] upon arriving in Ethiopia where Kepheus was king found the king's daughter set out to be devoured by a sea-monster. Kassiopeia, the wife of Kepheus, had engaged in a rivalry over beauty with the Nereids and had boasted to surpass them all. The Nereids had become angry, and Poseidon sharing their anger had sent a flood and a sea-monster against the country. The god Ammon had predicted that the danger would be relieved if Kassiopeia's daughter, Andromeda, were set out as food for the sea-monster, and so Kepheus was forced by the Ethiopians to fasten his daughter to a rock. On seeing her Perseus fell instantly in love and promised Kepheus that he would kill the monster if the king would give the rescued girl as his wife. Oaths were exchanged to this effect, and Perseus withstood the monster, killed it, and released Andromeda. (2.4.3)

Certain parallels are immediately clear: the claim of beauty which rivalled the gods' (the variant version in Hyginus [*fabula* 64] presents Andromeda more plausibly as the one whose beauty eclipsed that of Nereids), the anger of the gods, the disaster brought upon the country, the divine revelation of salvation by a sacrifice, the sacrifice of the beautiful daughter to a Beast (in this case even to the motif of the chaining in an isolated location), and rescue by a winged lover. Orual records that the Fox's words caused an icy shudder; well might she shudder in light of the full myth of Andromeda.

But there is more to the Andromeda myth that also fits into the story of Psyche. Apollodoros continues:

> But Phineus, the brother of Kepheus to whom Andromeda had been previously betrothed, plotted against Perseus. Perseus discovered the plot, and straightway turned Phineus and his fellow-conspirators to stone by showing them the Gorgon's head.[10]

Lewis selected for his story myths that turn on a set of triangular relationships. Rivalry for the love of the maiden is precisely what motivates Orual: "Did you ever remember whose the girl was? She was mine. *Mine*; do you not know what the word means? Mine!" (303). In both cases a third party intervenes in an attempt to prevent the course of true love, in Orual's case with considerable success, and the very masculine nature of Orual makes her a reasonable parallel with Phineus (or Agenor). And finally a female with a horrid face is a good description of both the Gorgon and Orual ("goblin daughter" [33]), and both have a baneful effect on others in their story.

From Andromeda we pass to Helen. Again the comparison is a natural one, since both Psyche and Helen are creatures of unsurpassed beauty, even to the point of assuming divine status. A cluster of allusions early in the novel brings Helen to our attention: the comment of the Fox ("prettier than Helen") noted above, his earlier observation "I could almost believe that there is divine blood in your family. Helen herself, new-hatched, must have looked so" (29),[11] and his subsequent allusion to *Iliad* 3.139ff., "Ah, no wonder ... if the Trojans and Achaeans suffer long woes for such a woman. Terribly does she resemble an undying spirit" (41).[12] But as with Andromeda, the Helen-myth has significant and unpleasant overtones and a comparison to Helen is hardly complimentary. She may in the *Odyssey* (4.560-69) and again in Euripides' tragedy *Orestes* (408 BC) be portrayed as immortal ("an undying spirit"), but in both cases comes immense destruction in her wake. With Helen come associations of great physical beauty, but also of human suffering for that beauty, of contention, infidelity, war, and death. In fact, Aeschylus in his tragedy *Agamemnon* (458 BC) relates the first two syllables of her name (*hele-*) to the Greek word for destruction (*helein*), "she, fittingly called *helenaus* ['destroyer of ships'], *helandros* ['destroyer of men'], *heleptolis* ['destroyer of cities']" – lines 689-90. Helen, Menelaos, and Paris form a triangle of the same sort as Orual-Psyche-the God, or that in the Andromeda-myth, with the difference that the prior relationship is the legitimate one. Also with Helen comes the link with the goddess Aphrodite (Ungit), for it is by her doing that Paris wins Helen; in certain vase paintings her son, Eros, is physically present at the famous Judgement of Paris and in others the first meeting of Paris and Helen is attended by Aphrodite (see Woodford 18-24). The resonances of the Helen-myth and *Till We Have Faces* are not so neat as for the Andromeda-myth, but again the alert reader will, with Orual, react uncomfortably at the comparison between Helen and Psyche.

In a less destructive version of the myth, Helen did not go to Troy with Paris; rather the gods sent a phantom to Troy, while the real Helen was taken to Egypt to await reunion with Menelaos. This theme seems to have been first worked out by Stesichorus, whose poem on Helen is part of the library at Glome (see below), and reused by Euripides in his play *Helen* (412 BC) and then by Lewis himself in *After Ten Years*.[13] Lewis' novel, if completed, would have presented Menelaos with both Helens, the daughter of Zeus who had remained ageless in Egypt and the phantom which had aged along with him, and forced him to choose between the 'phantom' and the 'real' Helen. But which one is the 'real' Helen? Like Helen, Psyche will be separated from her true husband and travel to distant places, and like Helen she will be reunited with him at the end.

The Fox's final comparison (16) takes us to the very first myth mentioned in the novel, "a tale of our Aphrodite":

> Then he deepened and lilted his voice and told how their Aphrodite once fell in love with the prince Anchises while he kept his father's sheep on the slopes of a mountain called Ida. As she came down the grassy slopes towards his shepherd's hut, lions and lynxes and bears and all sorts of beasts came about her fawning like dogs, and all went from her again in pairs to the delights of love. But she dimmed her glory and made herself like a mortal woman and came to Anchises and beguiled him and they went together into his bed. I think the Fox had meant to end here, but the song now had him in its grip, and he went on to tell what followed; how Anchises woke from sleep and saw Aphrodite standing in the door of the hut, not now like a mortal but with the glory. So he knew he had lain with a goddess, and he covered his eyes and shrieked, "Kill me at once."

Lewis' source is clearly the *Homeric Hymn to Aphrodite* (*c.*600 BC); the details of her approach at vv. 68-74 in particular correspond closely:

> So she came to Ida, the mountain of many springs, the mother of beasts, and went directly across the mountain to the hut. With her and fawning upon her came grey wolves and fierce lions, bears and swift leopards ravenous for deer. As she saw them she delighted in her heart and cast desire into their breasts, and all mated together two by two in the shadowy groves.

But the Fox does not exactly tell all that followed. In the original, Anchises does not in fact shriek, "Kill me at once"; rather, he asks Aphrodite not to leave him unmanned (185-90), since sleeping with a goddess may have ruined his sexual potency.

> Her body well clad, the noble goddess stood in the hut — her head reached to the sturdy rafter, while from her cheek shone a divine beauty — and roused Anchises from sleep and spoke and addressed him, "Get up, descendant of Dardanos — why do you slumber in unbroken sleep? — and see whether I look as I did when first I appeared unto you." So she spoke and he responded promptly from his sleep, but when he saw the neck and lovely eyes of Aphrodite, he was afraid and averted his gaze and covered up his fair face in the blanket and begged her, "As soon as I saw you, goddess, I knew you were a deity but you did not tell the truth. Now I beseech you, do not leave me to dwell among mankind as a living invalid, but be merciful, for a man does not enjoy vital vigour who goes to bed with immortal goddesses."
> (*Homeric Hymn to Aphrodite* 172-90)

Nor does the Fox quote Aphrodite's reply, "Take courage, Anchises, and do not be so afraid in your heart. You need not fear any harm from me or the blessed ones, because you are dear to the gods. You will have a dear son [Aeneas] who will be king in Troy ..." (192-96). In fact the story of Anchises and Aphrodite as told in the *Homeric Hymn* is a rare one among Greek myths, for here gods and men interact but the result is not destruction for the mortal (the usual outcome in Greek myth), but rather blessing.

By putting this story so early in the narrative, Lewis sets a sub-text for the novel that in this case also an encounter with Love (Ungit and her son) will not end in disaster, as one might naturally expect, but in glorious happiness.[14] In the original version of the story by Apuleius, Cupid and Psyche produce a child called "Pleasure"; in the *Homeric Hymn* Aphrodite and Anchises will produce a human hero, king in Troy and in later versions ancestor of Rome. Just as the myth of Anchises will culminate in a revelation of glory (171-75), so too Lewis' novel will reach a climax of revelation: Psyche has gone "to fetch the beauty that will make Ungit [Aphrodite] beautiful" and is herself revealed as "a goddess indeed" (317). Thus the reader who knows the story will realize that Love will not show a destructive aspect, but a benevolent one, that the ultimate outcome is going to be a revelation of divine (and mortal) beauty: "Goddess? I had never seen a real woman before" (317).

Aristotle, Sappho, and the library at Glome

Certain clusters of literary references also show a similar sort of resonance. Early in the story Orual admits that the Fox "was ashamed of loving poetry" and quotes three of his favourites (16-17):

> I had to work much at my reading and writing and what he called philosophy in order to get a poem out of him. But thus, little by little, he taught me many. *Virtue, sought by man with travail and toil* was the one he praised most, but I was never deceived by that. The real lilt came into his voice and the real brightness into his eyes when we were off into *Take me to the apple-laden land* or
> > *The Moon's gone down, but*
> > *Alone I lie.*
>
> He always sang that one very tenderly and as if he pitied me for something.

The first of the Fox's songs ("Virtue, sought by man with travail and toil") was identified by Schakel (186) with a passage from Simonides (late 6th/early 5th c. BC):

> There is a tale that Virtue dwells on unclimbable rocks and close to the gods tends a holy place; she may not be seen by the eyes of all mortals, but only by him on whom distressing sweat comes from within, the one who reaches the peak of manliness. (Campbell III fr. 579)

And in earlier versions of this paper I suggested another possibility: three lines from Hesiod (*Works and Days* 287-89 – early 7th c. BC), "vice may be had in abundance without trouble; the way is smooth and her dwelling-place is near. But before virtue the gods have set toil," cited by Plato on a number of occasions (*Republic* 364cd, *Protagoras* 340d, *Laws* 718e). But it has been pointed out to me that the allusion must be to a poem by Aristotle (4th c. BC), which we know was sung every day at his school, the Lyceum: "Virtue, thou whom men with toil / seek as their most precious spoil" – this is the opening of Lewis' own translation of the poem, "After Aristotle," published in the *Oxford Magazine* in 1956.[15] Orual is thus contrasting a poem sung on a solemn and serious occasion with the more romantic ones that the Fox really prefers.

The first of these ("take me to the apple-laden land") will be discussed below, as I suggest it comes from a classical source that was very dear to Lewis, while the other ("The Moon's gone down, but / Alone I lie") comes from a fragment of Sappho (fr. 168B): "The moon has gone down, the Pleiades are setting; it's midnight, the hour is passing, and I sleep alone." This presents some interesting resonances between Sappho and Orual. Both are women with a masculine aspect — Orual who can fight like a man, leads her own troops into battle, whose voice is "deep as a man's" (237), and Sappho described in one telling passage by Horace (*Epistles* 1.19.28) as "mascula Sappho." Both have a deep and intense love for a younger female; and both turn to writing to exorcise their demons. Sappho's most famous poem (31), begins "that man seems to me to rival the gods," and is another example of a triangular romantic relationship. *Her* girl is talking to *that* man while all Sappho can do is look on. And both "sleep alone" — there is no room for two on Orual's throne (221), nor, it seems, in her bed.

The other significant cluster of literary allusions comes in the inventory of the palace library at Glome (241). Orual proudly claims "eighteen works in all." Eight individual works are described. Most can be identified, and some display the same sort of resonance that I have outlined above. The reader will notice that Orual does not know the titles of the works, only what they are about:

(1) "Homer's poetry about Troy, imperfect, coming down to the place where he brings in Patroclus weeping." This scene occurs at Homer *Iliad* 16.2-3; the palace library thus had the first fifteen books of the *Iliad*.

(2) "Two tragedies of Euripides, one about Andromeda ...." The parallels between *Till We Have Faces* and the story of Andromeda have been set out above. This is an appropriate tragedy for the library of Glome, not just for the echoes between the myth and the novel, nor for the setting in a strange and distant land, but also because it has a happy ending. It is also a very nice touch that Glome possessed Euripides' *Andromeda*, while we do not.

(3) "... and another where Dionysus says the prologue and the chorus is the wild women." This is clearly *Bacchae* (produced after Euripides' death in 407 BC), and it makes a nice pair with *Andromeda*. In *Bacchae* a god appears in disguise to test a human, and the divine and mortal worlds interact with devastating repercussions. A human (Pentheus) is tested and is found wanting, and his destruction (like that of Psyche) comes through the hands of his family. In a letter to Arthur Greeves (3 February 1920) he tells of re-reading the play, "how quickly the terrible story happens ... when mortal wisdom met immortal passion" (*Letters* 1: 473).

(4) I suspect that the "useful book (without metre [i.e., in prose]) about the breeding and drenching of horses and cattle, the worming of dogs, and such matters" is a fusion of the minor works of Xenophon (*On Horsemanship, On Hunting, On Household Management*).

(5) "Some of the conversations of Socrates" could be either the dialogues of Plato, which could fairly be called "the conversations of Socrates," or Xenophon's *Memorabilia* ("Reminiscences [of Socrates]"). The former seems rather more likely in view of Orual's later knowledge of and quotation from Plato's *Phaedo* (292). Lewis was immensely influenced by Plato; in particular Plato's emphasis on the antithesis between the real and the temporal world and his theme of Love in *Symposium* seem appropriate here. It would be nice to think that the palace library included *Symposium* or *Phaedrus*, both of which are concerned largely with the goddess of Love and her son.

(6) The "poem in honour of Helen by Hesias Stesichorus," is particularly interesting, not merely because of the appropriateness of the Helen-myth (beauty, Love, the gods), but because Stesichorus is famous for his *Palinode* ("Recantation") about Helen. The story occurs in a number of

ancient sources; the following is the account in Plato (*Phaedrus* 243a):

For those who have erred in their version of a myth there exists an ancient means of purification. Homer [traditionally blind] did not know of this, but Stesichorus did. When he lost his eyesight through his slander of Helen, unlike Homer, he did know the reason; being a man of the Muses he recognized the cause and wrote as follows:

This story is not true / you did not board the well-benched ships / nor did you ever get to Troy

and when he had finished the *Palinode*, as it is called, he immediately regained his sight.

The second part of *Till We Have Faces* can fairly be described as Orual's "Palinode" — "I must unroll my book again. It would be better to re-write it from the beginning" (263), since there she puts things right with the gods and will be rewarded with a change in health — "You also are Psyche" (319). That Stesichorus' famous recantation about Helen was in the palace library is entirely appropriate and a hint of what will happen to our author.

(7) "A book of Heraclitus" is presumably his one attested work *peri physeos* ("On Nature").

(8) The "very long hard book (without metre) which begins *All men by nature desire knowledge*" is Aristotle's *Metaphysics*. Knowledge is what *Till We Have Faces* is all about: knowledge about the gods, about men, about herself. What, wonders Orual, thinking back to her glimpse of Psyche's palace, "is the use of a sign which is itself only another riddle?" (142). "Why must holy places be dark places?" (259). "I know now, Lord, ... you yourself are the answer" (319).

In light of the overall story, then, the presence of certain of these works in the palace library at Glome is entirely appropriate (Euripides' *Andromeda*, *Bacchae*, Stesichorus' *Palinode* in particular). It seems that Orual has unconsciously been collecting works about the nature of the universe and about the interaction between gods and men, perhaps to illuminate the holy and dark places that concern her so much.

A Source for "Maia"

My final classical reference is "Maia," the name that Psyche uses for Orual, "the old baby's name that the Fox had taught her" (75). It is used repeatedly by Psyche in the crucial scenes between the sisters: the encounter in the tower on the night before Psyche is "sacrificed" (77-84); their first meeting on the mountain (111-38); and the second meeting that leads to disaster (166-74). And it is used again in the glorious reunion, where Orual calls Psyche "goddess," to which Psyche replies with the old endearment from childhood, "But Maia, dear Maia, you must stand up" (316-17). "Maia" is a Greek term of address to an older woman, with the overtone of "nanny" or "nurse," but it can be the child's cry of "Mummy" (as at Euripides' *Alcestis* 393) and in one striking passage (Aeschylus *Libation-Bearers* 45) the chorus appeal not to "Mother," but to "Mummy Earth" (*Maia Gaia*). In view of the death of Psyche's mother at her birth and Orual's status as her virtual mother, it is a natural name for Orual and carries the irony that Orual will herself never be a mother. One of Orual's last recorded thoughts is her regret that she had not brought her nephew and heir to her "and learned to love him" (319).

But some have seen more here. Several critics detect in the "baby-name" a reference to *Maya*, the Hindu concept of "the illusion into which humans are brought by living in the material world" (Kuteeva 280), that sets off an essential antithesis between Orual's (and the Fox's) reliance on illusion and the reality that is foretold at the end of the novel.[16] Psyche is rooted in the reality of the true world, while Orual relies on what at the end of the novel is described as "the babble that we think we mean" (305). Myers sees in "Maia" an allusion to Maia, the mother of Hermes, "one of the lesser goddesses who became syncretized with the Great Mother" (*C.S. Lewis in Context* 197). Thus when Orual cries, "Lord, I am become Ungit" [287], the lesser Maia has become part of the greater whole. Schakel accepts the allusion to Maia, the mother of Hermes, but takes the name as meaning "simply 'mother' or 'nurse'" (188 n.4), while Howard elaborates on what he sees as the etymology of Maia "from the root *mag*, signifying growth or increase" (172-73). Thus it becomes an ironic name for Orual who is mother only of herself, "the thing she is big with, namely herself."

These are all ingenious interpretations, but I think the source of "Maia" is rather less complicated. I suggest that Lewis has in mind a powerful scene in Euripides' tragedy *Hippolytos* (428 BC), between Phaedra, wife of Theseus and inspired by Love with a fatal passion for her step-son, Hippolytos, and her old nurse whom she calls "Maia" (243, 311). This play was one that Lewis knew well and which played a considerable role in his return to Christianity in the 1920s. In *Surprised by Joy*, written shortly before *Till We Have Faces*, he relates how re-reading the *Hippolytos* brought him "once more into the land of longing," how Joy had returned with all its force (171-72), and there is a reference to the themes of Hippolytos in a letter of 1954 (*Letters* 3: 423-24). The dramatic and highly emotional scenes between Phaidra and her "*maia*," a younger woman with her older nurse, I suggest, lie behind the picture of Orual and Psyche in Lewis' novel. That the Fox taught Psyche the name "Maia" suggests that we should be looking for a Greek source.

Hippolytos too is a classical text that resonates with *Till We Have Faces*. It is a drama very much about the goddess of Love; in fact she opens the play. We see both her and her rival, Artemis the goddess of Chastity, interfere openly in the lives of humans with the predictable destruction that usually ensues. An older woman (nurse) interferes with the life of the younger Phaedra, just as Orual does in Psyche's, with good intent and fatal results. Their close relationship is the reason why Phaidra reveals the source of her trouble (325ff.), as it is the close relationship between Psyche and her "*maia*" that provides her greatest hurdle (315):

> Oh, my own child, my only love. Come back. Come back. Back to the old world where we were happy together. Come back to Maia.

The first of the Fox's favourite songs is *Take me to the apple-laden land* (17), a fair translation of the opening line (*Hippolytos* 743) of the antistrophe in the great chorus of escape, which follows the revelation of Phaidra's love to her step-son (literally, "I would hurry to the apple-bearing shore of the Hesperides"). In his autobiography, Lewis comments significantly on his re-reading of *Hippolytos*: "and in one chorus ... I was off again into the land of longing" (*Surprised by Joy* 217). Also *Hippolytos*, like *Till We Have Faces*, turns on a triangle of relationships, in this case Theseus, Phaidra, and Hippolytos. It seems that Euripides' *Hippolytos* was as important to the Fox as it was to Lewis.

I have selected certain of the major myths — Helen, Andromeda, Aphrodite, Hippolytos — that operate beneath the text of Lewis' novel, but there are others that might be investigated along the same lines. We get brief mentions of Antigone and Oedipus, Iphigeneia and Agamemnon, Orpheus, Odysseus, and Hermes, and each of these could be tied into the themes of Lewis' novel. Hermes is cited for his cleverness (150), but he is also the god who crosses the border between life and death, and would set off a particular resonance with the final scenes of the novel. Orpheus (237), like Psyche and Orual, went on a quest motivated by love to the underworld. Montgomery (63) explores the intriguing echoes of the quest of Orpheus in the mission of the children to the Underland in *The Silver Chair*. What is clear is that Lewis has used his classical allusions with great subtlety; he has selected myths that will resonate and serve as sub-texts for his own story, especially the tale of Aphrodite and Anchises, the first classical allusion in the novel, and one that will hint at the ultimate happy resolution.

NOTES

1. This paper appeared originally in a somewhat abbreviated form in *The Chronicle of the Oxford C.S. Lewis Society* 4.2 (2007): 5-20. I thank the co-editors of *The Chronicle*, Judith Tonning and Brendan Wolfe, for their permission to reprint that piece in an expanded form, and for their invaluable assistance, both in arranging my talk to the Oxford C.S. Lewis Society in October 2006 and in seeing the article through to print. I also thank both the audience at that talk for some very useful contributions and those who attended my briefer presentation of this topic at the C.S. Lewis conference at the Southeastern Baptist Theological Seminary in October 2007.

2. Lewis' own summary of Apuleius' story of Cupid and Psyche may be found in Hooper *Companion* 244-45.

3. Hooper (*Letters* 1: 268) points out that Lewis read the story in the Temple Classics edition of 1903, which included only the narrative of Cupid and Psyche.

4. These are quotations from the entries in his diary (*All My Road*) for 23 November 1922 and 9 September 1923. Some of the couplets are found in Hooper *Companion* 246-47.

5. From a crucial letter of 10 February 1957 to Clyde Kilby (*Letters* 3: 830-31), in which Lewis outlines the four levels of meaning that he, as the author, finds in his novel.

6. Letter to Katherine Farrer (2 April 1955) in *Letters* 3: 589-90.

7. Lewis will have got this term from R. Otto, *The Idea of the Holy* (published in English in 1923). See Myers, *Bareface* 168-74.

8. This must be the Great King and not a "ruler with headquarters at Byzantium" (so Myers *Context* 194). For the anachronism here see Storey 158-59.

9. Schakel has done some preliminary work along these lines: the "author expects a reader to recognize such explicit allusions and to draw relevant

parts of their original contexts into the story" (16). He comments briefly on Helen (16) and on Iphigeneia and Antigone (36-37), and shows also how certain biblical resonances operate in the same way. Myers likewise explores how Helen and Troy are used in the larger context of the story (*Bareface* 24, 38).

10. Hyginus 64 names the rival as Agenor and does not identify him as Andromeda's uncle. Hyginus, active at Rome in the late first century BC, wrote *Fabulae* ("Stories"), brief sketches of Greek myths, often based on dramas of the classical period.

11. The business about "Helen, new-hatched" has to do with the myth that Helen was born from an egg after Zeus seduced her mother, Leda, in the form of a swan. A 4th-c. BC Campanian vase shows a magnificently self-aware and "new-hatched" Helen – see Woodford 12.

12. In Homer the old men comment, "It is not without reason that the Trojans and well-greaved Greeks have endured such woes for so long a time over such a woman."

13. The fragment of *After Ten Years* is published in *The Dark Tower and other stories* 133-54, with a very useful afterword by R.L. Green and A. Fowler (155-58).

14. Schakel 17-18 takes the parallel further, finding in the Fox's next words, "It's only lies of poets, lies of poets, child," a significant undermining of the truth, "the first of many but mysterious occurrences which lie outside the domain of the Fox's understanding."

15. I owe this observation to Mark Edwards and Richard Jeffrey at a meeting of the Oxford University C.S. Lewis Society (October 2006). The poem is cited by Athenaeus 696 and Diogenes Laertius 5.7. Lewis mentions the poem at *Letters* 3: 696-97; his translation appears also in *Poems* 80-81.

16. See, for example, Hart 38; Sammons 133; Timmermann 505.

WORKS CITED

Hart, D. A. *Through the Open Door: a new look at C.S. Lewis*. University, AL: University of Alabama Press, 1984.

Hooper, Walter. *C.S. Lewis: a companion & guide*. London: HarperCollins, 1996.

Howard, Thomas. *The Achievement of C.S. Lewis*. San Francisco: H. Shaw, 1980.

Lewis, C. S. *All My Road Before Me*. Ed. Walter Hooper. London: HarperCollins, 1991.

—. *Collected Letters*. Vol. 1. Ed. Walter Hooper. London: HarperCollins, 2000.

—. *Collected Letters*. Vol. 3. Ed. Walter Hooper. London: HarperCollins, 2006.

—. *The Dark Tower and other stories*. Ed. Walter Hooper. London: Collins, 1977.

—. *Miracles*. New York: Macmillan, 1960.

—. *Poems*. London: Bles, 1964.

—. *Surprised by Joy*. London: Fontana, 1959.

—. *Till We Have Faces*. London: Collins, 1979.

Montgomery, P. Andrew. "Classical Literature", in Thomas L. Martin (ed.), *Reading the Classics with C.S. Lewis*. Grand Rapids MI: Baker Academic, 2000. 52-71.

Myers, Doris T. *Bareface: a Guide to C.S. Lewis's Last Novel*. Columbia, MO: University of Missouri Press, 2004.

—. *C.S. Lewis in Context*. Kent, OH: Kent State University Press, 1994.

Renault, Mary. *The Bull from the Sea*. London: Longmans, 1962.

Sammons, M. "The God Within: Reason and its Riddle in C.S. Lewis' *Till We Have Faces*." *Christian Scholar's Review* 6 (1976): 127-39.

Schakel, Peter J. *Reason and Imagination in C.S. Lewis: A Study of Till We Have Faces*. Grand Rapids, MI: Eerdmans, 1984.

Storey, I. C. "Between Myth and Reality: C.S. Lewis's *Till We Have Faces* as Historical Fiction." *Celebratio: Thirtieth Anniversary Essays at Trent University*. Ed. J. P. Bews *et al.* Peterborough, ON: Trent University, 1998. 154-64.

Timmermann, J. H. "The Epistemology of C.S. Lewis: Reason and Belief in C.S. Lewis' *Till We Have Faces.*" *Religion in Life* 46 (1977): 497-508.

Woodford, Susan. *The Trojan War in Ancient Art*. Ithaca, NY: Cornell University Press, 1993

Chapter Fifteen

Medieval Models of Loss in *Till We Have Faces*

Stephen Yandell

C. S. Lewis' voracious reading habit built for himself an extraordinary lens through which to view the world. He devoured any poetry, novels, myths, or fairy tales that appealed to his unique combination of literary and spiritual interests. These interests were indeed broad, but perhaps no topic lay more squarely at their center than the relationship of gods and men. He enjoyed finding the subject in any period of literature and was intrigued by every aspect of it, from humanity's initial fall to the varied paths characters took in seeking the divine. It also spoke to him at every stage of his spiritual journey; favorite works he discovered as an atheist, for example, proved just as intriguing to him after a Christian conversion.

This was precisely the driving force behind Lewis' passion for the Cupid and Psyche story. He loved the narrative the first time he encountered it in Lucius Apuleius's *The Golden Ass*, and a desire to tell his own version stayed with him throughout his life, coming to fruition with the publication of *Till We Have Faces* in 1956. The novel's setting is Classical, a pre-Christian country outside Greece, but the heart of the work is distinctly medieval. Lewis wanted to offer the tale from a human perspective, focusing on the reunion of a human soul with a personal God, and he turned to medieval works for inspiration. This came naturally, as it was the literature he loved and knew best, having taught it at both Oxford and Cambridge Universities.

Till We Have Faces often gets overlooked by readers of C. S. Lewis, though, for a variety of reasons. Fans of Lewis' fiction find it unlike anything else he wrote; it is not clearly fantasy, nor easily labeled modern or Classical. Others lament a theology that is odd and difficult. Medieval scholars, meanwhile, find it disconnected from Lewis' literary scholarship, such as *The Allegory of*

Love and *The Discarded Image*. While conceding immediately the first two points—the work's uniqueness and its challenges—I want to make a case here for the novel's clear, well conceived dependence on medieval literature for both its form and content. Few scholars have studied *Till We Have Faces* in terms of medieval literature, which is surprising since the Middle Ages informed almost everything Lewis wrote.

A handful of specific medieval texts served as the foundation of *Till We Have Faces*, and not simply because Lewis knew them well. They provided models of human relationships that no other period of writers had adequately explored. Specifically, Dante's *Divine Comedy* and *The Book of Margery Kempe* both address a kind of loss that intrigued Lewis as a storyteller and lay theologian. They explore ways in which a human relationship might suffer in the wake of one person's movement toward God, leaving the other behind. Although both works contribute to the form and subject matter of Lewis' novel, it is the fourteenth-century poem *Pearl* that offers the most complex and complete model for Lewis. In this work a family relationship is severed, bringing loss at multiple levels: spiritually, physically and emotionally. Understanding Lewis' debt to these three medieval works is crucial for readers hoping to understand the text's most important themes and its challenges.

Apuleius's Cupid and Psyche

We find the earliest version of the pagan myth of Cupid and Psyche in Apuleius's second-century Latin novel *The Golden Ass* (also called the *Metamorphoses* or *Transformations*). The tale of Psyche's reunion with Cupid, a "human soul in quest of salvation through union with the divine" (Kenney, *Golden Ass* xxv), has benefited from centuries of literary, mythological, and psychological interpretation, and the sheer number of retellings since Apuleius's day (his own version was based on a now-lost Greek original) attests to the power of its themes (Kenney, *Cupid* 12). However, "Cupid and Psyche" is secondary to the plot of *The Golden Ass*. It is the longest of a small number of narrative insertions in the work, spanning books four, five, and six, and is told by an old woman simply hoping to pass the time for a captured character.

To build on this core narrative and rewrite Apuleius is an idea Lewis had had "ever since I was an undergraduate and it's always involved writing through the mouth of the elder sister. [. . .] Tho' the version you have read was v.[ery] quickly written, you might say I've been at work on Orual for 35 years" (*Letters 3* 633). Through his editing of three volumes of Lewis' letters,

Walter Hooper chronicles the "long gestation" period of *Till We Have Faces*, arguing that it was most likely conceived with a reading of the original myth over the Christmas holiday in 1916 (*Letters 1* 268). In William Aldington's 1903 translation of Apuleius, Lewis found a new author to love.

Lewis' passion for an author tended to be based on the writer's ability to move him. If an author could handle the topic of God's relationship with humanity skillfully, any stylistic flaws might be overlooked. For example, Lewis held George Macdonald in the highest esteem ("I fancy I have never written a book in which I did not quote from him" *Anthology* 20), but he was also quick to concede Macdonald's faults: "few of his novels are good and none is very good" (*Anthology* 17). Similarly, Lewis found Apuleius's tale of Psyche mesmerizing, despite the Roman author's tendency to show "detestable faults of style" ("High and Low" 271). Nor did poor style in any way deter Lewis from sharing his discovery with Arthur Greeves. In a May 1917 letter he enthusiastically explains, "Apuleius [. . .] wrote the book in which the 'Cupid & Psyche' story occurs. I have found his complete works in the college library and their brooding magic no less than their occasional voluptuousness & ridiculous passages have made me feel that I must get a copy of my own. What lots I shall have to show you when I come down!" (*Letters 1* 304-5).

Psyche's path toward God, as Lewis discovered in his 1917 reading, is marked by a lengthy exile. Her difficult path, coupled with a betrayal by her own family members, spoke poignantly to Lewis in his years as an Oxford student. Continuing to struggle with his mother's death, Lewis the self-proclaimed atheist felt abandoned by God: "I maintained that God did not exist. I was also very angry with God for not existing" (*Joy* 115). At the same time he also found himself coming nearer to God, a situation as absurd as "the mouse's search for the cat" (*Joy* 227). The death of his mother was a devastating physical abandonment, and shortly afterward he discovered emotional abandonment by his father. The strained relationship between Lewis and his father has been adequately treated in Lewis' biographies, but it is worth noting here that for a time Lewis' anxiety impacted his relationship with everyone close to him: "If I woke in the night and did not immediately hear my brother's breathing from the neighboring bed, I often suspected that my father and he had secretly risen while I slept and gone off to America—that I was finally abandoned" (*Joy* 39). Much of the same pain later appeared in the character of Queen Orual. When Lewis turned his pen to creating this protagonist at the end of his life, she came to embody loss on multiple levels.

Lewis' Tale of Orual

Soon after its publication in 1956, Lewis came to understand the difficult reception *Till We Have Faces* would have. As he explained dejectedly to a friend, "it has had had a less favourable reception not only from critics but from most friends than any I ever wrote" (*Letters 3* 829). The book's reception today shows a similar disconnect from his earlier writings. Some readers feel distanced by Lewis' storytelling choices: a pantheon of gods, human sacrifice, an unlikable narrator, and themes couched in ambiguity. Literary critics, however, tend to identify *Till We Have Faces* as the best display of Lewis' maturity as storyteller and theologian. Chad Walsh calls it a "surging breakthrough of an inwardness that Lewis had striven for years to suppress" (178). The novel also allows Lewis to delve into character depths he had not previously attempted. C. N. Manlove goes as far as to argue that *Till We Have Faces* "is his first book to be centrally concerned with a relationship" (189).

Two book-length studies of the work, Peter Schakel's *Reason and Imagination in C. S. Lewis* and Doris Myers's *Bareface*, have been particularly useful in defending the novel's centrality to understanding Lewis. Schakel feels the book "is Lewis' finest imaginative work [. . .], the culmination of efforts Lewis made in a number of works throughout his life to use similar images and imaginative structures to resolve [the] tension [between reason and imagination]" (x). One of Myers's strongest contributions to the scholarship lies in acknowledging its ambitious use of multiple levels of meaning—a book that tells a story which is simultaneously more literal than any other he had told before, and more mythic: "the originality of Lewis' approach is to ignore allegory, to deemphasize the mythic literary tradition, and to treat it as something that could, perhaps did, really happen" (5).

More recently, scholars have pointed to the significant influence Joy Davidman Gresham had on Lewis' development of the novel during 1955 when she read drafts and suggested revisions. Karen Rowe, for example, recognizes Gresham's presence as contributing to a different kind of writing for Lewis; she praises the novel's "portrayal of a woman with various roles and societal pressures forced upon her." She complicates any easy reading of a feminist agenda, however, by making clear that Lewis ultimately argues "the only true solution to finding rest in a restless world is when Orual and Psyche are made one with each other and with the god" (152). All of these scholars have, like Lewis, identified the centrality of humanity's relationship with the divine in the Cupid and Psyche story, not lettering the context of a pre-Christian barbarian country get in the way. The ability of Christian truths to emerge in the storytelling of societies much older than Christ is something Lewis mused throughout his life.

Lewis was equally interested in exploring the kinds of intimacy he found associated with gods and humans. The marriage of Cupid and Psyche suggested for Lewis a kind of closeness found in the "Bride of Christ" imagery invoked in II Corinthians 11:2. Paul describes his having promised the Church "in marriage to one husband, to present you as a chaste virgin to Christ." Similarly, Revelation 21:2 describes the Church as "coming down out of heaven from God, prepared as a bride adorned for her husband." The binding of the Church to Christ in holy union represents a split for an individual from the world, and Psyche's marriage to her husband, taking her away from her initial family, represents a similar loss on three levels: a physical loss (Psyche dies while being offered up as a sacrifice), an emotional loss (Orual's emotional dependence on Psyche is shattered), and a spiritual loss (Psyche's perfection is taken away from Orual).

Dante's Beatrice in the Divine Comedy

Perfection such as Psyche's has long fascinated medieval authors. The medieval poet Dante Aligheiri is arguably Italy's greatest author, and in the early fourteenth century he spent the final decade of his life writing the three-part epic the *Divine Comedy*. 100 cantos narrate the journey taken by Dante, his first-person narrator. First he is led by the roman author Virgil down through the circles of Hell and up the Mountain of Purgatory. At the top of Purgatory, Dante then finds Beatrice, a woman Dante had loved in his childhood and whom Virgil has requested to take over as guide. She accompanies him through the Spheres of Heaven, where he eventually comes before God.

Dante's real-life relationship with Beatrice Portinari mimics couples who were popularized in the literature of the courtly love tradition during the High Middle Ages. Dante had only met the girl a few times, and just as in the courtly tradition, fell in love with her immediately, never married her, but came to love her in a very deep, spiritual sense. Her death at the age of 24 also devastated him. While he endured political exile for the final nineteen years of his life, Dante continued to build in his head the importance of this relationship. Her perfection and grace simply grew, taking on increasingly important spiritual significance. This love is most fully treated in an earlier work, a collection of poems called *La Vita Nuova* (*New Life*). Familiarity with the *Divine Comedy* is something Lewis found essential for anyone hoping to understand medieval literature. After classical works, which top Lewis' list for works any medieval student should know, he says, "and after that the two things to know really well are the Divine Comedy and the Romance of the Rose. The student who has really digested these [. . .] has the game in his hands" (*Letters 2* 142).

The *Divine Comedy* models a key aspect of *Till We Have Faces*'s central theme: death separates two humans bound in a deep, spiritual love. Dante's work also serves as a model for important forms in the novel: a first-person narrator describing his personal spiritual journey, and the use of spiritual guides as purveyors of truth. The first of these, Dante's love for Beatrice, is revealed in Orual's passionate, obsessive love for her sister Psyche. Just as Beatrice represents perfection in every sense for Dante (physically, emotionally, spiritually), so does Psyche for Orual, and for all of Glome. Even as an undergraduate Lewis felt inspired by the depth of Dante's love; Beatrice represents for the Italian poet a longing for something both earthly and spiritual. Lewis' own encounters with *sehnsucht* (longing, joy, and pain) made the relationship quite relatable for him. In a diary entry of 1922 he writes of his admiration for the focus and intensity displayed by Dante, arguing that anyone in love "might write tolerable songs, but it took a man of one affair to write the Divine Comedy" (125-6). Dante's depiction of Beatrice also remains emblematic in literature for not merely love, but also a search for perfection.

Perhaps no member of the Inklings was better able to appreciate such metaphysical forms of love than Charles Williams, the London editor who joined the writing group in the early 1940s. After marrying the woman he adored, re-named "Michal" after King David's wife, Williams grew increasingly fascinated with Dante and Beatrice and made their love the subject of his scholarly work *The Figure of Beatrice*. In it he argues that Beatrice "seems to [Dante] something like perfection—though, of course, he knows quite well that she is not" (35). For Dante, Beatrice is both personal and celestial: "What Dante sees is the glory of Beatrice as she is 'in heaven'—that is, as God chose her, unfallen, original; or (if better) redeemed; but at least, either way, celestial. [. . .] The high and glorious Beatricean quality of Beatrice is the hope of the blessed" (27). Williams understands that Beatrice's larger-than-life character transcends gender ("her high threats produce a philosophical demonstration of the nobility of man's nature" 72), and even transcends any single form of relationship: "Beatrice is not only a type of the love-relationship; she is a type of every relationship" (190).

Lewis was equally fascinated by the transcendence of Beatrice and describes the natural, infectious beauty of Psyche with language that echoes

Dante: "It was beauty that did not astonish you till afterwards when you had gone out of sight of her and reflected on it. [. . .] She made beauty all round her. When she trod on mud, the mud was beautiful; when she ran in the rain, the rain was silver" (22). Similarly, the love Psyche inspires from others also transcends gender. As her infatuation with Psyche grows, Orual admits that "I wanted to be a wife so that I could have been her real mother. I wanted to be a boy so that she could be in love with me. I wanted her to be my full sister instead of my half sister. I wanted her to be a slave so that I could set her free and make her rich" (23). Just as Dante's personal exile takes his loss of love (through death) to a heightened level, so does Orual eventually realize that she has spent her final years in exile. Cupid's cryptic words make sense only at the end of her life: "Now Psyche goes into exile. Now she must hunger and thirst and tread hard roads. [. . .] You also shall be Psyche" (173-4).

Dante's love for Beatrice represented for Lewis both a natural love for the divine and for perfection, and also for a more dangerous, obsessive love for secular, temporal things. Orual's love for Psyche is equally complex. Despite the growing selfishness that Orual displays, the natural love she displays for her sister cannot be dismissed. As Gilbert Meilaender reminds us in *The Taste for the Other*, "Orual's love for Psyche and others is not mere selfishness. It is natural affection at its best. [. . .] Yet there is something in that love that cannot co-exist with the gods who sit in judgment upon Orual. Almost inevitably she finds herself thinking of the gods as her great rival" (174).

Margery Kempe's Book

A second key medieval work that readers of *Till We Have Faces* should be familiar with is *The Book of Margery Kempe*. This spiritual autobiography chronicles the remarkable life of a mayor's daughter who experienced visions of Jesus. Margery grew up in the English city of Bishop's Lynn, northwest of Norwich, in the late fourteenth century. She married John Kempe early in life and at age twenty gave birth to the first of fourteen children. Divine revelations changed her life, but because she could not read or write, she had to dictate her life story to two scribes in her later years in order for these truths to be remembered. She refers to herself as "the creature" throughout her text and opens her book with an account of the eight-month mental breakdown that afflicted her immediately after her first child's birth. Images of "devils opening their mouths all alight with burning flames of fire," she explains, tormented her until the sudden appearance of Christ restored her fully to health (41).

The miracle of Christ speaking to Margery brought about not only her conversion, but also an ongoing devotion that manifested itself in peculiar ways. She is best known today not for the intimacy she sought in her relationship with Christ, but for weeping loudly (and publicly) at the thought of Christ's crucifixion, fasting as frequently as possible, and trying desperately to abstain from sex with her husband so that she could remain pure for Christ. These features had been popularized by many female mystics in the late Middle Ages, but were taken by Margery to an unprecedented extreme. They were also a source of confusion, anger, and embarrassment for her husband, creating stress throughout the marriage.

Christ continued to speak to Margery throughout her life, and although the validity of her visions has been debated, as well as the degree to which she was perhaps consciously creating the role of mystic for herself, the strength of her voice remains her defining characteristic. The sincere passion with which she devoted herself to Christ has not been challenged, and the single remaining manuscript we have of her life story is a remarkable testimony of a woman defying many social pressures and demanding to define herself in her own words. Her account is the earliest autobiography surviving in English, and its insights into late medieval life for a middle-class woman are unparalleled among historical documents.

The discovery of Margery Kempe's text in the twentieth century is as remarkable a story as her life. Very few medieval manuscripts that were previously unknown have come to light after 1900, and when Hope Emily Allen, a Robert Rolle scholar, stumbled upon the single surviving copy of Margery's *Book* in 1934 while doing research in a Lancashire library, scholars were shocked. This same year Lewis was completing work on *The Allegory of Love* (later published in 1936), and although the male-dominated field of medieval literature took years to consider the text seriously, the discovery certainly would have piqued Lewis' interest. Even with only a passing knowledge of it—and it does not seem important enough for him to discuss it in his literary scholarship or letters—Lewis would have enjoyed finding the same central theme in Margery that was beginning to take shape in his idea for the story of Psyche's sister: the turmoil created when one half of a close relationship chooses to pursue God over everything else. Both texts allow strong female protagonists to relate personal life stories at the end of their lives and in their own voices; and simply on a narrative level *Till We have Faces* appears to owe its two-part division to Margery's account. In each text the first part makes up approximately 85 percent of the entire work, and the second part makes up 15 percent.

Margery expresses passion for Christ with an intimacy that Psyche also expresses for the god of the Mountain. As Orual explains of her sister, "Psyche [. . .] was half in love with the Mountain. She made herself stories about it. 'When I'm big,' she said, 'I will be a great, great queen, married to the greatest king of all, and he will build me a castle of gold and amber up there on the very top'" (23). Similarly, Margery describes Jesus as the perfect husband: "Then our Lord said in her mind, 'I thank you, daughter, that you would be willing to suffer death for my love [. . .]. I shall never be angry with you, but I shall love you without end. Though all the world be against you, don't be afraid, for they cannot understand you" (65). Later, Christ explains to her, "We are united together without end. To me you are a love unlike any other, daughter, and therefore I promise you that you shall have a singular grace in heaven, daughter. [. . .] I shall say to you, my own blessed spouse, 'Welcome to me, with every kind of joy and gladness, here to dwell with me in joy and bliss, which no eye may see, nor ear hear, nor tongue tell, nor heart think, that I have ordained for you" (86, 88).

At no point does Margery seek to dissolve her marriage, but her movement emotionally away from her husband becomes increasingly stressful for John, understandably. We see the same frustration in Orual having to contend with a sister who places God—a new intimate companion—before herself. Remaining in her marriage becomes the central conflict of Margery's story; she is unsure how to deal with the relationship with her husband while being wholly in love with Christ. Believing that any sexual contact was sinful, she spent much of her life trying to convince her husband to break off sexual relations with her. At one point she even makes an agreement with John that she will pay off his debts and eat meals with him again on Fridays if he will no longer demand conjugal relations (60). His lack of understanding for her divine love frustrates her, though. Just as Psyche is frustrated with Orual's inability to recognize her marriage to Cupid, Margery describes an evening when her husband reveals how little he understands her love for God:

> It happened one Friday, Midsummer Eve [1413], in very hot weather—as this creature [Margery herself] was coming from York [. . .] that her husband asked his wife this question: "Margery, if there came a man with a sword who would strike off my head unless I made love with you as I used to before, tell me on your conscience—for you say you will not lie—whether you would allow my head to be cut off, or else allow me to make love with you again, as I did at one time?" "Alas, sir," she said, "why are you raising this matter, when we have been chaste for these past eight weeks? [. . .] Truly I would rather see you being killed, than that we should turn back to our uncleanness." (58)

Unlike Lewis' novel, though, Margery's account comes to no answer. The spiritual rift between Margery and her husband remains unresolved, and no reunion can take place between the humans.

When Lewis turned to writing his novel in the 1950s this medieval work clearly would have suggested itself in terms of its central theme, its narrator, and its two-part division, but it perhaps also posed a challenge for an author wanting to tackle a dilemma which has plagued human relationships literally for centuries. Lewis concedes the challenge of providing such an answer while describing his new novel's main concern: "It is the story of every nice, affectionate agnostic whose dearest one suddenly gets 'religion', or even every luke warm Christian whose dearest gets a Vocation. Never, I think, treated sympathetically by a Christian writer before" (*Letters 3* 590).

Pearl

The same conflict lies at the heart of *Pearl*, a poem Lewis knew well; he lectured on it and mentions it several times in his literary research, including *The Allegory of Love* (252, 286) and in literary essays such as "*De Audiendis Poetis*" (7) and "The Genesis of a Medieval Book" (18). *Pearl* comes to us in a single surviving manuscript, Cotton Nero A.x, Art. 3 in the British Library, and it includes, among other things, three other poems believed to be by the same author: *Sir Gawain and the Green Knight*, *Cleanness*, and *Patience*. Its author remains anonymous, and we refer to him alternately as the *Pearl*-poet or the *Gawain*-poet. Scholars continue to speculate on the degree of training he must have had in ecclesiastical, legal, and other matters, but ultimately they agree on a few conclusions: the author was a contemporary of Chaucer's and wrote not in London, but the north-west midlands of England. *Pearl* has also been called the most skillful example of poetry from the late fourteenth century's Alliterative Revival. During this period poets purposefully mimicked older poetic forms like Anglo-Saxon verse which used a great deal of alliteration, a repetition of initial consonant sounds in words.

Through 101 stanzas, grouped into twenty sections, the poem tells a remarkably compelling story. It opens with the narrator, a jeweler by trade, lamenting his loss of an expensive, small pearl. He searches in a garden and eventually lays down to sleep on a small mound where he might have dropped it. We soon realize that the story is not merely that of a jeweler and a lost pearl, but also a father who has lost his two-year-old daughter in death, and it is on her grave that he has come to mourn. The dreamer awakes in an Eden-like garden, a scene which Lewis found throughout medieval poetry, especially in dream visions such as *Pearl* and Chaucer's *Book of the Duchess*. Lewis had borrowed this same imagery in writing the opening of *The Silver Chair*, when Jill arrives in Aslan's Country: "level turf, darting birds with yellow, or dragonfly blue, [. . .] and emptiness. There was not a breath of wind in that cool, bright air. It was a very lonely forest" (11).

After wandering a while the dreamer comes to a small stream, across from which he is amazed to see his young daughter standing, now in full royal gowns. Lewis follows this plot device almost exactly in describing Orual's discovery of her lost love. Orual comes to a valley stream, and the far side, where Cupid's palace lies, represents an afterlife where only Psyche can dwell. Orual is forbidden from residing here, just as the father in *Pearl* cannot cross over to be with his now-deceased daughter.

The rest of *Pearl* consists largely of the extended theological debates between father and daughter. The father is initially overjoyed to see his daughter, but is soon confused over why he cannot join her on the other side of the stream (which he does not realize represents death). Casey Finch translates the Middle English as follows:

> More marvelous than man could tell
> Rose ridges from that riverside;
> Above that beauteous brook and dell
> Climbed a crystal cliff with light supplied.
> And seated below that citadel
> Was a child, a maid of noble blood.
> She wore all white. And very well
> I recognized this marvelous maid!
> Like glints of gold in wood inlaid,
> So shone that fair one on the shore.
> I doted on her face, delayed,
> And the more I knew her, more and more. (157-68)

His emotions soon turn to anger, frustration, and jealousy as he tries to understand why his daughter does not seem to miss him, and why she, who has served God for a far shorter time than he, has been granted such abundant reward.

Roles are quickly reversed as the daughter begins parenting the father, explaining a series of difficult concepts. Divine logic, Pearl reminds her father, differs from human logic. Just as Christ teaches in the Beatitudes, the last shall be first in the kingdom of God. She also explains that she is one of many, many brides of Christ (whom the dreamer is eventually able to see in the distant city of New Jerusalem), but that Christ loves each one completely, intimately, and individually. Finally, he must also be convinced that two cities of Jerusalem can exist simultaneously: both a secular one and spiritual one. These are all divine mysteries, and we, as audience members, are being educated on important spiritual topics alongside the narrator. It helps that we have already had to get used to multiple narratives being told concurrently: that of a jeweler and lost jewel, of a father and his daughter taken too soon, and of humanity's split from God.

Just as we see the reversal of roles in *Pearl*, Lewis describes how Psyche's ability to rise in maturity over her older sister is one of the things that most infuriates Orual. When Orual visits the imprisoned Psyche, she explains that "I realizes somewhat slowly that all this time she had been petting and comforting me as if it were I who was the child and the victim. And this, even in the midst if the great anguish, made its own little eddy of pain. [. . .] "I believe you are not afraid at all," said I, almost, though I had not meant it to sound so, as if I were rebuking her for it" (67, 70).

The narrator continues to feel sorry for himself, however, wondering when he can be reunited with his daughter, but she makes clear that she is no longer his; she belongs to God now as his bride, and the dreamer will be able to join her on the other side of the stream only after he has died:

> "O jeweler," said that gem so clean,
> "You jest! Or is this lunacy?
> Three things you've said to me, I glean.
> All three are false, pure foolery.
> You speak not knowing what you mean;
> Your words are thoughtless! Witlessly
> You guess I'm in this garden green—
> How little mortal eyes can see!—
> And claim that in this lovely lea
> You'll linger long. You last aver
> You'll wade this water easily.
> You can't at all, my joyless jeweler!" (289-300)

The Pearl-maiden tells the parable of the workers in the cornfield (in which each laborer is paid equally by the landlord, despite having arrived at different times to the work) to make clear that God rewards his children as he sees fit, not according to human notions of fairness. Rather than conceding God's authority, the dreamer continues to rant about the injustices of the divine. Like Orual, the dreamer knows enough about the divine to plead his case with what seems a reasonable argument:

> Then more did I speak out my mind.
> "Your story seems unreasonable!
> God's righteousness rules all mankind
> Or Holy Writ is a foolish fable!
> In Psalms you shall the saying find,
> Indeed quite indisputable,
> 'By You are *earned* rewards assigned,
> O cherished King unchangeable!'
> If one worked more in toil and trouble
> Yet you're rewarded first, then for
> Less work more wealth is payable.
> So more is less and less is more!" (589-600)

The Pearl-maiden's response shows an exasperation with her father, as if he were a child. She is Christ's spouse, and she knows him intimately:

> "But *more* and *less* within this site
> Are one," replied that righteous maid.
> "Though differently does He requite,
> Here equally each one is paid.
> What He allots, though harsh or light,
> Here equally each gift is weighed.
> As water from a wondrous height
> Flows freely in a fine cascade,
> So freely at our feet is laid
> Each gift; who loved the Lord in life
> With precious prizes thus is paid,
> For God's good grace is great enough." (601-12)

The dreamer leaves his daughter to climb to the top of a nearby hill, taking in the majesty of the New Jerusalem, but is soon overcome with an overwhelming feeling of longing and joy. He rushes down to the river and attempts to cross it, and in this forbidden action he is awakened by God and sent back to the earthly garden. However, the dreamer awakes transformed. He has been humbled by God and the lessons taught by the Pearl-maiden; he also vows to continue serving God while he is alive.

Even a cursory familiarity with *Till We Have Faces* should allow one to see the structural similarities between the two works. In both, an older family member loses a younger one prematurely to death. Psyche joins the Shadowbrute in the intimacy of marriage after being sacrificed on the mountain. She dwells in a mountain palace, just like the Pearl-maiden, while Orual is left behind to negotiate a selfish, festering jealousy. A confrontation between the family members allows each author to script crucial theological debates for his audience, but it is ultimately only through divine intervention that both Orual and *Pearl*'s dreamer are transformed.

Dreams play an important role in *Till We Have Faces*, just as in *Pearl*, and the most important ones take the form of *oracula*—one of five types of medieval dream categorized by Macrobius in his fifth-century *Commentary on the Dream of Scipio*. In the Middle Ages, this form of dream was considered one of the forms of divine revelation, meaning that, as Lewis explains in *The Discarded Image*, it was both true and spiritually useful (64). *Oracula* were characterized by an authority figure from the dreamer's life navigating him or her through the relevant revelatory material, and for Orual, this includes her father, the Fox, and eventually Psyche herself.

Both *Pearl* and *Till We Have Faces* are told from the protagonist's first-person perspective, the primary subject requiring a spiritual education, and role reversals prove crucial for this education. Discussion between the two family members reveals an immaturity on the part of the protagonist. In Lewis' novel the key hierarchies get turned on their heads: the youngest sister takes the role of comforter to the older sister; she faces death with greater maturity; and she transcends humanness more quickly. The same qualities of strength and independence, partnered with a submission to the divine, were a part of Joy Davidman's personality, and they find their literary equivalent in the Beatrice, Margery Kempe, the Pearl-maiden, Psyche, and eventually Orual.

Lewis also tried to emulate *Pearl*'s alliterative style to a small degree. The style emerges typically when the work is most poetic. Lewis' translation of Fox's verse, for example, favors l-alliteration:

> "Take me to the apple-laden land [. . .]
> Alone I lie [. . .]" (9)

Similarly, when Orual speaks to Psyche at the end of the novel, Lewis shifts the queen's voice radically. A repetition of initial consonant sounds signals the transformation from prosaic to poetic: "Oh my own child, my only love. Come back. Come back. Back to the old world where we were happy together" (304). And later, "You have seen [. . .] when men open the shutters and broad summer morning shines in [. . .]?" (306). These alliterative aspects of the novel represent spiritual growth and help signal Orual's transformation.

In addition to sharing similarities in form, both stories employ basic themes that are revealed through the negotiation of complex theological issues. Primarily, this is seen in humanity's relationship with God—an intimacy that is both loving and devouring, majestic and intimate (49). Lewis also helps reveal a God that has both masculine and feminine characteristics as part of its wholeness: both a strong husband and compassionate wife; a judging parent and forgiving lover; an Old Testament icon and New Testament flesh-and-blood person. Such imagery of the divine was appearing with increasing frequency in the fourteenth-century, but can appear shocking to twenty-first-century readers. The writings of mystics circulated at the time of the *Pearl*-poet, for example, and Julian of Norwich's "Jesus-as-Mother" imagery in *Showings* is one of the most well known examples of such creative metaphors. By taking as his primary subject the general divide between humanity and divinity, however, Lewis used difficult, perhaps muddled metaphors of the divine as something to weave into the story rather than to solve definitively.

Just as Orual's journey becomes one of learning (to understand herself, God, and the world around her more accurately), so is *Pearl*'s central conflict ultimately about the protagonist having to confront his own fundamental misunderstanding of his surroundings. As A. C. Spearing explains of the poem,

> It is in this area, of his adequacy to respond to and understand his visionary experience, rather than in the status of the experience itself, that an important element of the questionable enters the poem. The Dreamer carries into the supernatural world of his dream the values and expectations which belong to his natural waking life on earth, and the resulting contrast between the Dreamer's materialism and the spiritual nature of the world in which he finds himself is a central motive of the whole poem. [. . .] He persistently fails to understand what he sees and learns there. (119, 122)

A stream separates Psyche from Orual after the sacrifice, and this gap appears tangibly in *Pearl* as well. A stream with "bonkes brent" (steep banks) keeps the two family members from reuniting (106). As it does for Lewis, the divide in *Pearl* functions in many ways. It is not merely geographic in nature (the close bank / far bank), but also temporal (present life / afterlife), spiritual (fallen / reunited, death / life), and hermeneutic (secular comprehension / divine knowledge).

Perhaps Lewis' most significant use of *Pearl* in his own novel is an adoption of something we might label "medieval loss." We understand *Pearl* most fully through four levels of reading, most famously articulated by Dante. An allegory will, ideally, function on four levels, and these were used most often for Biblical exegesis in the Middle Ages: the historical level (real-life events enacted in a literal narrative), typological level (Biblical or historical "types" prefigure later events), tropological level (moral enactments), and anagogical level (a mystical narrative pointing to end times, heaven, and the afterlife). In *Pearl* one is being told two literal narratives: the story of a jeweler and jewel, as well as a father and daughter. Both describe real-life physical and emotional loss. At the same time, the poem represents a typological representation of the split between God and man—humanity's loss of God. At a moral level, the poem focuses on the dreamer, whose pride has taken away his identity—a spiritual loss of self. And finally, anagogically, the poem reveals an end-times narrative in which the dead have been taken from Earth—a spiritual loss of hope. The poem ends triumphantly by restoring each loss, however: the father find his lost Pearl, comes back to God, confronts his own pride, and realizes life after death means a joyous reunion in the New Jerusalem.

One of the fullest explanations Lewis provided for *Till We Have Faces* acknowledges a similar multiplicity in narrative layers. In a 1957 letter to Clyde Kilby he writes:

> The 'levels' [of the novel] I am conscious of are these. 1. A work of (supposed) *historical* imagination. A guess at what it might have been like in a little barbarous state on the borders of the Hellenistic world with Greek culture just beginning to affect it. [. . .] 2. Psyche is an instance of the *anima naturaliter Christiana* [soul by nature Christian] making the best of the Pagan religion she is brought up in. [. . .] She is in some ways like Christ [. . .] because every good man or woman is like Christ. [. . .] 3. Orual is [. . .] an instance, a 'case,' of human affection in its natural condition: true, tender [. . .] but in the long run, tyrannically possessive and ready to turn to hatred when the beloved ceases to be its possession. [. . .] 4. [The case when] someone becomes a Christian, or, in a family nominally Christian already, does something like becoming a missionary or entering a religious order. The others suffer a sense of outrage. What they love is being taken from them! (Lewis, *Letters 3* 830-1)

Lewis' numbering here does not follow the Dantean scheme, but central to the success of the novel is Lewis' maturity at showing transformation—a movement from loss to fulfillment—at multiple levels. At the historical or literal level, Lewis clearly understands the intimacies of human relationships that need mending due to loss. Loss is explored in the relationships between parents and children, siblings, and friends; and nowhere else in his fiction does Lewis come close to this range of complexity in character development while presenting a diversity of relationships. Loss on a typological level is explored in the novel in terms of humanity's greatest dilemma: the post-lapserian separation from God. At a tropological or moral level, Lewis lays out for his readers many of the personal barriers that individuals must be overcome in their path toward God: pride, selfishness, and jealously. And as an anagogical narrative, the novel provides readers with a hopeful vision of the future, envisioning what humanity's reunion with God may look like, and what a restored relationship with God can entail. Orual's transformation thus models restoration after multiple kinds of loss. We find a restoration of relationships with others, with God, with self, and with an eternal hope.

Although scholars have had very little to say about *Till We Have Faces* in terms of medieval literature, these three medieval texts provide, to varying degrees, foundational support for Lewis' project. In each of them we find, in addition to borrowed narrative forms, the central conflict for Lewis' novel. As Lewis confronts problems that underlie humanity's relationship with the gods, he reveals complexities behind individual human relationships. These three medieval authors show that the human side of the equation is much more complicated than Apuleius was willing to explore, and this proved to be exactly the kind of conflict—abandonment and loss—that Lewis wanted to explore.

Although Dante's *Divine Comedy* and *The Book of Margery Kempe* focus on different kinds of loss in human relationships (in Dante a physical split and in Margery a spiritual one), *Pearl*'s father-daughter relationship proves the greatest influence for Lewis. In this work alone, not only among medieval literature but also among several subsequent centuries of English literature, did Lewis find a combination of loss in human relationships that spoke to the problems he wanted to address in *Till We Have Faces*. The Pearl-Maiden's death marks the physical loss her father must deal with; he also experiences an emotional loss as she turns her most intimate allegiances to God, and a spiritual loss as she reveals to him how irrational his human-centered logic appears to God. Similarly, Orual experiences abandonment and loss at all of these levels before coming to God. Familiarity with all three texts thus reveals to us forms and themes that may be new to a majority of Lewis readers but which Lewis would have known intimately. Dante, Margery Kempe, and the *Pearl*-Poet allow us to understand Lewis better and, perhaps most importantly, to appreciate the complexities that make his most ambitious work of fiction so successful.

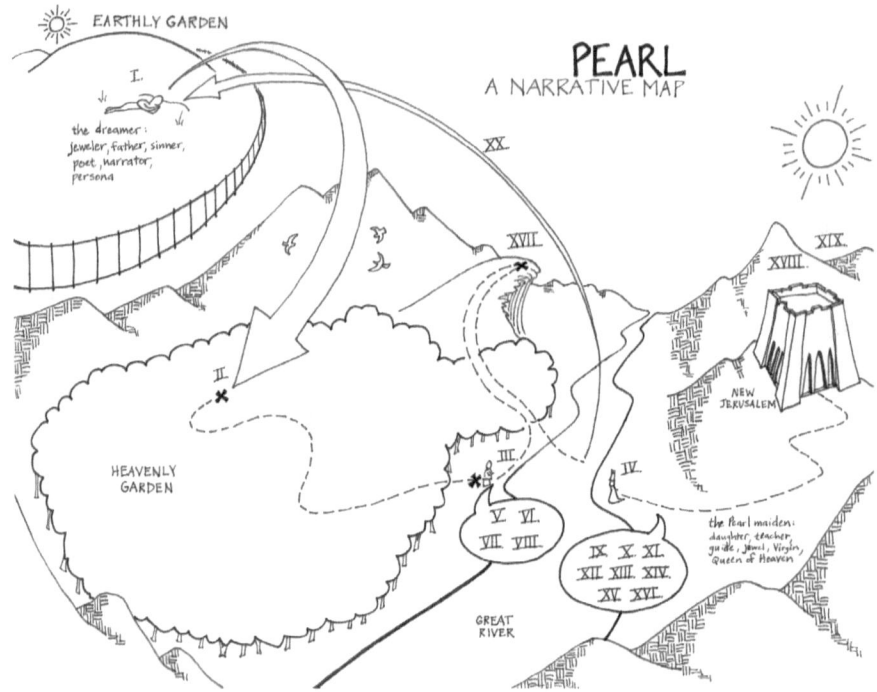

WORKS CITED

Finch, Casey, trans. *The Complete Works of the Pearl Poet*. Berkeley: U of California P, 1993.

Kenney, E. J., ed. *Cupid & Psyche*. By Lucius Apuleius. Cambridge: Cambridge UP, 1997.

—. *The Golden Ass*. By Lucius Apuleius. New York: Penguin, 1998.

Lewis, C. S. *All My Road Before Me: The Diary of C. S. Lewis*. Ed. Walter Hooper. New York: Harcourt Brace Jovanovich, 1991.

—. *The Allegory of Love: A Study in Medieval Tradition*. Oxford: Oxford UP, 1988.

—. *The Collected Letters of C. S. Lewis Volume 1: Family Letters: 1905-1931*. Ed. Walter Hooper. San Francisco: HarperCollins, 2004.

—. *The Collected Letters of C. S. Lewis Volume 2: Books, Broadcasts, and the War: 1931-1949*. Ed. Walter Hooper. San Francisco: HarperCollins, 2004.

—. *The Collected Letters of C. S. Lewis Volume 3: Narnia, Cambridge, and Joy: 1950-1963*. Ed. Walter Hooper. San Francisco: HarperCollins, 2007.

—. "De Audiendis Poetis." *Studies in Medieval and Renaissance Literature*. Cambridge: Cambridge UP, 1980. 1-17.

—. *The Discarded Image: An Introduction to Medieval and Renaissance Literature*. Cambridge: Cambridge UP, 1987.

—. "The Genesis of a Medieval Book." *Studies in Medieval and Renaissance Literature*. Cambridge: Cambridge UP, 1980. 18-40.

—. *George Macdonald: An Anthology*. London: Geoffrey Bles, 1946.

—. "High and Low Brows." *Selected Literary Essays*. Cambridge: Cambridge UP, 1980. 266-279.

—. *The Silver Chair*. New York: Macmillan, 1980.

—. *Surprised by Joy: The Shape of My Early Life*. New York: Harcourt Brace Jovanovich, 1995.

—. *Till We Have Faces: A Myth Retold*. New York: Harcourt, 1984.

Manlove, C. N. *C. S. Lewis: His Literary Achievement*. London: Macmillan, 1987.

Meilaender, Gilbert. *The Taste for the Other: The Social and Ethical Thought of C. S. Lewis.* Grand Rapids: William B. Eerdmans, 1998.

Myers, Doris T. *Bareface: A Guide to C. S. Lewis' Last Novel.* Columbia: U of Missouri P, 2004.

Rowe, Karen. "*Till We Have Faces*: A Study of the Soul and the Self." *C. S. Lewis: Life Works and Legacy Volume 2: Fantasist, Mythmaker, & Poet.* Ed Bruce L. Edwards. Westport: Praeger, 2007.

Schakel, Peter J. *Reason and Imagination in C. S. Lewis: A Study of Till We Have Faces.* Grand Rapids: William B. Eerdmans P, 1984.

Spearing, A. C. *Medieval Dream-Poetry.* Cambridge: Cambridge UP, 1976.

Walsh, Chad. *The Literary Legacy of C. S. Lewis.* New York: Harcourt Brace Jovanovich, 1979.

Williams, Charles. *The Figure of Beatrice: A Study in Dante.* New York: Noonday P, 1961.

LIST OF CONTRIBUTORS

Michael E. Travers (editor) is Professor of English at The College at Southeastern in Wake Forest, North Carolina and a Research Fellow of the L. Russ Bush Center for Faith and Culture at Southeastern Baptist Theological Seminary. He holds the Ph.D. from Michigan State University and is the author of three books: *The Devotional Experience in the Poetry of John Milton* (Edwin Mellen, 1988), *Encountering God in the Psalms* (Kregel, 2007) and co-author (with Richard D. Patterson) of the forthcoming *Face to Face with God: Human Images of God in the Bible* (Biblical Studies Press).

Contributors

Gregory M. Anderson is the Senior Pastor of Union Church Hong Kong. He has lectured on C.S. Lewis in Asia, Europe, and the US. His work on Lewis has been published in journal articles and book chapters. Greg has served as a visiting assistant professor at Wheaton College, and pastor of churches in England, South Dakota, and Ohio. He was educated at Wheaton, Princeton Seminary, Yale University, and the University of Minnesota.

Justin D. Barnard currently serves as Director for the Carl F.H. Henry Center for Christian Leadership at Union University in Jackson, Tennessee and holds an appointment as Scholar-in-Residence for the Fellows Program at Second Presbyterian Church in Memphis, Tennessee. He holds an M.A. and Ph.D. in philosophy from Florida State University.

Steven D. Boyer holds the Ph.D. from Boston University and currently serves as Professor of Theology at Eastern University in Saint Davids, Pennsylvania. He is the co-author (with Christopher Hall) of *Through a Glass Darkly: Theology and the Mystery of God* (Baker, forthcoming).

Byron Brown received his Ph. D. from the University of Florida in 1981. He is currently a Professor of English at Valdosta State University. He has published articles in composition studies and British Romanticism.

James T. Como holds the Ph. D. from Columbia University and is professor of rhetoric and public communication at York College (CUNY). In 1968 he founded the Speech and Theatre disciplines there, and in 1969 was a founding member of the New York C. S. Lewis Society. His books (*Remembering C. S. Lewis* and *Branches to Heaven: the Geniuses of C. S. Lewis*), articles, radio interviews, television appearances and lectures here and abroad are widely known. His latest book is *Why I Believe in Narnia: Thtirty-three Essays on the Life and Work of C. S. Lewis* (Zossima Press, 2008).

Elizabeth Baird Hardy holds a Master's Degree from Appalachian State University and is Senior Instructor of English at Mayland Community College in Spruce Pine, North Carolina, where she was named the 2006 Outstanding Faculty member. In addition to authoring the book *Milton, Spenser, and the Chronicles of Narnia: Sources for the C.S. Lewis Novels,* she is a professional storyteller and collaborates on a variety of projects with her husband, award-winning historian and author Michael C. Hardy.

David S. Hogg is Associate Professor of Theology and Medieval Studies at Southeastern Baptist Theological Seminary. He is the author of *Saint Anselm of Canterbury, the beauty of theology* (Ashgate, 2004) and a member of the Medieval Academy of America. He holds the Ph.D. from St. Andrews University (Scotland), the M.Div. from Westminster Theological Seminary.

Walter Hooper became Lewis' secretary just prior to Lewis' death in 1963. Thereafter he was invited to edit Lewis' literary remains. He is the co-author, with R. L. Green, of *C. S. Lewis: A Biography,* author of *C. S. Lewis: A Companion & Guide* and editor of *The Collected Letters of C. S. Lewis* (3 volumes). He is Adviser to the Estate of C. S. Lewis and lives in Oxford with his cat, Blessed Lucy of Narnia.

Samuel Joeckel completed a Ph.D. in English from Claremont Graduate University and currently serves as Assistant Professor of English at Palm Beach Atlantic University in West Palm Beach, Florida. His articles on a host of subjects—disability studies; Samuel Johnson and happiness; William Cowper and the problem of evil; Christianity and postmodernism; and C.S. Lewis and Platonism—appear in *Christian Scholar's Review, Christianity and Literature, The Kentucky Review, Quodlibet,* and *Mythlore.*

Bradford C. Mercer is the Senior Minister of Westminster Presbyterian Church in Greenwood, MS. He holds an M.A. in Theology from Reformed Theological Seminary, and an M.Phil in Historical Theology from the University of Wales, UK.

Michael Muth received his Ph.D. in medieval philosophy from Duke University. He is presently Associate Professor of Philosophy at Wesleyan College in Macon, GA. Besides C. S. Lewis, his research interests include the writings of Bonaventure, medieval bestiaries and medieval views on nature, and virtue ethics.

Kip Redick is an Associate Professor of Philosophy and Religious Studies at Christopher Newport University. He received his Ph.D. in communication from Regent University and his professional interests include spirituality of place, media ecology; visual, religious, and environmental rhetoric; film studies; and argumentation theory. His specific research interest centers on the study of wilderness trails as sites of spiritual journey.

David Rosenberg is the co-founder of and currently teaches within the Humanities department at Providence Hall, a Classical Christian preparatory school in Santa Barbara. He holds a Ph.D. in German Language and Literature from the University of California at Santa Barbara. Dr. Rosenberg has published an article on the history of the discourse of "national psychology" in the German literature and culture journal *Monatshefte*.

Sanford Schwartz teaches English at Penn State University. The author of *The Matrix of Modernism* and other studies of modern literary, cultural, and intellectual history, he is currently completing a study of C.S. Lewis's Space Trilogy (forthcoming from Oxford University Press).

Ian C. Storey received his PhD in Classics from the University of Toronto, and since 1974 has taught in the Department of Ancient History & Classics (Trent University, Peterborough, Ontario), where he is Full Professor and Principal of Otonabee College. His special area of academic interest, apart from the life and fiction of C.S. Lewis, lies in ancient Greek drama, especially the works of Euripides and Aristophanes. He has published *Eupolis. Poet of Old Comedy* (Oxford 2003) and *A Guide to Ancient Greek Drama* (Blackwell 2005), and his *Euripides' Suppliant Women* will be appearing from Duckworth Press in 2008.

Dr. Stephen Yandell is a member of Xavier University's English Department in Cincinnati, Ohio. He teaches medieval literature primarily, but also offers a range of courses on "Tolkien and his Medieval Sources," "Spiritual Fantasies," and the Inklings. He also studies political prophecy and medieval translations of Biblical narratives and is co-editor of a collection on medieval political prophecy entitled *Prophet Margins: The Medieval Vatic Impulse and Social Stability* and translator of the Middle Welsh tale "Math Son of Mathonwy" for *Medieval Literature for Children*.

Name & Subject Index

Names Index

Abbott, Edwin, 216 (n6), 220
Adey, Lionel, 226, 234
Aeschliman, Michael, 35, 64, 65, 76, 92, 102
Aeschylus, 242, 248
Albertus Magnus, 231
Alexander, Samuel, 202, 215 (n3), 220, 240
Anderson, Gregory M., 5, 6, 105, 121
Anscombe, Elisabeth, 107, 108
Apuleius, 238, 239, 240, 244, 250 (n2), 255, 256, 257, 271, 273
Aquinas, 10, 231, 232, 233
Aristophanes, 164, 279
Aristotle, 54, 61, 105, 111, 121, 231, 244, 245, 247
Arnold, Matthew, 39
Auden, W. H., 43
Augustine, Saint, 4, 7, 10, 11, 64, 76, 98, 104, 110, 210

Bacon, Francis, 67, 68, 70, 76
Barfield, Owen, 16, 18, 19, 21, 23, 24, 25, 26, 27, 30, 141, 156
Barth, Karl, 193
Beethoven, 36, 205
Beevor, Anthony, 36, 48
Berger, Peter, 167, 168
Bergson, Henri, 8, 201, 202, 203, 204, 205, 206, 207, 208, 209, 210, 211, 214 (n2), 215(n4),
   216 (n5), 218 (n12), 221, 222
Bertodano, Helena de, 187, 188, 198
Blake, William, 21, 190, 217 (n11), 221
Bloom, Harold, 121
Bowler, Peter, 215 (n3), 221
Boyd, Fr. Ian, 19
Brown, Capability, 145
Brown, Edwin, 106, 121
Burke, Edmund, 143, 144, 145, 146, 154, 156
Burson, Scott R., 94, 95, 98, 102

Calvin, John, 10, 93, 102, 116
Carnell, Corbin Scott, 138, 139, 140, 156
Carson, D. A., 99, 100, 102
Chaucer, Geoffrey, 10, 229, 231, 264, 265
Chesterton, G. K., 19, 35, 37, 101, 102
Christensen, Michael, 116, 121
Christopher, Joe, 23, 76, 182, 205
Coghill, Nevill, 19, 23
Cohen, Patricia, 79, 87
Collins, Lady, 26, 27
Colson, Chuck, 23, 29
Como, James T., 3, 26, 28, 29, 33, 122
Cunningham, Richard, 45, 48
Curtius, Ernst Robert, 142, 156

Dante, 10, 256, 259, 260, 261, 270, 271, 274
Darwin, Charles, 71, 73, 76, 221
Davidman, Joy, see Joy Gresham
Dawkins, Richard, 71, 74, 76, 84
Deleuze, Gilles, 214, 221
Dennett, Daniel, 71, 73, 74, 76
Descartes, Rene, 68, 69, 70, 71, 76
Detienne, Marcel, 162, 163, 168
Dewey, John, 35, 36, 39, 46, 48
Dorsett, Lyle, 106, 118, 121, 234
Dougherty, Judy B., 36, 48
Driver, Godfrey R., 109
Dunbar, Nan, 29, 205
Dundas-Grant, 23
Dyson, Hugo, 23, 192

Edwards, Bruce, 110, 121, 122, 123, 274
Edwards, Michael, 110, 121
Eliot, George, 28, 30
Eliot, T. S., 106, 215 (n4)
Erasmus, 227
Euripides, 163, 168, 238, 240, 242, 246, 247, 248, 249
Evans, C. Stephen, 78, 87

Farrer, Austin, 1, 13, 16, 18, 20, 23, 25, 28, 99, 102, 105, 106
Farrer, Katherine, 250 (n6)
Finch, Casey, 265, 273
Flick, Alexander Clarence, 33, 48
Ford, Paul, 182
Frame, John M., 93, 94, 96, 102
Freud, Sigmund, 71, 78, 79, 83, 192
Frye, Northrop, 213, 221, 228, 229, 233, 234

Galileo, 69
Gibb, Jock, 20, 26
Glyer, Diana Pavlac, 105, 121
Goethe, Wolfgang von, 188, 189, 192, 195, 196, 197, 198, 205
Gombrich, E. H., 143, 145, 156
Goodell, Henry, 33, 48
Green, Roger Lancelyn, 23, 25, 28
Greeves, Arthur, 26, 77, 79, 87, 106, 216 (n5), 239, 246, 257
Gregoire, Reginald, 33, 48
Grenier, Cynthia, 187, 198
Gresham, David, 14
Gresham, Douglas, 14, 108, 121
Gresham, Joy, 15, 239, 258, 268
Grudem, Wayne, 96, 102
Guerlac, Suzanne, 215 (n3), 221

Habermas, Jurgen, 46, 48
Hardie, Colin, 29
Harrison, Jane, 167, 168
Hart, D. A., 251 (n16), 252
Hartocollis, Peter, 78, 87
Harwood, Alfred Cecil, 16, 18, 23, 25, 26, 29
Harwood, Daphne, 29
Havard, "Humphrey", 23
Hays, Richard, 117, 121
Heck, Joel, 121
Heidegger, Martin, 215 (n3)
Heine, Heinrich, 189, 198
Helm, Paul, 94, 96, 102
Herrick, James, 110, 121

Hesiod, 245
Hitchens, Christopher, 74, 76
Hitler, 36
Hobbes, Thomas, 71
Hoekema, Anthony, 95, 102
Homer, 142 143, 246, 247, 251 (n12)
Hooper, Walter, 1, 2, 11, 13, 17, 30, 43, 48, 61, 87, 103, 106, 121, 122, 135, 137, 156, 157, 182, 213, 220, 234, 250 (n2), 252, 257, 273
Horace, 245
Howard, Thomas, 248, 252
Hulme, T. E., 215 (n4), 221
Hume, David, 37
Hunt, John, 143, 156
Husserl, Edmund, 215 (n3)

Jacobs, Alan, 108, 121
Julian of Norwich, 269
Jung, Carl, 78, 79, 88

Kempe, Margery, 256, 261, 262, 263, 268, 271
Kenney, E. J., 256, 273
Kierkegaard, Soren, 215 (n3)
Kilby, Clyde, 26, 30, 250 (n5), 270
Kirkpatrick, William T., 29, 35, 237
Koch, Sigmund, 80, 87
Kort, Wesley, 182
Kuhn, Thomas, 219 (n16)

Lane, Belden C., 146, 154, 156
Lawlor, John, 19, 29
Lepensie, Wolf, 48
Lewis, C. S.,
 The Abolition of Man, 27, 37, 64, 65, 66, 69, 71, 72, 73, 76, 129, 135, 234
 All My Road before Me: The Diary of C. S. Lewis, 1922-1927, 27, 30, 87, 216 (n5), 220, 252, 273

The Allegory of Love: A Study in Medieval Tradition, 9, 20, 30, 172, 182, 255-256, 262, 264, 273
"Bulverism", 39, 126, 135
"Christian Apologetics", 5, 11, 92, 103
"Christianity and Culture", 92, 103
The Collected Letters of C. S. Lewis: Books, Broadcasts, and the War: George Macdonald: An Anthology, 273
God in the Dock, 11, 22, 23, 30, 61, 103, 122, 135, 156, 205, 220
"The Grand Miracle", 205, 220
A Grief Observed, 101, 103
"High and Low Brows", 273
The Horse and His Boy, 95, 103, 147, 156, 164, 173, 182
"The Humanitarian Theory of Punishment", 40, 48
"Is Theology Poetry?", 10, 11, 202, 205, 220
The Last Battle, 95, 103, 147, 156, 182, 185, 186, 198
"The Laws of Nature", 103
"Learning in War-Time", 48
Letters of C. S. Lewis. Ed. and with a Memoir by H. W. Lewis, 20
Letters to Malcolm, Chiefly on Prayer, 15, 20, 103, 107, 109, 122, 126, 135
The Lion, the Witch, and the Wardrobe, 8, 95, 103, 139, 147, 156, 170, 172, 174, 175, 179, 180, 187
The Magician's Nephew, 95, 103, 147, 156, 170, 171, 173, 175, 176, 177, 178, 182
"Meditation in a Toolshed", 126, 135
"Membership", 125, 130, 131, 135
Mere Christianity, 4, 5, 11, 91, 96, 97, 98, 99, 103, 109, 122, 182, 203, 205, 216 (n6), 220

Miracles, 37, 96, 98, 103, 107, 127, 135, 208, 215 (n3), 216 (n6), 217 (n7), 220, 240, 252
"Modern Theology and Biblical Criticism", 86, 87
"Myth Became Fact", 138, 140, 156
"The Novels of Charles Williams", 211, 214, 220
On Stories and Other Essays on Literature, 76, 92, 103, 156
"On the Reading of Old Books", 38, 119, 122
Out of the Silent Planet, 8, 64, 92, 148, 156, 201, 206, 207, 208, 210, 217 (n8), 218 (n15), 220, 222
"The Parthenon and the Optative", 39, 48
Perelandra, 8, 26, 86, 95, 103, 128, 131, 132, 135, 137, 148, 150, 151, 156, 195, 196, 197, 198, 201, 202, 203, 206, 207, 208, 209, 210, 213, 217 (n9), 218 (n12), 220, 222, 237
The Pilgrim's Regress: An Allegorical Apology for Christianity, Reason, and Romanticism, 38, 79, 81, 86, 87
Poems, 17, 18, 20, 22, 97, 103, 251 (n15), 252
A Preface to Paradise Lost, 9, 105, 110, 122, 176, 177, 179, 182, 210, 220
Prince Caspian, 147, 156, 162, 164, 166, 174, 182, 237
"Private Bates", 41, 48
The Problem of Pain, 11, 31, 96, 98, 103, 128, 135, 191, 196, 198
"Prudery and Philology", 41, 49
"Psycho-Analysis and Literary Criticism", 83, 87
Reflections on the Psalms, 4, 5, 11, 105, 106, 107, 108, 111, 115, 119, 120, 122, 123, 127, 135, 202, 207,

216 (n6), 220
"Rejoinder to Dr. Pittenger", 5, 11, 89, 103, 109, 122
"A Reply to Professor Haldane", 64, 76, 103
The Screwtape Letters, 18, 26, 43, 98, 103, 126, 129, 130, 135
"Sex in Literature", 40, 49
The Silver Chair, 95, 103, 147, 157, 182, 237, 250, 265, 273
"Sometimes Fairy Stories May Say Best What's to Be Said", 103
Spenser's Images of Life, 182
Studies in Medieval and Renaissance Literature, 21, 182, 234, 273
Studies in Words, 83, 87
Surprised by Joy: The Shape of My Early Life, 7, 11, 14, 15, 30, 78, 79, 87, 91, 95, 103,138, 157, 166, 167, 168, 182, 192, 198, 205, 216 (n5), 220, 249, 252, 273
That Hideous Strength: A Modern Fairy-Tale for Grown-Ups, 37, 64, 74, 128, 135, 195, 196, 198, 201, 210, 211, 212, 213, 219 (n15)
They Stand Together: The Letters of C. S. Lewis to Arthur Greeves (1914-1963), 26, 27, 77, 87
Till We Have Faces: A Myth Retold., 2, 7, 9, 10, 96, 104, 137, 151, 155, 157, 223, 237, 238, 240, 242, 246, 247, 249, 252, 253, 255, 256, 257, 258, 260, 261, 262, 267, 268, 270, 271, 273, 274
"Transposition", 84, 87, 108, 122, 129, 135, 216 (n6), 220
"Vivisection", 40, 49, 132, 135
The Voyage of the "Dawn Treader", 147, 150, 157, 182, 237
"The Weight of Glory", 7, 11, 140, 155, 157, 159
"Why I Am Not a Pacifist", 54, 55, 61

"Willing Slaves of the Welfare State", 42, 49
Lewis, C. S. and Don Giovanni Calabria. *The Latin Letters of C. S. Lewis*, 182
Lewis, Warren ("Warnie"), 13, 14, 15, 16, 19, 20, 21, 24, 25, 29
Lombard, 233
Longinus, 43, 143
Lovejoy, Arthur, 212, 221
Luther, Martin, 10, 93, 104, 116

Manlove, Colin, 182, 258, 273
Manwaring, Elizabeth W., 143, 145, 157
Maritain, Jacques, 204, 205
Marshall, I. Howard, 96, 104
Mascall, E. L., 51, 52, 55, 57, 58, 59, 60, 61
McLachlan, H. J., 104
Meacham, Steve, 187, 198
Mead, Marjorie Lamp, 30, 107, 122
Meilaender, Gilbert, 92, 93, 104, 261, 274
Milton, John, 8, 9, 10, 105, 169, 175, 178, 179, 181, 183, 190, 195, 209, 210, 217 (n5), 221, 277
Moberly, R. W., 117, 122
Monod, Jaques, 74, 76
Montgomery, P. Andrew, 250, 252
Moore, Janie, 14, 27, 28, 108
Morgan, C. Lloyd, 202, 222
Moulin, Leo, 33, 48
Myers, Doris T., 248, 251 (n8, n9), 252, 258, 274
Nicholson, Marjorie Hope, 143, 157
Nietzsche, Friedrich, 189, 190, 191, 192, 195, 196, 198, 215 (n3)

Otto, Rudolph, 139, 140, 141, 149, 154, 157, 250 (n7)
Otto, Walter, 162, 168
Oursel, Raymond, 33, 48

Name Index

Paxford, "Fred" (gardener at the Kilns), 15, 21
Péguy, Charles, 204, 205
Pindar, 205
Pinnock, Clark, 94, 98, 104
Piper, John, 114, 122
Plato, 70, 77, 81, 116, 119, 155, 157, 216 (n6), 231, 245, 246, 247
Plutarch, 239
Pope John XXIII, 22
Pope John Paul, II, 24
Price, Merdith, 173, 183
Pullman, Philip, 8, 185, 186, 187, 188, 190, 191, 193, 194, 195, 197, 198, 199

Raine, Kathleen, 21
Renault, Mary, 239, 252
Reppert, Victor, 37, 110, 124
Reumann, John, 109, 122
Robinson, Ian, 226, 227
Robinson, J. A. T., 17, 30
Rowe, Karen, 258, 274

Sammons, M., 251 (n16), 252
Sappho, 244, 245
Sayer, George, 15, 29, 106, 107, 122, 183
Schaefer, Henry F., 64, 76
Schakel, Peter J., 245, 248, 251 (n9, n14), 252, 258, 274
Schiller, Friedrich, 188, 189, 192, 199
Schopenhauer, Arthur, 36, 166, 168
Schroeder, Gerald, 85, 87
Schwartz, Sanford, 8, 201, 222, 279
Shakespeare, 10, 96, 164
Shamdasani, Sonu, 78, 87
Shaw, George Bernard, 35, 205
Shelley, Percy Bysshe, 205, 217-218 (n11), 222
Socrates, 240, 246
Southron, Jane Spence, 38, 49
Spearing, A. C., 269, 274
Spenser, Edmund, 8, 169, 170, 174, 181, 182, 183

Steiner, Rudolph, 16
Storey, I.C., 9, 10, 237, 251 (n8), 253

Thorson, Stephen, 141, 157
Timmermann, J. H., 251 (n16), 253
Titian, 205
Tolkien, J. R. R., 16, 23, 24, 25, 108, 121, 183, 192
Tracy, Steven, 132, 135

Van Leeuwen, Mary Stewart, 132, 136
Vanauken, Sheldon, 92, 104
Virgil, 116, 142, 143, 259

Wain, John, 114, 122
Walls, Jerry L., 94, 95, 98, 102
Walsh, Chad, 258, 274
Ward, Michael, 10
Wartofsky, Alona, 187, 199
Wells, H. G., 8, 35, 201-213, 218 (n15), 222
Westblade, Donald J., 104
Whitehead, Alfred North, 203, 215, 222
Williams, Charles, 168, 183, 210, 211, 213, 214, 216 (n6), 218 (n14), 220, 260, 274
Williams, D. T., 106, 107, 123
Williams, Rowan, 188
Willis, Peter, 143, 156
Wilson, A. N., 107, 108, 123
Wittgenstein, Ludwig, 108
Woodford, Susan, 242, 251 (n11), 253
Wren, Christopher, 205
Wright, R. K. McGregor 94, 98, 104
Wright, Tom, 117, 123

Subject Index

Acta Apostolicae Sedae, 22
American Psychological Association, 80
Apologetics, 4-5, 9, 10, 15, 16, 21, 22, 105, 107, 108, 109
Apologist, 4, 5, 34, 35, 38, 46, 92, 113
Arcadia, 142
Argument from Desire, see longing
Arminian, Arminianism, 94, 98, 99, 100
Atheism, 84
Atonement, 95
Augustinianism, 92, 98, 100

Baal, 127
Bacchus, see Dionysius
Beautiful, the, 143, 144, 148
Beauty, 129
Bles, Geoffrey, publisher, 20, 26
Bodleian Library, 15, 19, 28

Calvinism, Calvinists, 91, 93, 95, 99, 100
Capital Punishment, 52
Castlereagh Hills, 138, 139, 151
Chora, 137, 138, 146, 154
"Christian Hedonism", 114
Church of England, 106
Collins, publisher, 26, 28
Comedy, 161, 167
Common Prayer, Book of, 106
Compatibilism , 93, 95, 96, 98, 99, 101
Creation, Christian Doctrine of, 126, 208
C.S. Lewis Company, 26
Culture , 2-3, 4, 6, 9, 33, 35, 36-39, 45, 46, 63, 92, 133, 188, 189, 191, 202, 237
Cupid and Psyche, myth of, 9, 238, 239, 244, 250 (n2, n3), 255, 256, 258, 259

"Darkest Zeitgeistheim", 79, 80
Darwinian, 8, 203, 204, 206, 207, 208, 213
Darwinism, 202-205, 208, 213, 214 (n1)
"Death of God" movement, 17
Diary (of C. S. Lewis), 27
Dionysius, 161-167

Eerdmans Publishing Company, 22
Egalitarianism, 125, 130, 133
Epistemic moral certainty, 51, 55-58
Equality, 128, 130, 131, 208
Ethos, 105, 120
Evangelism, 92
Evil, 7, 8, 40, 67, 96, 97, 112, 151, 164, 169, 171, 173, 177, 178, 180, 181, 189, 202, 209, 210, 219
Evolution, incl. "creative" and "emergent" evolution, 8, 193, 201-213, 214 (n1), 215 (n3)
Exegesis, 111, 225, 270
Exegetical Proofs, 115

Faerie Queene, The, 169, 175
Faith, 80, 110, 111, 191, 196
Fantasist, C.S. Lewis as, 33
First things, 127
Free will, see human responsibility
Free Will Defense, 96
Freudian, 85

Gender , 2, 6, 125, 133, 173, 217 (n4), 260, 261
Gender hierarchy, 125
Gender relations, 125
Gnostic, Gnosticism, 141
Gothic Romances, 211-212, 214, 218 (n14)
Grace, 96, 98

Guardian, The, 19, 185

HarperCollins, publisher, 28
Hierarchy, 6, 125, 126, 128, 129, 131, 132, 133, 173, 179, 212, 215 (n4)
His Dark Materials trilogy, 185-188, 190
Human responsibility, 5, 91, 93, 94, 96, 97, 99, 100, 101
Humor, Incongruity Theory of, 166-167

Imagination, 10, 80, 83, 86, 92, 110, 113, 138, 139, 141, 143, 144, 146, 154, 166, 167,
    219 (n16), 229, 232, 240, 258, 270
Inequality, 129, 130, 132
Inklings, 260

Jesus College, Oxford, 21, 22, 23, 25
Journey narratives, 137, 153, 260
Joy, see longing

Kilns, the, 14, 20, 24

Landscapes in Lewis' writings, 6, 137, 138, 139, 141, 142
Laughter, 161, 166, 167
Lewis Estate, 23, 25
Libertarianism , 93, 94, 96, 97, 99
Lilith, 173
Logos, 105, 120
Longing, 4, 6, 7, 8, 10, 38, 77, 79, 81, 82, 83, 84, 85, 128, 138, 139, 140, 141, 150, 151, 152, 153, 154, 155, 159, 171, 192, 193, 231, 249, 260, 263, 267
Lysistrata, of Aristophanes, 164

Maenads, 162-166
Magdalen College, Oxford, 109
Magdalene College, Cambridge, 15
Magic, 66-67, 171-172

Materialism, 4, 79, 202-205, 208, 210-212, 269
Meaning, 92
Medieval Model (also "cosmology"), 92, 206, 209, 219 (n16), 255-256, 270
Medieval Period, 9, 189, 225-233
Middle Ages, see Medieval Period
Midsummer Night's Dream, A, 164
Molech, 127
Monarchy, 125
Monotheism, 114
Moral Argument, 4
Moral Law, 92
Myth, mythic, mythopoeia, 78, 92, 117, 137, 138, 139, 140, 141, 142, 146, 148, 150, 151,
    154, 155, 165, 167, 187, 192, 212, 219 (n15), 229, 233, 237-251, 255, 257, 258

Natural Philosophy, 65, 69
Nature, 127, 137-155, 207, 208, 216-217 (n7)
Nazi Death Camps, 126
Nazi Germany , 72, 75, 130
New England Anti-Vivisection Society, 132
New English Bible, 107
New York C.S. Lewis Society, 25
N.I.C.E., 74, 210, 212
Nicene Creed, 126
Numinous, 137, 139, 140, 141, 142, 147, 150, 152, 154, 240

Obscenity, 41
Old Western Man, 40
Omnipotence, divine, 91, 93, 94, 97, 101, 211, 230
Omniscience, divine, 93, 230
Open Theism, 94, 98

Pacifism, 54, 59, 60
Paradise Lost, 169, 175-181, 195
Pathos, 105, 115, 120

Pearl Poem, 10, 264-272
Picturesque, the, 143, 145, 146
Platonism, 119, 203, 209
Poetry, Psalms as, 110
Predestination, 95, 96, 99
Psalms, Christological prophecy in, 115
___, connivance in, 114
___, death in, 112
___, Imprecatory, 112
___, nature in, 114
___, praise in, 114-115
___, second meanings in, 113, 115-116, 118
___, truth in, 113
___, worship in, 113
Psychology, 4, 78-80, 85, 86
Public Philosopher, C. S. Lewis as, 34-47

Rational Argument for God, 4
Rationalism, 78, 79
Rationality, 152
Reader-response, 233
Reason, 80, 86, 152
Rhetoric, 105, 110, 111, 119
Romantic, Romanticism, 34, 35, 38, 45, 46, 92, 140, 167, 177, 189, 192, 206, 210, 245

Science, 3-4, 63-75, 80, 84
Scientism, 4, 36, 64
Scripture, 100, 101, 116-117, 141, 161
Second things, 127
Second Vatican Council, 18, 22
Sehnsucht, see longing
Shadowlands, 7, 148, 185, 186
Shadowlands, the movie, 28
Socratic Club of Oxford, 5, 92, 107
Sovereignty of God, 5, 91, 97, 99, 100, 101
Soviet Union, 75
Spirit of the Age, see zeitgeist
Sublime, the, 142, 143, 144, 148, 154

Tao, the, 65, 74
Theologian, C. S. Lewis as, 4, 33, 258
Theology, 86, 229-230
Time Magazine, 17
Topos, 137, 138, 146
Truth, 86, 101, 129, 175, 178, 191, 230, 240

Wadham College, Oxford, 20
War, justice of, 51, 52, 55, 58, 59
Wheaton College, IL, 28
Women, view of in Lewis' writings, 161, 186, 258
Worldview, in Lewis' writings, 226, 227, 230

Zeitgeist, 226, 227, 228, 232, 233

Other Titles from Zossima Press

Why I Believe in Narnia:
*33 Essays and Reviews
on the Life and Work of C.S. Lewis*

by **James Como**
292 pages ISBN 0972322175

Reading *Why I Believe in Narnia* provides a panoramic view of C. S. Lewis' multi-faceted genius and its application in fields as diverse as social criticism and children's literature. *Why I Believe* gathers essays and reviews that span Prof. James Como's many years as a preeminent Lewis scholar, to which the author of *Remembering C.S. Lewis* and *Branches to Heaven* has added several new entries. Chapters range from reviews of critical books, documentaries and movies to evaluations of Lewis's books to biographical analysis. In addition to close-up looks, Como reflects on the "big picture" of the most important contributions Lewis has made, not just in literature, but as a social philosopher and reformer. For the serious student of C. S. Lewis, *Why I believe in Narnia* is an invaluable tool for appreciating the breadth and depth of Lewis' thinking.

C.S. Lewis & Philosophy As a Way of Life

by Adam Barkman
ISBN 09723221-6-7

C. S. Lewis, world famous Christian apologist and author of children's novels, is rarely thought of as a "philosopher," despite his university training and teaching philosophy for several years at Oxford, where he debated some of the world's most renowned philosophers. C. S. Lewis's long journey to Christianity was essentially philosophical – passing through six different stages. This journey, as well as every philosophical topic Lewis discussed, such as metaphysics, natural theology, epistemology, logic, psychology, ethics, socio-political philosophy, and aesthetics is explained here in detail. Barkman incorporates previously unexplored treasures from Lewis's unpublished philosophy lectures, lecture notes, and hand-written annotations from copies of philosophical books such as Aristotle's Ethics and Augustine's City of God.

Owen Barfield once said that "What Lewis thought about everything was evident in what he wrote about anything." *C. S. Lewis and Philosophy as a Way of Life* is the definitive book on "what Lewis thought about everything," which is to say, his philosophical underpinnings. Way of Life is must reading, consequently, for anyone wanting to understand Lewis' theological and literary writings.

> Adam Barkman addresses a yawning gap in the secondary literature, placing C.S. Lewis the philosopher within a broad and richly-textured historical and intellectual context. His command of the material as well as his scope and focus make *C.S. Lewis and Philosophy as a Way of Life* indispensable.
>
> James Como, author of
> *Remembering C.S. Lewis* and *Why I Believe in Narnia*

Fourteen essays that truely place MacDonald in context. Important, challenging, and exciting.

This comprehensive collection represents the best of contemporary scholarship on George MacDonald.
  Rolland Hein

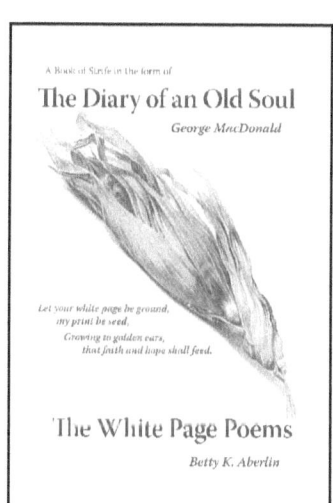

Daily reflections by two poets from different times and places, but with a common love.

Betty Aberlin's close readings of George MacDonald's verses and her thoughtful responses to them speak clearly of her poetic gifts and spiritual intelligence.
  Luci Shaw

www.ingramcontent.com/pod-product-compliance
Lightning Source LLC
Chambersburg PA
CBHW031235290426
44109CB00012B/306